John Hodges,

I hope you enjoy my book!

All my best,

Christine

RESILIENT

Childhood
Adversity to
Cambridge
University

CHRISTIAN AUSTIN

ISBN 978-1-0681681-0-9

This is a work of nonfiction. The events described are based on the author's memories and experiences. Some names and identifying details have been changed to protect privacy.

Published in the United Kingdom by Christian Austin.

The first six years of life sets the stage for who we become later in life. Christian had some poor role models for respectful and healthy relationships growing up. Resilient walks us through some of the ways early childhood abuse and trauma can lead to a horrendous life of prison and rehab. Christian then brings us hope, as his authentic self was uncovered over time, and doors started opening up for him. Now he is shedding light in the darkness for others to see that anyone can turn their life around. Thank you Christian for sharing this inspiring story with the world.

— Patti Ashley, PhD, LPC

RESILIENT is a deeply authentic book. It is raw and unfiltered and sometimes shocking but it's honest, has integrity, and doesn't wear a mask. It doesn't play games with the reader and doesn't lie, doesn't pretend. It's about real people, often the ones who don't make it in life, hurt people who have spirit and character, true outsiders, the kind that the British class system shits out. I was thinking yesterday that now I've finished it I miss it. That's the highest praise I can give a book. You know, like it's over…and there's a grieving process cos you can never read it for the first time again.

— Jerry Hyde, Rock & Roll Therapy

This book is dedicated to the far too many friends who never got the chance to become who they might have been—and to my mother.

A Note from the Author

This book holds scenes and memories of childhood abuse, sexual trauma, addiction, suicide attempts, and the loss of friends to overdose. I share them not to shock or disturb, but because they are part of a life that has been lived deeply, endured fully, and—against the odds—redeemed in unexpected ways.

Some passages may weigh heavy on the heart. If you carry your own scars, read gently. Step away if you need to. Come back when you're ready.

This is not just a story of brokenness. It is also one of music, resilience, and fellowship—of hope stitched together in the quiet hours—and of a man who, brick by brick, clawed his way out of the dark.

In every man, heredity and environment have combined to produce a creature of certain abilities and desires—including a deeply ingrained need to function in such a way that his life will be MEANINGFUL. A man has to BE something; he has to matter.

—Hunter S. Thompson, in a letter to Hume Logan New York, 22 April 1958

Table of Contents

Prologue

With zero reluctance I climbed into the boot of the car and settled onto the bedding provided for me. I needed to escape this island no matter the cost. I was not going back.

After watching scores of police scouring the island's ports and ferry terminals on the television news this past week, my accomplices and I had agreed I'd leave my hideout and attempt the crossing today. As each day passed, the searching of cars had become increasingly blasé, and it seemed the authorities thought I'd already made good my escape.

I could be back on the mainland within two hours.

The boot lid was gently closed. Near darkness, muffled gusts of wind and the acrid bite of diesel assailed my senses. Both front doors slammed one after the other, the engine fired into life, and I felt the car roll forwards and gain speed.

"You okay?!" Cookie shouted over the engine noise.

"Yeah, I'm good."

"Cool. Don't make a sound unless I speak first. We'll have you back on the mainland in no time."

Two thoughts flashed through my mind: *These guys are risking a hefty prison sentence for me*, and *Who would next open the car's boot?*

The car slowed as we approached the ferry terminal. The sound of Cookie and Tony talking to one another, a long blast from a ship's horn, and the crying of seagulls all seemed distant echoes from within my confined space.

The tone of Cookie's voice changed.

"The queue's moving," he said. "Here we go."

The car once again crawled forward, and I heard other voices. Ferry staff were guiding cars on to the boat's deck, and I listened while unconsciously holding my breath. Were they going to search the car or ask for the boot to be opened?

Relief washed over me when the engine was cut and I heard Cookie's voice, "You okay, man? We're gonna go up to the bar and have a beer. Keep yer head down, yeah?"

There wasn't much else I could do other than keep my head down.

* * *

As my life would have it, I'd had an appearance in Newport Magistrates Court a week previously. It was 14 December 1987, and the hearing had been committed to Crown Court, which meant my crimes were deemed too serious to be dealt with by the magistrates' court. It also meant I'd been remanded to Camphill Prison once again. The worst of it was I'd be handed over to the custody of the Prison Service instead of the police for future court appearances—bad news because the police security at Newport magistrates court was a lot laxer than that of the Prison Service.

I'd been arrested with my then girlfriend, Denise, during a crime spree stretching from the Isle of Wight to Cornwall and I'd been returned to face the music. Each time I appeared before the magistrates they remanded me for a week or two while evidence was collated. I was up on charges of car theft and credit card fraud—my *modus operandi* around this time.

The jailer at Newport magistrates court was named Ron, an old boy who was close to retirement. He stood at six feet tall—the same as me—wore a copper's uniform without a hat, had a full head of silver hair, and a mischievous sparkle in his sharp grey eyes. He was a lovely soul simply waiting to collect his pension—not one of the malicious types. He'd let you have a phone call, or find a lighter for your cigarette, that kind of thing.

When I'd first been brought in, after the journey in the police van from Cornwall, there'd been a red asterisk on the cell-board beside my name denoting I was an escape risk. Over the subsequent weeks and months of appearing before the magistrates Ron and I had become friendly. And slowly, over those weeks, he'd grown more relaxed around me.

When leaving the magistrates' court after each appearance, the exit from the courthouse opened on to the pavement of a normal street. From the courthouse door to the waiting police van there were only four footsteps. This was extremely rare and a blessing for me. Usually, a courthouse or a police station has a gated courtyard and the gate to the street is never unlocked while prisoners are outside the building. It would only be unlocked once the prisoners were securely locked in the van. This was why December 14 was my last chance to escape before the Prison Service's increased security of being handcuffed at all times.

The day of my escape was a cold one. It was also an early finish for the courts so when Ron opened the door to the street it was still daylight. I remember my words as I rubbed my hands together:

"Is it cold out there, Ron?"

"It's bloody freez…"

He didn't finish the sentence. As he opened the door, I placed my right hand on the wall and gave a powerful thrust while breaking into a run. I was fleet and determined to escape.

It *was* bloody freezing. The cold was burning my nostrils and throat as my feet pounded the pavement. I could hear the sound of Ron giving chase and I pumped my legs faster, increasing the distance between us.

I spotted a stream along the side of the road and aimed for it. I leapt across it, slipped on the grass, fell, regained my footing then headed down a side street. After fifty yards, I took another turn. When I looked back there was no sign of Ron. It was after two o'clock and I knew it would be dark in an hour or so. I also knew there'd soon be coppers everywhere and I wouldn't have a chance of evading them. I needed to find a bolthole of some kind. I continued scanning my surroundings but saw little opportunity for cover, simply terraced houses. I had to find somewhere fast. My breathing was becoming more laboured and painful, and I felt I was burning the last of my stamina.

I rounded a corner and there, ahead of me, stood an enormous red brick viaduct. With its arches decreasing in height due to a rising embankment, the right-hand end disappeared into a grassy incline. I scrambled up this slope and found the final arch was around three feet tall and several feet wide. I crawled into this opening and remained there slowly regaining my breath knowing, once it became dark, I needed to find my friend Cookie's house.

After waiting an hour or so—expecting to be discovered every moment—I climbed a fence tangled with tall weeds situated at the rear of my hideaway. I now needed to find Albany Road. I'd not contacted Cookie during this prison stint, so his name wasn't on my prison correspondence list. This meant the police wouldn't be aware of our connection and I'd be in the clear if only I could reach the safety of his house.

I had no idea how near or far I was from Albany Road so couldn't believe my luck when I asked a passerby for directions.

"Sure, Albany Road's that left over there," he said, pointing back the way he'd come.

A hundred yards away. I found the door number I was looking for and knocked.

The door opened and my good friend exclaimed, "Hey, Christian. I thought you were banged up."

"I was," I replied, "I escaped."

"Quick, come inside, it'll be on the radio and the telly.

"You're joking," I replied.

"Seriously, this is the Isle of Wight where nothing ever happens—it'll be on the TV."

Shit, I thought, *that's all I need. How the hell am I gonna avoid capture if I'm all over the news?*

Cookie turned on the radio and, true to his word, I was the main headline. A news presenter alerted Hampshire County a prisoner had escaped and was now loose somewhere in Newport. He gave my description and warned I shouldn't be approached.

Next, he turned on the TV and, again, the presenter on *Coast to Coast* read out exactly the same spiel.

As he focused on the newsflash, I could see Cookie hadn't changed a bit since we'd last done time together. He had the same dark thatch of unruly hair framing his thin face, was still built like he'd never ceased pumping the weights he'd loved to throw around the prison gym, and his intense brown eyes fixed on me and sparkled childishly as he listened to the TV presenter describe the fugitive in his living room.

"Wanna cuppa tea?" he asked. "There's some hash in that tin next to you—skin up. You ain't going far for at least the next few days. The ferry terminals'll be watched and all cars 'n' lorries'll be searched. They know those are your only escape routes. You'll have to stay in my spare room in another house but it's not far. I'll drive you there in a while.

"What a hornet's nest you've stirred up. I love it."

We smoked the spliff together and drank sweet tea while watching the newscast. Cookie's partner, Julia, came downstairs with one of their two kids and sat down in an armchair beside a Christmas tree covered in fairy lights and decorations with a pile of glittering presents beneath it. It was easy to forget it was Christmas; there hadn't been much festivity in Camphill prison, and it felt surreal to no longer be there.

Cookie kissed Julia goodbye, said he'd only be a short while, then drove me to my new residence. He unlocked the front door, and I followed him up the stairs into a large cold double room. Once inside, he flicked on an electric bar fire and instructed me to only leave the room to use the toilet.

"The other rooms are rented out to different lodgers, but it's best if you stay in here as much as possible."

The room was sparsely furnished with only a double bed covered in a tiger-skin-patterned blanket, a TV on a desk, and a black office swivel chair. Cookie left the room briefly returning with some cold beers then handed me tobacco, cigarette papers, hash, and a lighter.

"Keep your noise down and watch the trouble you've caused on the telly. You'll be safe here until things calm down. I'll come see you tomorrow and we'll figure out how to get you off the island." Then he was gone.

I switched on the TV and found the right channel then cracked open the first beer I'd had in months.

The next news round came up and there I was again: "Escaped prisoner, Christian Austin. Six feet tall, dangerous, not to be approached." The "not to be approached" suited me fine. No mugshot, thankfully, simply the description and then live footage of coppers in bright yellow hi-visibility coats searching cars and lorries at the ferry terminals. It looked very windy and cold. I took another sip of the beer and a toke on the spliff smiling at the irony of being in this warm and cosy room.

I slept well that night, it was the first time I'd slept in a proper bed for many months. I awoke in my own time then washed and returned to my room without encountering any of the house's other occupants.

Cookie turned up after a couple of hours and handed me a coat and a scarf.

"Here, put these on," he said. "We'll go to mine to use the phone and have some breakfast."

Arriving at his house, we found Julia cooking while the two kids were sat in front of the television watching Christmas movies. It felt refreshing to be in this house surrounded by the trappings of Christmas, far removed from the barren cells and cold corridors of HMP Camphill, the nonstop jangling of keys, the loud echoes of voices and shouts, and the many prison officers.

After we'd eaten, Cookie handed me the telephone, and I rang a good friend's number from memory. The phone was answered and I said, "Simon, how you doin'?"

"Yeah, I'm good. Well done, you! You got 'em running around in circles, man. You okay? Do you need anything?"

Ah, good friends. You can't match that kind of response. I always found it insane how I could live in the criminal/junkie world and need to watch my back with so many people and yet there were those I'd spent years with who were completely staunch. I could probably count those staunch ones on the fingers of one hand and Simon was one of them.

"Aww, thanks, Simon. Yeah, could you post me a hundred quid to this address..."

He promised to send me the money right away.

"Nice one. I need to stay here on the island until the heat dies down—my mate here reckons about a week or so—then I'll come see you. Thanks, you're a diamond! Speak soon."

Cookie returned me to my room and the next week found me doing little other than watching the news, drinking beer, smoking spliffs, and simply enjoying no longer being in prison.

* * *

But how had I arrived at this place, a fugitive on a small island off the south coast of England being hunted by most of Hampshire constabulary?

All lives are built from different episodes and experiences and—just as in the pages of this book—each follows one and leads to another, all with varying degrees of significance.

1

Little Man
(Tom Waits)

I first began trying to destroy myself at around eleven or twelve years old. This would have been in 1974 or 1975 and the form this initial self-destruction took was sniffing solvents—glue, shoe conditioner, Tippex thinners, anything I and my equally dysfunctional companions could get our hands on.

Today, at sixty years old, this feels painfully sad. I'd only inhabited my world for a little over ten years and had already decided I wanted to check out due to my life experience up to that point. I'd also already had a brush with the law.

My first memory of stealing is from when I was six or seven years old. I watched my father one morning in the hall of our Clapham flat in southwest London. It wasn't fully light yet, but I saw him take money from the gas meter, put it in his jacket pocket then leave the flat, softly closing the door behind him.

Once enough time had elapsed and I felt certain he wasn't going to return, I went to the meter and copied exactly what I'd seen him do. I quietly drew the cash box out so as not to alert my mother and siblings, emptied a load of coins into my hand then replaced it. Not long after this my mother prepared me and two of my siblings for school and I made a beeline straight for the sweet shop on Abbeville Road.

"Sherbet," I said to the shopkeeper. "Blue, yellow, and red," I said, passing over all the coins I had. He handed me lots of bags of the coloured crystals that I filled my pockets with, then I left the shop.

It wasn't long before I was not only the most popular but also the most conspicuous kid in the school—there'd never been so much sherbet in the playground of Bonneville Junior in all its history.

Not long afterwards, I was collared by one or two of the teachers. My new friends weren't too close-lipped about the source of the sherbet, and I was quickly nicked. Other details of that day elude my memory but, I'm certain that stunt earned me one of my worst hidings up until that moment.

My second recollection of being caught stealing is also worth a mention. It was at this point I should have realised a life of crime was not for me.

I was in the playground of a different school, one that catered for kids whose mums needed to work through school holidays, and it wasn't long before I became bored. Leaving the school I walked along the pavement, the road beside me filled with teeming London traffic. There were some blocks of high-rise flats on my right, and I headed towards them. At the bottom of these flats were many small sheds allocated to various tenants. I began searching around these sheds and soon came across a bicycle, the perfect antidote to my boredom. I pulled the bike out, jumped on it and promptly cycled back to the school playground to parade it before my friends. It wasn't long before one of the playground guardians approached the group of children surrounding me and asked me where I'd got the bike from.

"My friend lent me it," I replied, jumping on the bike to make my escape, "I have to take it back to him."

Later in my criminal career I became adept at escaping those determined to detain me but, at this point in time, I hadn't honed these skills. I was an amateur, so was captured.

The bike was left on the pavement, leaning against the fence and I was hauled off to one of the school offices for interrogation.

"Right, Christian, can you tell me where you got the bike from?" This was directed at me by a tall woman dressed in a light-coloured blouse and brown tweed skirt. Perhaps she was the headmistress as she possessed an air of authority over the teacher who'd pulled me from the playground.

"I was loaned it by a boy from the flats down the road," I responded. "He's gonna think I've stolen it if you don't let me take it back to him."

"We can't just let you ride away from the school. There's traffic everywhere so very dangerous, and you're in our care. I'll ask you again as I don't believe you. Where did you get...?"

There was a rap on the door and a policeman was ushered into the room by yet another teacher.

"Good morning, I was passing the school on patrol with my colleague and noticed my son's bicycle leaning against the fence outside."

Oh crap, I thought, *here we go.*

"This boy says he was loaned it by a boy from some flats nearby," announced the lady in the tweed skirt.

"That's not likely. The bike was in our shed with the door closed so it's more likely this boy took it from there."

"Did you take the bike from a shed?" he asked me.

I could do nothing other than stick with the fabrication I'd already confected, and my defence crumbled when the policeman said I was lying because the bike had been in a shed behind a closed door.

My guardians handed me over to his custody. He drove me to Abbeville Road police station where I was placed in a cell with the door left ajar because I was a minor. My mother couldn't leave work early, so I sat on the cell's bench swinging my legs and reading graffiti I mostly didn't understand until she came to collect me.

2

Another Brick in the Wall
(Pink Floyd)

I wasn't born in the UK. My first breath was drawn in the maternity ward of a British military hospital in Cyprus where my father was stationed—such outposts peppered around the world are considered British territory, hence my holding a British passport.

My father was English and my mother is Scottish. I say "my father *was* English" because he was found one morning in 2005 face-down in his garden pond a few miles outside Downham Market in the county of Norfolk. His shoes had been abandoned on the steps leading from the back door and I know very little else on the matter. I knew him too little, ultimately too much, and I swear I had nothing to do with his premature demise, despite sometimes wishing such an end for him. I even have a solid alibi.

However, I'm getting ahead of myself.

My mother and father were neither wealthy nor poor. They were both single children whose parents *were* financially well off but, for reasons I still don't understand, none of that money trickled down to their children until after their respective parents left this world.

My grandmother on my mother's side attained the position of one of the first female accountants in Scotland—a profession traditionally populated by men—and in the 1940s was able to move from Dundee to London and send her only daughter to study at the prestigious South Hampstead High School. By my mother's reckoning she was a domineering matriarch of Victorian values and as such my mother's freedoms were limited.

I never met my grandfather on my mother's side as he'd died before my birth. I was told he'd been in the RAF during the Second World War, but no more. These stories of my mother's past are as rare as diamonds, so I know little of our family history.

As for my father's parents, my grandfather had worked for the Shell Oil company travelling to different destinations for many years, mostly in the Middle East and the Caribbean, with his wife raising their son wherever they found themselves. When they wanted to speak privately in front of me and my siblings, they'd speak in Arabic.

I vaguely remember these paternal grandparents from my early years, up until they disowned their daughter-in-law and grandchildren after I stole a gold-plated Dunhill lighter during one of our visits to their quaint cottage near Exeter. I'd guess I was six or seven years old.

A bigger scandal than my theft of a lighter, however, was their only son was gay. Gay in the 1960s: a criminal offence punishable with prison time.

And, like many gay men during those times, he needed a smokescreen. Enter my mother. Although, to be fair, I think both my mother and father latched onto the first person who could help them escape their mutually domineering parents, something only possible through early marriage—this family history has been gleaned from my sisters over many years and is not something I was aware of in my youth.

My father then attempted to suppress his feelings towards men by attempting to settle down, producing four children and trying to embrace family life (although the first son, my elder brother, was born with special needs).

This suppression of feelings resulted in unexpected and dangerous consequences. He took to the bottle to keep those feelings inside and this, in turn, led to domestic violence and misery for the whole family.

My mother was beaten, and I heard her screams from the bedroom throughout my early years and often witnessed the violence my father doled out to her. I was beaten, my special needs brother was beaten, we were all beaten, and our home had a permanent atmosphere of tension and imminent violence.

These memories are from our first-floor council flat in Clapham, Southwest London, where my parents settled after their return from Cyprus.

My father was variously a hairdresser and a dog breeder, which meant there were always dogs in our flat and with dogs come dog leads…

I can feel the fear now…and the pain of the dog lead used to beat me. Sometimes the leather end, sometimes the chain end, depending on the extent of my father's drunkenness and wrath. I'd invariably end up trapped in the corner of one of the rooms in the flat, trying to make myself as small as I could but it was futile, the lashes would rain on me and wound me and all I could do was await the abatement of his fury. My father: Despot. Demon. Fucked-up mortal. Fucked up due to the 1960s' UK laws around homosexuality that led him to hide his "aberration" under the guise of a heterosexual marriage with four children. Children who suffered at his whim. I hear my own, my mother's and my siblings' screams each time we are beaten with his fists, kicked by his feet, or whipped with his dog leads.

I remember watching my mother having her nose broken on one occasion, her face covered in blood. She then raised her arms to protect her head and face from the cast-iron kettle hurtling towards her down the hall that smashed into her side and resulted in three broken ribs.

I and my siblings had opened the living room door a crack after hearing my mother's screams and had witnessed this beating doled out by our father. I don't think he realised we were witness to this event he was so consumed with his own anger.

I recently spoke with my younger sister about this incident and she told me our father had straightened my mother's broken nose himself, which I'd either forgotten or not witnessed. My poor mother endured many similar beatings and has never lived with another man since...living the life of a single woman for over fifty years.

These violent incidents and their attendant screams became the soundtrack to the years we spent living in our Clapham flat and, today, I feel many of these events are hidden deep within my mind. There were plenty of them yet mostly I recall them as one single blurred tapestry.

The most consequential outcome of these difficult beginnings was—having learnt the art of self-sabotage from my father—my becoming both protagonist and antagonist in my life over the next few decades.

I emulated my father's actions when stealing that bicycle, those actions I'd witnessed when he'd stolen from the gas meter, but there was also an element of attention seeking in my behaviour. A phrase I've heard many times over the past fifty years comes to mind today: *Negative attention is better than no attention*. Maybe that was the case, or perhaps I was crying out for help but couldn't state outright to anybody what was happening within the walls of our flat.

My father taught me violence is a perfectly normal phenomenon that always surrounds us. I learned I was not worthy of love and was to be hated, which ultimately engendered a feeling of worthlessness deep within me, and this created a kernel of self-hate that festered and almost destroyed me over the next few decades.

My mother, despite all the travails visited upon her, was a foil to this insanity. Over the course of my story, it will be seen she's an incredibly strong woman although these experiences inevitably and irreparably damaged her emotionally.

The doctors said my brother would never walk or talk. My mother defied them by teaching him to do both. I can't begin for a moment to imagine the frustration, sadness, and tears she went through both receiving my father's punishments and bringing up us four children in that Clapham flat, but she did an outstanding job.

She taught us all to speak, walk, run, cycle, read and write. She instilled an insatiable thirst for knowledge in me, a thirst that has never left me and is still alive today. She also tried her best to stop my thumb-sucking, which was a manifestation of my obvious insecurity, but I didn't manage to quit this until my fourteenth year.

Spelling was one of my best subjects while being taught at Bonneville Junior school and I always got high marks in such tests. Art, too, was something I excelled at. I remember copying a drawing of a Tyrannosaurus Rex skull that was very advanced for my years—my teachers couldn't believe I'd managed to copy every nuance of the original.

However, there was an enormous chasm between my learning abilities and my behaviour. I'm certain the teachers had some idea why I was so messed up and, in today's educational institutions, such behaviour would be flagged resulting in a home visit from the social services; not so back then.

Due to my lessons at home, I brought violence to the playground. Often before the first class had begun, a crowd of children would form a circle around me and whichever boy I'd have an altercation with. Fists and feet would fly with total disregard for my personal well-being. Sometimes I'd beat my opponent and often I'd lose but there was always fighting, fighting, and more fighting that, ironically, resulted in receiving more punishment at home from my tutor in violence. As will be seen, a cycle of violence that accompanied me through my formative, teenage, and adult years, always to my own and others' detriment. I was taught the art of self-sabotage by my very accomplished father.

Today I am aware of the existence of two Christians, a duality that has followed me from that terrible Clapham flat: the one created and taught by my mother, the other by my father. Christian 1, devouring all available knowledge and propelling himself towards a successful academic or occupational career; and Christian 2, hellbent on an early grave or a life sentence in prison.

There's still an ongoing war between these two sides of the same coin, a war that becomes progressively easier to win the older I get. This contretemps will become evident as I relate my sixty-year journey.

My early memories of Clapham are nebulous, like indistinct whispers. I have little recollection of my relationship with my three siblings. I guess my focus was on my survival and desperately learning how to negotiate not only my six-year-old landscape but also the contours of my father's erratic psychology…my survival depended on being able to gauge his moods and this skill would stand me in good stead later on in school playgrounds, care homes, borstals, and prisons.

This perpetual cycle of fighting and breaking the rules, interspersed by periods of successful learning and recognition of my intellectual abilities, was interrupted by the Greater London Council deciding it was time the flats we lived in were given a long-overdue renovation.

I have little recollection exactly when my father moved out of our flat. I think my mother had begun divorce proceedings and no doubt I wasn't the only one pleased at this development. It was around this same time my mother was informed she and her brood would be relocated to a town in Hampshire called Farnborough. She was told she could either await the completion of the flats' renovation and return or stay in the house she was being relocated to. This house had four bedrooms and a back garden, and my mother decided to stay. Not only was the move to a more desirable property, but her youngest son was completely "off the rails" and perhaps a geographical cure was just the thing required; however, it was too late. Christian was beyond redemption by this point.

Now, not only did I need to leave my friends behind, but I also had to start anew in a strange town. The first event I recall was my going out on my bicycle (a tenth birthday present) to investigate my new surroundings where I was set upon by a gang of kids around my own age. I'd been oblivious to these kids approaching.

"Hey, nice bike," one of them commented.

"Gissa go on it," asked another.

I placed my foot on the pedal to cycle away from what felt like trouble when the boy who'd spoken first pushed me causing me to lose my balance. I and the bike both fell to the floor and I landed heavily.

"Why'd you do that?" I asked, making to get up onto my feet. A foot pushed me back down and the second boy grabbed my bike's handlebars, dragged it away from me then jumped into the saddle and began to ride in circles around all five of us.

"'Cause it's our bike now, that's why." This was the first boy again, evidently the leader of this small gang.

I watched helplessly as they sauntered away from me, the boy on my bike happily continuing to cycle in circles around the other boys. I remained sitting on the ground, knowing there was nothing I could do that wouldn't result in a beating from four boys.

"Welcome to your new home, Christian," I quietly said to myself, forcing back warm tears.

* * *

We'd moved to a place called Caswell Close on a Greater London Council (GLC) estate named Prospect Estate and never was a more ironic misnomer given. This was a part of London's "overspill" scheme that consisted of moving London's overcrowded population into purpose-built housing projects in the suburbs.

I would be trapped in its tight clutches for the next twenty years.

The GLC estate was populated from every different borough of London. There was a potpourri of different people and accents who had only one common denominator: they were all families who'd left London to start a new and different life. My mother had her own reasons for relocating there and I'm sure there were as many other reasons as there were families. I'm also sure some returned to their eventually renovated flats…we didn't.

My antics at my new school didn't simply continue, they increased exponentially, developing in a colourful arc from delinquency to criminal activity, spurred on by the new friends I eventually did make. Friends who were just as dysfunctional as I was who'd been raised in homes just as screwed-up as mine.

My new school didn't only have a tarmac playground as my former school had, it also had a well-tended field of green grass. One of my first acts of violence that found me outside the headmaster's office awaiting a good caning was pinning down one of my fellow pupils on this lush grass and repeatedly punching him in the face. I've no recollection of why we began fighting but very quickly the predictable bunch of blood-thirsty kids formed a ring encircling us and we flew at one another.

My hapless opponent didn't stand a chance against the pent-up anger raging deep within me. All the beatings from my father, every lash of the dog lead, every punch and kick were lying dormant awaiting this moment, and that livid force now burned down from my shoulders and through my arms into this boy's face. He was pinned to the ground, and I kept punching and punching, completely out of breath from the exertion, until somebody alerted the teachers and they came to his rescue. This was only the first of many altercations while I was at Farnborough Grange junior school and, writing of these events today, I can perfectly see all the reasons I was becoming increasingly out of control. I'm certain my mother also made the connection between my behaviour and that of her now absent husband.

There was still an element of thirsting for knowledge throughout this period. This took the form of reading boys' adventure books by Willard Price: *South Sea Adventure, Amazon Adventure, African Adventure, Underwater Adventure*. Boys' pulp fiction—although I was headed for an entirely different *Pulp Fiction* at this point. Just as reading gave me an escape route later on through my prison years, these books helped me escape my reality when in my Farnborough bedroom in the evenings.

* * *

The event that was to change the course of my young life involved the continuing expansion of Prospect Estate. This whole housing construction project was an endless sprawling carpet of flat-roofed houses, many of which were yet incomplete.

One weekend a few of my friends and I broke through the fence surrounding this construction area and began lobbing stones through the windows of the big machines sat around looking like so many muddy yellow monsters. We smashed all their windows with absolute glee and then fired many red-and-white-spiked surveyors' poles through the aluminium sides of the site cabins. I guess we were so intent on this happy destruction, we lingered far too long.

The police had been called and we were all collared.

3

Road To Nowhere
(Talking Heads)

As if my mother's life thus far hadn't been tragic enough, she was diagnosed with multiple sclerosis. I recall this only in hindsight because I'd imagine my siblings and I were far too young to be privy to such terrible news.

Regardless, she was working fulltime, raising four children alone, and she'd somehow contracted a degenerative disease affecting the brain and nervous system.

Many social workers now came and interviewed me and my mother endlessly. Reams of paper were filed in reports on my home circumstances, the condition of my mother's health, my behaviour versus my intelligence/ potential, and a date was then set for a juvenile court appearance.

There was no doubting I was a highly intelligent kid. But, at twelve years old, I was so uncontrollable it was decided I'd be placed in council care until the age of sixteen years old. To salve my mother's conscience the social workers assured her they'd try and get me placed in a school similar to Dawlish College, the naval training school in Plymouth, Devon. I can't blame my mother for swallowing this line—I mean, Christ, she didn't know where her life might be in six months or whether she'd even still have a life to live.

The whole process of locking me up that day lasted only an hour or so, but it would have far-reaching consequences for me, my relationship with my mother and family, and my behaviour for many years to come.

I wasn't immediately placed in a secure environment. My mother brought me home and a date was set for me to be driven by a social worker to an assessment centre named Fairfield Lodge in Southampton. The day arrived, I said goodbye to my siblings, climbed into an Austin Cambridge with my mother, the social worker, and a suitcase filled with clothes then we set off for my new home.

As well as reading boy's adventure books at that time, I also enjoyed building Airfix models—plastic construction kits of WWII fighter planes, bombers, battleships or tanks. I'd spend hours following the instructions with my tongue poking from the corner of my mouth in concentration, then I'd glue all the parts together until the model was complete and finally, once the glue had dried, paint the thing then place it on my bookshelf or hang it from the ceiling.

I remember my mother bought me an Airfix BMW motorbike kit as a present to bring to the "home" with me. I'll also never forget it was a typically wet English day.

We all three of us entered the assessment centre and were ushered into an office where the head member of staff received us. After some formal greetings and offers of tea, while struggling to hold back my tears, I said goodbye to my mother and was led upstairs by another member of staff to my new room. It contained a single bed, a wardrobe, and had deep blue curtains hanging at the window. This person then left me there and explained I only needed to retrace our steps back downstairs if I needed anything.

I realised this window would look out onto the car park where we'd recently pulled up. I walked over and looked down at the rain falling and splashing on the ground, and saw the Austin Cambridge was still in its parking space. I waited for a final glimpse of my mother before she left.

It took some time for the social worker and my mother to appear. My mother looked up and saw me at the window then waved goodbye as she got into the car. I watched the rear lights recede as it pulled out of the car park and joined the flow of traffic. There was a lump in my throat too large to swallow.

Warm tears spilt from my eyes while cold rain ran down the window's glass, and I clung tighter to my Airfix model and firmly stuck my thumb in my mouth. I couldn't allow the desperate racking sobs to break free of my body as I was determined not to show any weakness in my new home. I was twelve years old and was now totally alone.

Fairfield Lodge held roughly twenty kids, a mix of boys and girls. They ranged in age from ten to sixteen years old, all came from dysfunctional homes or were orphans and ninety percent of them, including me, were fuckups before their lives had barely begun. Each kid was there for assessment to determine the most appropriate care home to send them on to. The staff all seemed pretty okay to me and, unlike the home I'd eventually be sent to, there were no screams in the night from sexual or physical abuse.

Incredibly, the kids aged from fourteen years were allowed to smoke cigarettes and could buy tobacco when they spent their canteen money each week. I'd begun smoking on "Cancer Corner" outside Oak Farm School a few months earlier but was now dependent on handouts from the older kids or on collecting cigarette butts to make roll-ups.

The home was a secure unit with doors and windows always locked. There was, however, a large back garden we could play in with an enormous cargo net hanging from an imposing oak tree not far from the back fence for swinging and playing on. I noted this with interest.

This cargo net was perfect for my first escape from care. Along with a couple of boys I'd become friends with—Andrew and Robbie—I scrambled up the net, played around a bit then leapt for the back fence. My friends quickly joined me on the other side, and we sprinted off towards the golf course.

Using all our cunning to stay away from the main roads, we eventually found our way to Southampton city centre. When evening came and the light began to dim, we scouted around for somewhere that might have cigarettes, food, and money we could help ourselves to. The boys I'd absconded with were more experienced at burglary and stealing than I was because, up until this point, I'd only been involved in criminal damage, not acquisitive crime.

"Right, where can we get fags, food, and money?" Robbie asked.

"I've no idea," I said. "You're the ones who come from here."

"I know," offered Andrew, "the lido is bound to have all those things. It's only five minutes from here and it'll be closed now."

We made our way to the lido, an outdoor swimming pool, and arrived there within ten minutes. After discovering a means of entry, we scouted the place to ensure no one else was around. It seemed we were alone. There was an open window just above the water level at the blue painted edge of the pool, which meant one of us would need to enter the water and see if it could be opened.

"I'll do it," Andrew volunteered. "Just keep an eye out and warn me if anyone turns up, yeah?" He quickly stripped to his pants and entered the water.

Robbie and I kept our ears and eyes open while he swam to the window and tried to open it enough to climb within. Security guards and camera technology really weren't common in the 1970s, so we weren't disturbed.

There was a clicking sound and Andrew looked up at us both from the water and smiled.

"Yes, I got it," he whispered.

He opened the window a couple of feet below us and climbed in.

Within moments he reappeared.

"Here, grab these."

Andrew began passing cartons of cigarettes up to us. We reached down and grabbed them then he returned shortly with carrier bags full of sweets, fizzy drinks, and food—pasties, pies, and sandwiches. He passed these up then climbed back out through the window and into the pool.

We pulled him up from the pool edge and he quickly got dressed.

"There's some money in the bags as well. I didn't bother with coins."

Leaving the same way we'd entered, we headed towards the large central park area where we'd be less visible to passing traffic, especially police cars. My friends informed me we were close to Southampton's Civic Centre, the administrative hub of Southampton and the location of the police station and the cells we were determined to avoid.

A road ran through the park so we followed it, soon encountering rows and rows of modular metal-framed market stalls set up. Most of them were skeletal frames while some had fake grass laid on them ready for fruit and veg traders to place their wares on the following morning. We collected some of these blankets of fake grass and made a shelter around one of the modules then smoked cigarettes, ate some food and sweets, and drank fizzy drinks. After counting the notes, we found we had thirty or forty pounds between us.

Using the fake grass blankets above and below us we spent a night sleeping restlessly then left our temporary base as dawn broke. We wanted to be gone before the market traders arrived as we knew this would result in our downfall.

I decided I was going to head back to Farnborough to see my friends. We split the proceeds between us, and I said goodbye to Andrew and Robbie and wished them both luck.

* * *

I caught a train to Farnborough and headed straight for my mother's house then walked in through the back door as if I'd returned from a day at school.

"Hi," I said when my mum entered the kitchen. I'd arrived home hungry so was making a sandwich.

"Christian, you scared the life out of me! What are you doing here?"

"I ran away with a couple of the other boys. We went to Southampton first but then I decided to come home. I don't like it there. I wanna come home."

"But you can't live here anymore. You know that. The courts have said you need to stay in care until you're sixteen."

That was the first and only time I went back home after absconding. My mother cooked me some dinner and then called the police.

The car pulled up into the same car park my mother had dropped me off at a few weeks previously. I have no real idea what I expected to happen when I arrived home but my mother calling the police probably wasn't on the list. At this point, she had a faith in the system and the way things worked. It would prove this faith was much misplaced.

* * *

There were four of us—Billy, Danny, Smudge, and me. We'd had enough and had decided tonight was the night we'd escape.

As if the muffled cries of Paul and Kenny being sexually assaulted by the night watchman most nights weren't reason enough to want to leave, Mr. Mitchell's appearance in the early hours of that morning, lashing out at anyone unfortunate enough to be within range of his leather belt, had strengthened our mutual resolve to abscond. Sure, we'd all been deemed uncontrollable delinquents and been removed from our homes, but that didn't justify our being treated this way and surely didn't give our 'carers' *carte blanche* to do whatever they wanted to us.

The reason for Mr. Mitchell's 3 a.m. visit to the main dormitory was a late-night burglary. The tuck shop had been broken into, sweets, crisps and chocolate had been stolen, and he was beyond livid—the dormitory door had flown open, the lights came on in a bright flash, and the school's headmaster had begun screaming for everyone to get out of their beds.

This was Winton House, Winchester, in 1976. My first 'care' home.

We waited for cover of darkness and then left via the rear of the school, slipping out of the back gates and across a railway bridge in the direction of the city centre.

It felt good gaining distance from that terrible place with each step we made. I'd had nothing to do with the burglary of the tuck shop and had no idea who'd been responsible, but the pure anger of Mr. Mitchell was fresh in my mind, and I'd be happy never to see him or his school again.

We approached the bus station and found everything was quiet. It was probably nine or ten in the evening and dark with very little traffic around. We discovered a squat building with a small garden behind it and, while two of us kept an eye out for anyone approaching, the other two crept round the back to try and gain access within.

I found a rusting pair of garden shears lying against the back wall and tried to prise the wood-framed window open. One of the glass panes cracked and I froze but it didn't break so there was no resultant crash of glass on the footpath below. I was able to raise the catch and open the window then I climbed inside.

I heard a brief, sharp, whistle. Stop. Hold everything…including my breath. Someone was nearby and one of the boys was warning me to be quiet.

We were operating like a pack of wolves or wild dogs hunting prey, each of us an independent unit within the pack, each looking out for the others. With good reason, we had no trust in adults or authority and, over the past two years, had become our own teachers—learning how to fight and fend for ourselves in a world we'd been condemned to where it was hard to know who could and couldn't be trusted. I'd been regularly absconding with fellow delinquents over these past several months and, although each escape only lasted for a few days or weeks, each one began with the need to steal money for the items we needed most: food, cigarettes, and sweets.

Another brief whistle gave the "all clear." I climbed in through the window and found myself in a small office. I opened the three desk drawers and, in the last one, hit the jackpot: a cash box. Yes! I drew it out from the drawer, shook it, felt the weight of coinage inside then handed it out through the window to Billy.

"Just gonna find some tools to break it open with and I'll be with you," I informed him as he quietly took the cash box from my hands. I scrabbled about in the other drawers but there only seemed to be stationery and nothing in the form of screwdrivers, hammers, or anything likely to open a locked metal box.

I gave up and climbed back out through the window. Billy was trying to jam the garden shears into the side of the box but struggled to keep it steady.

"Here, let me stand on it to keep it still while you break into it. Don't fuckin' stab me, okay?" I whispered to him. After three or four whacks with the shears, Billy said, "Stay right there…think I got it."

I felt something give beneath my feet and he hissed, "Yes, it's open."

"Grab what's in it and let's go. Quickly."

He emptied the box of its contents, stuffing them into his pockets, and then we left the shadows and crossed the street to join the other two boys. We continued towards the city centre, staying in the shadows where possible and ducking into driveways or alleys whenever we heard a vehicle approach. We were four young teenagers and definitely a target for a police car driving past as our absence from Winton House would have been noted and reported by this time. We headed in the direction of the train station where we jumped the fence and walked along the train tracks to the next, much quieter, station thirty minutes along the line.

* * *

We spent the night sleeping fitfully in the shelter of this station, named Shawford. It was the next station along from Winchester in the direction of Southampton, which is where we were headed. Two of our party hailed from there and, knowing my mother would call the police on me, I agreed on Southampton too. Upon waking early in the morning, we shared an occasional cigarette between us until there were no more then waited for the first train.

We'd counted the proceeds from our theft and discovered we had a little over £300 between us—£75 each. In 1976, this was a king's ransom. We had the equivalent of £500 each in today's money at thirteen/fourteen years old…but no provisions.

"Train's coming, boys," Smudge called out, and we all jumped up excitedly to await its approach. We'd feel a lot safer once we were on board, clack-clacking our way further and further from Winchester and those seeking to detain us.

We paid the guard the sum for four tickets and found ourselves in Southampton city centre within the hour. Once we'd bought some food and cigarettes, we were all laughing and joking, slapping each other's backs, feeling a lot less at risk now we were far from Winton House.

We walked past the Civic Centre with some trepidation and I'm certain our steps would have become faster to escape its glare. The next sight to greet us was the Red Funnel ferry service. I think it dawned on all of us at the same time this was our destination—it feels today as though the Red Funnel sign was flashing at us in glowing neon.

"That's it—the Isle of Wight! Come on, who's up for some of that?"

"Of course!" cried Danny. "Yes—we're on holiday. That's where people go on holiday, right?"

We purchased tickets and were told the next ferry would be in ninety minutes' time, so we went for a stroll along the quayside. After finding a spot where we could hang out and wait without attracting attention to ourselves, we sat on the quay, kicking our legs, smoking cigarettes, eating food and sweets, laughing, and joking. We spent the ferry crossing on the top deck with the raw freedom of the wind and spray spattering our young faces.

The ferry docked in Ryde, and we jumped on a double-decker bus that would take us all the way across the island to Yarmouth. Not one of us had ever been on the island before so we had no idea where to head to…just followed our noses. This was during the summer months so the weather was fine and dry. We sat on the top deck and watched the countryside flash past us outside the bus windows. Cows, horses, and sheep grazed in the lush green fields, giving little attention to the bus as it slid past them, tractors slowed down our passage until they turned into open gateways, and we worked our way across this southernmost island of the UK.

Gradually, a large cluster of buildings appeared on our right-hand side and grew in size until we could discern their purpose. Like long red ships with tall chimneys and windows peppering their sides, these were Her Majesty's Prisons Parkhurst, Albany, and Camphill—a veritable colony not far from the island's administrative centre, Newport.

All four of us were silent as the bus continued west. None of us broke this silence, for we all had a presentiment this was our future laid before us. I'm not sure I knew about these prisons being on the Isle of Wight at that stage of my life, but I was aware of the stories back in the care homes, stories with the names of those who had "come of age" and climbed the hierarchical ladder to Winchester Prison and Portland borstal, among others.

The way UK law worked in the 1970s, delinquent boys (and girls) could not be locked up in a prison cell until the age of fifteen years. Once this age was attained, the magistrates' court could lock one up for a period commensurate with the severity of ones' crimes but, until that time, we could abscond and create mini crime waves as often as we liked only to be returned to the home from whence we'd escaped.

The prison complex became hidden from view as the bus continued towards Newport town and Danny broke the uneasy silence:

"Fuck that for a game of soldiers."

The remaining three of us laughed at this but a sense of unease had swept over me, and it took a while to shift. I'm certain the others all felt a similar sensation. We knew we would eventually graduate to prison… it was simply a case of "when?"

In fact, most of the boys I spent the years 1975-1978 within the council care system with were all waiting for me in the prison estate once I myself came "of age."

* * *

"The Harbour Lights" was the name of the café we landed at once we arrived in Yarmouth. Situated next to the ferry terminal, it had offerings of food, drinks, and pinball and fruit machines—which to us pretty much amounted to heaven. We ordered a huge plate of food each and wolfed the lot down while laughing and beaming at one another. Once the food was gone, we moved to the fruit machines. The lady behind the counter asked, "Why aren't you boys at school?" and we fed her a line about being on holiday with our parents.

"They've gone to the pub and left us to wander around the place and find our own fun," we assured her while asking her to break yet another ten- or twenty-pound note into coins.

"They also seem to have given you a lot of spending money," she added with obvious scepticism.

Had we been a bit less excited by the flashing lights of the machines, we may have done the sensible thing and moved on to a different venue.

Shortly, a couple of policemen walked into the place and stopped our playing on the machines.

"Good afternoon, boys. We'd like to ask you a few questions," announced one of them.

"Like where you're from and why you aren't at school?" asked the second policeman.

"We're on holiday with our mums and dads," I responded, "they're in a pub somewhere here in town and we have to meet them in two hours."

"And where is your hometown?"

"We're from Portsmouth," I lied.

"Do your parents know you're all here in this café?"

I said they did.

"Okay, I feel something isn't right here. You seem to have lots of cash, and I don't believe this yarn about your parents being here in town. You're coming to the police station with us and this lady will tell your parents where to find you *if* they come looking for you, okay?"

We were led outside and loaded into the back of a police van then they drove us to the local police station where they could separate us for questioning and, more importantly, search us.

We all had the paper money stuffed inside our underwear so their initial search in the café only produced hands full of shrapnel—the cash we were feeding into the hungry machines. Now, inside the police station, they instructed us to strip. Five-, ten-, and twenty-pound notes began to accumulate on the tiled floor as the four of us undressed and one of the police officers gathered all the notes as evidence. Next came the tedious questioning in the interview room:

"What's your name?"

"What's your home address?"

"Where did you get the money from?"

"Where are your parents?"

"Why aren't you at school?"

We'd all been trained well so responded only with "No comment" to each question they fired at us. We knew it was pointless anyway—we'd been nicked; four boys were on the missing list from a care home in Winchester, and a bus station office had been burgled one mile and half an hour away from the school they'd absconded from.

After questioning, we were locked in individual cells, then fed some dinner (which was nowhere as good as the food the Harbour Lights café was serving), and I lay down on the hard mattress to try and sleep.

Sometime later, the sound of the hatch in the metal door rattling open woke me and a voice said, "Wake up, you'll be leaving us soon."

Another short while later a key turned in the lock and I was led back to the custody suite where I joined my three friends, all smiling and looking as though they'd also been sleeping off a fruit machine hangover.

We were returned our possessions one at a time—minus the cash—and each of us signed to say we'd received them. We were then bundled back into the police van to be driven to Cowes, the island's main port. I was interested to see how we'd be ferried across The Solent— surely not locked in the van?

It wasn't long before I discovered we'd be ferried across in a police launch. How bloody exciting…and it really was.

This launch was like a huge speedboat with the rear three-quarters of the craft open-plan. There was a simple cabin behind a windscreen at its front end. The captain of the launch called us to the mini-cabin and showed us the navigation screen glowing a bright orange.

"You see the centre of the circle, boys?"

"Yes," we all agreed, completely in awe of this whole thrilling experience, bouncing and sliding across the waves towards Southampton.

"Well, that's us...in the centre. And you see the map moving around us? That's the coastline and all the dots you see are other vessels and obstacles to be avoided. I can navigate just by looking at the screen."

"Wow!" We were all impressed by this and, looking back today, that experience alone made the whole escapade worthwhile.

It was dusk when we'd embarked, and it was growing dark as we approached Southampton's docks. I once again enjoyed the salty sea air and the wind whipping my face, although this time with a distinct absence of freedom. It really didn't matter as these adventures I experienced served a couple of purposes.

On the one hand, they were a wonderful release from the day-to-day ennui of whichever approved school I happened to be residing in at the time and, on the other—unbeknown to me at that time—I was learning the most valuable life lesson ever, one the fellow junkies and criminals in my hometown never learned: that no matter where I am in the world, no matter how little I have in my wallet or my pockets, everything will be fine...I'll be okay.

I one hundred per cent attribute these early adventures as a training ground for my future escapes from my hometown when I'd had enough of the drugs and crime; my following the convoys to various festivals all over the UK in the eighties; sojourns to France, Portugal, or Italy for months with just a guitar or saxophone and a sleeping bag.

I find it ironic it took such a circuitous route to arrive at a freedom those from my hometown never discovered. I've given this plenty of thought since escaping the drugs-crime nexus: had I not become the delinquent youth the authorities felt it necessary to remove from society, I'd probably still be trapped in that hometown looking like the near-skeletons I used to inject drugs with all those years ago—those who never had the experience of absconding from care homes as I did and never learned everything will be okay if you trust and have faith in yourself—or, worse, beneath the ground after a heroin overdose like so many of those I grew up with.

Unlike those former companions and despite 'wasting' the first half of my life in prisons, I've travelled throughout many European countries as well as to North Africa and Asia; lived in the country of Georgia for the best part of a year (until a global pandemic forced me to change countries); learned to speak in different languages—mostly French along with a little Italian and Georgian; I've played music to thousands of people on various stages including the UK's iconic Glastonbury festival; and succeeded in attaining a master's degree in criminological research from University of Cambridge, regularly placed within a list of the top five universities in the world.

* * *

My catalogue of absconding soon brought me before the headmaster of Winton House. I was led into the office and shown a folder packed full of yellow sheets of paper.

"You see all these forms, Austin? Every time you abscond from here, one of these forms is filled out and today I've decided enough is enough. You're being moved next door to Ashbourne Lodge for reassessment."

In some way I felt relief wash over me. I'd also had all I could take of the nocturnal screams and various forms of regular abuse occurring in Winton House. I went to my room and packed my belongings and was then escorted on foot to the big house next door. This place had blocks screwed to the sash windows and therefore could only be opened four inches or so. I spent a month or two there and was then told I'd be going "somewhere you won't want to escape."

This almost turned out to be the case. St. Edward's school near Romsey had thirty horses, stables, and courses on horse management, bricklaying, and carpentry. This is also where I first learnt a little guitar and finally stopped sucking my thumb—at fourteen years old. I was now surrounded by thirty new boys and could no longer deal with the embarrassment of such a childish habit. So, overnight, I stopped.

There was more an emphasis on nurturing the wayward child at this school and the staff possessed an enthusiastic attitude towards the potential for change. There were cinema screenings in the main hall on weekends and even occasional discos where girls from a Salisbury school would arrive to dance and mingle with us.

During the summer months many of the boys interested in the horses would trek across the New Forest for hours on end with capable riders among the staff leading us. We'd be instructed by these leaders when to walk, trot, and canter and those confident enough could jump fallen trees and small hedges. This was so far removed from my previous experience of care homes and I thoroughly enjoyed these halcyon days in the sweltering heat, cantering on my favourite dappled grey, Simba, with the wind in my long chestnut coloured hair—a colour that was the middle ground of the blond hair of my youth changing to the dark brown of my late teens/ early twenties.

I remember a trek where a transit van loaded with bell tents, a small marquee, lots of sleeping bags, and catering equipment preceded the group. When we arrived at the pre-arranged spot on horseback, we'd pitch these tents and decide who would share with who while the staff members erected the marquee and filled it with the paraphernalia required for an outdoor kitchen. We stayed in the forest for perhaps five days and each day we'd all ride out in a different direction leaving one or two members of staff at camp to prepare an evening meal. We'd return from the trek famished, clean up, eat, then collapse into our sleeping bags filled with an exhaustion only a full day's riding can produce.

I stayed at St. Edwards for eighteen months before I got itchy feet and then, along with two other residents, Marcus, and Tommy, decided I'd had enough, and we absconded together. This sounds as stupid to me today as it was forty-five years ago but this penchant for self-sabotage would continue for many more years.

Marcus hailed from Elephant and Castle in London. Like me, he was tall for his fifteen years but any similarities ended there as he was more solidly built, had hair that hung to his shoulders in untameable blonde waves, and buck teeth that seemed to prevent his mouth from fully closing. This gave the impression he was a little simple, but nothing could be further from the truth—his mind was sharp and he possessed a quick wit.

He'd assured us there were plenty of places in his neighbourhood the three of us could stay. We figured the best time to flee would be the weekend because there'd be less staff on duty, and it would take longer for our absence to be noticed. Despite gaining respectable grades in my exams and being held up as a credit to the school (I attained 97% for a CSE in technical drawing, the second-highest grade in Hampshire County), I was itching for adventure. We made sure we had the most important provisions: tobacco, cigarettes, a lighter—the Holy Trinity of any fifteen-year-old delinquent—and some food we'd purloined from the kitchens.

Heading out through the stable yard, I said goodbye to Simba who I felt so much love for...the last I ever saw of her.

On through the stables and beyond to the trail that we always took when going out on a hack. This track eventually led to Plaitford Common where we could walk uninterrupted for miles with only occasional horse riders or walkers to be found. It was a fifteen-mile walk to Southampton where we would catch a train to London, blagging the ticket collector any way we could.

We successfully avoided any scrutiny at Waterloo train station and were then free to roam the streets of London. This station was the last risk for us, the last place our escape plans might be foiled. Then we headed for Elephant and Castle.

We made it to a place that belonged to a friend of Marcus. The next few days were spent meeting some of his friends and hanging out. We wandered around his neighbourhood enjoying this newfound sense of freedom and the wonderful feeling of being in control of our own time with no staff to tell us what to do. We also somehow needed to support ourselves.

After breaking into a couple of places around Vauxhall to earn some cash we decided to raid an off-licence Marcus said he'd done before. He'd nicked a couple of hundred quid from there and assured us it was an easy target. We turned up at the place and Tommy stood guard while Marcus and I went round to the back to find a way in.

We must've been stupid to return somewhere Marcus had hit previously. Before we knew it the place was teeming with coppers. I could hear Tommy crying, "Get off me," and Marcus and I both ran in the same direction straight into the arms of more coppers. They'd seen us looking suspicious from afar and had given us the rope to hang ourselves with.

We were brought to West End Central police station and after a few hours I was shown to an interview room where a legal aid lawyer was already sat at the table.

"Hello, Christian."

He stood up as he greeted me then sat back down and began shuffling through several papers on the desk.

"Okay, I'll explain what will occur once we're called in to the courtroom. You'll be remanded in custody by the magistrates until a Crown Court date can be set, which can take two or three months. This means you'll remain locked up in a remand centre.

"Once we're given a date, I'm certain you'll receive a custodial sentence. Now you're fifteen years old, I'm guessing you'll be sent to borstal. I honestly can't see an alternative outcome and I'm afraid there's no way to sugarcoat it."

* * *

The lawyer was right. At Marylebone magistrates court the following morning, I and my fellow defendants were informed our actions, coupled with our previous criminal records, dictated the charges were too severe to be dealt with by that court so we would be remanded in custody while awaiting a date to be set for a Crown Court appearance.

At the end of the day's court sessions all remanded prisoners were escorted from their cells to a waiting "sweatbox." This was the term given to the white vehicles containing small cubicles for the transportation of miscreants from courts to prisons and police stations and back again.

The sweatbox drove through London, stopping at several prisons to deposit prisoners of different ages—some would get dropped at Wormwood Scrubs, some at Wandsworth, others at Brixton, depending on the route. I was totally new to this game so had no idea then what any of these prisons were called. I was sat on the plastic bench of my small cubicle with a locked door inches from me on my left and a small blacked-out window on my right through which I could view the world I'd been removed from. It was still daylight outside and I could see many people walking the streets.

For the under-twenty-one-year-olds riding this sweatbox the destination was Latchmere House. This was a remand and allocation centre situated close to Richmond, West London. Remand means being incarcerated while waiting for court documents to be processed and delivered by the police and Crown Prosecution Service, and by one's own lawyers for the defence. Allocation refers to prisoners under observation after sentencing to ascertain which type of prison was most suitable for them—potential escapees, control problems, and violent offenders would be allocated to a category B prison; a white-collar criminal would usually be sent to a category C or even category D prison; a life-sentence prisoner, or lifer, would be sent to a category A prison for the first few years of their sentence.

We all stepped down from the sweatbox steps and followed the officers to the prison reception where we were processed. We were made to strip and hand over our clothes and were then searched for contraband. We changed our clothes for a uniform. Unconvicted prisoners—i.e., those who hadn't either pled or been found guilty—were given brown-coloured jeans and jacket with a blue and white striped shirt, convicted prisoners were handed blue jeans and jacket with the same shirt.

"Shoe size?"

This was directed at me, at my own naked self.

"Size nine," I informed the screw.

He drew a pair out and handed them to me along with socks, pants, shirt, the brown suit, and a towel.

"Name and date of birth," said the next screw. "Home address… religion…dietary requirements?"

I answered the questions and was then directed to a booth where I could dress. Once a bunch of us had all received our kit and dressed, we were told to follow a different screw through a door. He allowed us all to pass through, then led us across a large yard and down an alleyway with an enormous fence running along either side. This was my new world; I'd better get used to it. And I did—I became periodically used to it for the next twenty years.

Following the screw, we were dwarfed by robust fences. We had been since leaving the reception building. I use the word "robust" with good reason. I could have thrown myself at one of these fences and it may have given an inch or two, no more. Twelve feet high with large coils of razor-wire atop each of them, these fences and wings and the cells and the dining room I'd be introduced to over the coming days would replace the world I had once inhabited. A world I wouldn't return to for more than a year.

I learned quickly what a dog-eat-dog world I'd now landed in. Fortunately, we were all in individual cells, so I was alone. I made my bed with the bed-pack provided then hit the light and slept. It had been a long day.

4

Too Much Too Young
(The Specials)

I awoke to the sounds of banging and clanging, keys jangling, voices echoing. It was all hard surfaces outside my cell door, nothing to soften the blow. Cell doors were being opened along my corridor and the hubbub grew with each door opened. More and more young men spilling into the corridor and heading for the recess. As I became increasingly familiar with these surroundings, I became less fearful and more confident but, to begin with, I was green and scared, mainly due to my being in the London prisons area and not in the south of England prisons where I would have encountered acquaintances from the care homes.

My door was opened, and I was able to observe my new world.

The first thing I noticed was how many black guys there were, it had been the same on the sweatbox the day before. There weren't many black people in Farnborough, nor in the care homes I'd frequented as they were in the "sticks." This was a new dynamic for me. There had been a similar demographic in Clapham but that was several years ago—my world had become ninety percent white since that time.

All these black guys were speaking in a Caribbean patois. I'd soon get used to this and I'd learn to understand it too. Survival dictates one needs to learn a lot quickly in prison and, if you don't learn fast, you're liable to sink. I couldn't understand back then why there were so many black people in prison, but I wasn't a criminologist in 1978. Now, being familiar with the writings of Löic Wacquant and Elizabeth Alexander, I understand perfectly well why such a disproportionate number of black people were and are incarcerated within the Greater London area.

There is a glaring correlation between the mass incarceration of black people and countries who were heavily invested in the transatlantic slave trade. Using the US, Britain, and Brazil as prime cases, a trend is evident, a trend that has been growing steadily over decades. As an example, in the US "the white-black incarceration gap has grown rapidly in the past quarter-century, jumping from one for four in 1980 to about *one for eight today*," Wacquant, 2009, p. 197 (italics in original). In the US, this trend ensnares large numbers of Latinos as well as blacks.

In all three examples these prisoners are predominately sub-proletariat and are trawled from the ghettos of Brixton and Stockwell, Chicago and Detroit, and the *favelas* of Rio de Janeiro. My contention would be it takes generations, not decades, to eliminate the dark stain of inherent racism from a society and, just as with McDonald's, Krispy Kreme donuts, crack cocaine, knife crime, and reality television, everything across the Atlantic sooner or later finds itself in our laps. Hence the disproportionate numbers of blacks in the UK's carceral system.

In the seventies and well into the eighties each cell in every prison in the UK was equipped with a chamber pot or, in prison parlance, a pisspot. The cell door was locked in the evening, and it wasn't unlocked until morning, except in an emergency. So, prisoners had to piss in a pot during the night and "slop-out" in the morning. I picked up my pisspot and headed to the recess where I discovered a queue of young men waiting to empty their pisspots into a big sink with a tap above it.

The pervasive smells throughout the corridors, cells, and recesses of my new home were overwhelming and stomach-churning, and there was no evading them. They could almost be tasted: the acrid bite of cheap and nasty disinfectant blended with the noxious reek of floor polish, piss, bleach, body odour, and the waft of cooking food drifting insidiously from somewhere nearby.

I observed plenty of screws standing at strategic points around these stinking corridors and recesses. There's always a sense of tension in the air in prisons and the screws have a hell of a job ensuring that tension doesn't spill into violence between two prisoners or, even worse, against themselves—"pressure cooker" is the term most often used, and I've heard no better description.

As in most societies' pecking orders, prisons are about both struggle and dominance. I noticed several different prisoner types early on. A radar for trouble was something I'd had to develop in both my school and care home environments from an early age and this talent would now serve me well.

Firstly, I saw there were those who could be summed up as victims. They'd move aside for anyone who intimidated them, and one could practically smell the fear emanating from their whole person. The next level was almost as scared and timid as the last but—if push came to shove—they could bully some tobacco or canteen goods from the real victims. Next were those I'd regard as floating in the middle. These were followed by those who acted tough and would lean on all previous types but crumble at the slightest sign of aggression. There were also those who could handle themselves, who could easily destroy all from the preceding types, and had the swagger that accompanied that confidence. Finally, there were those who didn't need swagger—these guys had the respect of everyone because they were known drug dealers or gangsters from their respective parts of London. One didn't fuck with them.

I followed this platoon of inmates along the corridor, out into the open and across a yard to the dining hall. All prisoners dined together, which I found surprising, but there were an awful lot of screws around the yard and in the dining hall, probably a ratio of one to ten. However, the deterrent that prevented a full-scale prison riot wasn't the ratio of screws to inmates, it was the hefty prison sentences doled out for such actions. There was a minority of prisoners who didn't give a fuck and would happily become involved in a riot, but these were the nutters. Most inmates had loved ones, families, girlfriends—termed "stakes in conformity" in the world of criminology.

I'd guess there were a couple of hundred inmates sat down eating. They all resided on different wings so the dining room experience was the only time many inmates were assembled and could exchange contraband. After eating, inmates were escorted back to their respective wings and locked in cells. There was little work available and those who did manage to gain employment found themselves in the laundry, the kitchens, or sweeping the various yards, wings, and corridors.

I spent my time reading as much as possible. I don't remember how my book collection began, but I'd imagine I would have borrowed a book from a neighbour—no doubt a not very good book—then the choice would have broadened with my branching further out along my corridor and making new acquaintances. We were all locked in our cells for twenty-two hours per day so I would read a book every day or two. My mother would also send me books through the post, and this was my only real distraction from the drudgery of prison life.

I managed to get into trouble within a week or two, trouble with a fellow inmate.

The problem arose in the dining hall. One lunchtime we were sat down eating and one of this group decided it was time to test me. He said something derogatory to me, which was intended as a test, evidently the moment I had to stand up for myself and gain respect—or forever become a victim. I chose the former. There was a palpable electricity in the air and anticipation on everyone's faces as the contretemps played itself out. This guy was in the fourth or fifth level of the hierarchy and I was a rookie inmate, therefore the outsider.

"Right, I'll see you in the recess," the inmate sneered at me. This was where all fights took place in Latchmere House. An inmate or two would keep dog (keep watch) while the fight progressed with as little noise as possible. I returned to my cell, and I could feel the fear in my stomach. This was the moment—post-fight—I'd either be considered a prisoner who could look after himself or one whose tobacco, food, and canteen money would be open season for all.

The time until our doors were next unlocked couldn't go slowly enough. I wasn't prepared for this, I didn't want to fight this guy, I wished I could be somewhere else at that point. Spending my formative years in Clapham, I was now considered a bumpkin by these Londoners. The moment I opened my mouth and said I was from Farnborough, Hampshire, it was evident I wasn't one of them. My South London accent had been diluted by my time away, so I couldn't pretend I was one of them. The odds weren't in my favour, and I knew I'd be regarded by all spectators as the losing horse in this race.

The stalls were open. The key turned in my door's lock and the race was on. I headed towards the recess, my heart in my throat. I could hear its beating pounding in my ears so much I was deaf to the usual hubbub in the corridor. I turned into the toilet area and there he was—the guy planning on smashing me to a pulp so he could keep his reputation intact and walk with his head held high. He was a similar height to myself, that is around six feet tall, and he was more thickset than me—I've always been slim with not much muscle. I inched towards him. I was no stranger to fighting—after all, I was always fighting in the school playground and care homes. The sense of necessity overtook my fear, and I advanced into the fray.

My assailant threw a fist at me. It wasn't well-aimed and glanced off my jaw leaving a dull ache. I jabbed at his face and missed the mark altogether. A couple more punches were thrown by each of us, and I felt the red-hot pain of his fist connecting with my left temple, then another fist hitting my right shoulder. This was a much weaker punch, which confirmed what I'd already surmised—he was right-handed. Okay, I'd need to watch his right fist more than his left.

We flew at one another again and this time fell into a clinch where neither was prepared to let go. Short but ineffective punches stalled for time while adrenalin-fuelled thoughts flashed through different strategies. I lunged forwards and the weight of my body slammed my contestant into the tiled wall with a blunt thud. The clench was broken so I connected a right followed by a left to his torso that left him open, then I flew at him with a head-butt. I felt pain in the top of my forehead where I'd connected with his cheekbone. This was it. I had him now. All I need do was not allow him any leeway. I'd felt what a blow that head-butt had been, and I could sense the shock from the hushed crowd as they realised I might have a chance at this shitty little title of 'who could hold his head the highest' this afternoon.

He threw another punch at me, but it was wild. I could see he was shocked and surprised that I wasn't the walkover he'd anticipated. I moved forward, going in for the kill. The secret to fighting I learned over the years is confidence. I believe we all enter a fight with apprehension, and all fights are cerebral, physical, and political. This fight was concerned with territory, boundaries, and status in the same way a dog fight is. I landed a right hook to the side of his head, followed through with a jab and then he sealed his own fate while protecting his face and head with his arms:

"Okay, no more. Enough...enough."

It was over. In a few moments and as many words, my position in the hierarchy was established. I'd been scared and had convinced myself he was tougher than me, that I'd come off worst. The confidence had come once the adrenalin, and cortisol began to pulse through my veins.

Back in my cell with the door locked behind me I was jubilant. Prior to the screw locking the door, there was still a chance he could've returned to attack me with a weapon, or with a couple of his friends. Now I was safe and, though I'd still need to watch my back around him, I'd won my first major challenge in prison and would stand out among these guys for the next while as someone not to be messed with—in many ways the most important attribute a prisoner can possess; it meant I got to keep my shit.

* * *

The day of my sentencing in Knightsbridge Crown Court arrived so I was up early, keen to discover what the day held for me. I was quickly ushered into a sweatbox that left the prison to make its drops around central London. Arriving at Knightsbridge, I was handed over to the custody of the court screws who then placed me in a holding cell with other prisoners also anxious to discover their fates.

"Austin, your barrister's here to see you!" came from the jailer opening our cell door. He guided me through several corridors then opened a door to an interview room.

My barrister was standing before a desk and appeared to me like a character from a courtroom drama. He stood a little taller than me and was wearing a silver wig made up of strange curls, plaits, and black bows of silk, a long black gown, and incredibly shiny black shoes. A bundle of papers wrapped with red ribbon beneath his arm completed his legal justification and I felt suitably impressed.

He firmly shook my hand, asked me to be seated, then informed me of the day's likely procedure and outcome.

"Christian, I'll be as honest as I can with you. This doesn't look good. I can see from your past criminal record you've been a thorn in the authorities' side for several years now and, in my opinion—and based on my experience—I think these latest offences will earn you a custodial sentence. Due to your still being age fifteen, borstal is most likely. Generally, a sentence of six months to two years is doled out of which you'd serve a minimum of nine months, depending on your behaviour. I advise you to plead guilty as the evidence against you is overwhelming."

I was entirely in agreement with him. I wanted the fiasco over as quickly as he did so I could get to borstal and start serving my time.

A short while later, I was led up two flights of concrete stairs to the courtroom. Entering a large wood-panelled chamber I saw the judge sat on a raised dais front and centre looking old and sullen with a grey wig on his head. Above and behind him was an enormous royal coat of arms with the crowned lion and unicorn on either side of a colourful shield with *Dieu et mon Droit* etched on a scroll beneath. I was directed to a dock in the centre of the room and there, on either side of me, were representatives of the prosecution and defence. This all looked extremely expensive and pretentious to a young delinquent of only fifteen years. It felt as intimidating as it was supposed to and once the case against me began, I was lost within seconds. Apart from being asked to give my name and date of birth, there was little else I understood.

I was asked whether I pleaded guilty or not guilty and this I understood because I'd anticipated the question. Then they were once again speaking with that clipped British accent you associate with Spitfire pilots in black and white films.

"Will the prisoner rise?" The policeman next to me indicated I should stand.

"Having pleaded guilty to the charges against you, it is my duty with the power invested in me to sentence you to six months to two years in borstal. Take him away."

Despite my barrister and fellow remand prisoners priming me for this likely outcome, I felt a weakness in my knees and a churning in my stomach. Up to two years in teenagers' prison. Not Latchmere House but borstal. I must have been holding a hope somewhere within I'd be given one final chance but, no, this was the end of my freedom for a long time.

I was led back downstairs to the cell and then ten minutes later the door opened again, and I was told I had a visit. The policeman showed me to a booth with a glass screen and my mother was sat behind it. I could see she was upset even though we'd both been warned of this likely outcome. There were no tears—I'd guess my mother had shed her quota of tears back in the Clapham flat as I've never seen her cry since those terrible days.

"I brought some cigarettes and snacks for you and gave them to the jailer. He said he'll give you them after our visit. Try to stay out of trouble and not make things any worse, okay? And see if you can get on any courses…some kind of training."

My mother was always thinking of my future and practicalities while I knew my focus would simply be on my survival in my new environment. I think we both realised the chances of my staying out of trouble were slim although I assured her I'd try my best. All I wanted to do was escape this nightmare, get in the car with her and go home but a different path had been laid out before me long ago back in our flat in Clapham. Possibly even earlier when she had walked down the aisle with that man called my father. Who knows where I'd have been sat at fifteen years old if she'd chosen a different man as her husband? Probably not in the cells located in the underbelly of Knightsbridge Crown Court.

Damn my life, I thought, why the fuck does my life need to be so fucked up? Christ, gimme a break, will you? But there was no Christ, there was no God, there was only this reality—me separated from my mum by a sheet of plexiglass shortly before being driven to Wormwood Scrubs awaiting allocation to whichever borstal was deemed best suited to my temperament.

The jailer said the visit was over, so we said our goodbyes. "Send my love to everyone," I said as my mum left.

That was it. What else could I say? I'd been sent down the drain and wouldn't see any of my friends at home for at least another year. The jailer gave me a couple of packs of Peter Stuyvesant (my mother's brand) and some sweets and this final gesture from my mum made me want to cry again. Jesus, my mum loved me and must have regretted her decision to marry that man because of all the hell he'd created for the whole family. But how do you change the trajectory of disaster?

Once the day's sentencing was finished those of us returning to various prisons were placed back in a sweatbox and driven to Lambeth's holding cells. This was a huge hub with an underground car park capable of holding many huge sweatboxes, each of which could in turn hold twenty prisoners. This is one of those places Joe Public walking the streets above has no idea exists. Only those privileged enough to be in the system were privy to such knowledge. The King's Cross station of London's penal system.

I found myself to be one of the youngest in a cell of ten or twelve young men from London. They could all relate to one another's different areas and all spoke a common tongue. I was an outlier in more than one respect. I was fifteen years old and knew none of these people, or the criminal friends they found they had in common as they chatted. I was out of my depth, and I had the booty everyone wanted: cigarettes. As soon as they were spotted everyone wanted a cigarette and, despite trying my hardest to share one or two or three, it was impossible. In an instant I had no cigarettes, not even the packets. They were all stolen from me, and I could do nothing against these older men ranging from sixteen to twenty-one. I wasn't feeling so tough at that point, and yet again I could feel tears rising and wished I was at home with my mum and my sisters, but instead I was on my way to Wormwood fucking Scrubs' B-wing with a bunch of guys who'd just turned me into a victim. After the lifebuoy of seeing my mum I'd once again entered the ocean of sink-or-swim, and I'd better get over the fear and get my shit together. This would need to be one step at a time and my radar for danger needed to be finely tuned. Necessity and survival made this my new priority.

The reception into The Scrubs as it was known wasn't dissimilar to that of Latchmere House. Similar questions from the same faces in the same uniforms with the same detached attitudes. Some of these screws had been doing this shit for years and it showed. They were now on the slow slide down to their pensions and couldn't give a toss. Then there were the other faces, those of the inmates—some scared, young, fresh-faced like me. We were kept separate from the over twenty-ones. This was a prison for adult males situated not far from White City, northwest London, and named after the parkland it was surrounded by. B-wing was built from the same red London brick as all the other wings and was dedicated to young offenders awaiting allocation to different borstals.

We were each handed our new uniforms—this time mine was the blue of the convicted prisoner—and our bed-packs and were then led through a labyrinth of corridors and locked doors to our respective cells. I was shown into my cell and my name card was placed in the slot outside the door with my religion and "Borstal Allocation" marked on it. There were two beds in the cell and a window high up the back wall. A few minutes later another prisoner was shown in and, unbelievably, it was one of my aggressors from Lambeth's holding cell.

The moment the door was closed, he sought to establish his supremacy over me and my possessions, current and future.

"When you get paid all your shit's mine, you hear?"

Instant rage and indignation filled my being—because this guy had watched me crumble before a gang, he assumed he could dominate me too. A fire raged inside me, and I had supreme confidence I'd take this little shit down in seconds. I had to, my whole future in this cell and all subsequent prison cells, dining halls, and corridors depended on my actions in that moment. I threw myself at him with fists flying. There was no escape for either of us and he quickly realised he'd made a grave error. I remained above him, pummelling him with punches for as long as it took for him to cede defeat. I only retreated once I was certain we had an understanding. I could see in his eyes he understood, and he was scared.

It was at this point that I could have taken advantage of our isolation in this cell together. I could have beaten him senseless as my revenge for the gang behaviour at Lambeth, or I could've turned the tables and demanded his possessions were mine. But I didn't. I didn't operate that way.

By this point in my life, I never went in for that stamping on the opponent's head once they were down, that gratuitous violence. Violence was merely a protective mechanism to be used when cornered, not for bullying. Neither was the leaning on somebody for their possessions my kind of thing. Today, I'd put that down to my mother instilling a sense of fairness in me from an early age.

Aside from this incident, there is little else I remember from those days in the Scrubs. I was told by fellow inmates that I'd probably be allocated to Portland borstal as it was remote and considered the "dustbin of the South." I'd be deemed a control problem due to my absconding record and my general attitude towards screws.

They weren't wrong.

5

Ball and Chain
(Janis Joplin)

All seven wings of Portland were named after different luminaries from the naval tradition. The house we'd arrived at was Hardy House, the induction house. There were also Nelson, Grenville, Benbow, Raleigh, Drake, and Rodney. Over the next four years I would become familiar with three of these houses, with the addition of one extra: E-Hall. This was the name of Portland's solitary confinement block.

Hardy House was a vast improvement on Wormwood Scrubs. Firstly, it was much more modern with cleaner recesses, cells, and dining facilities. It was the wing where we would reside for the first week or two while being taught the rules of the borstal and shown its grounds. During these first days, the chaplain would visit each new prisoner to determine his state of mind and the degree of his religious belief, and each prisoner would also see a welfare officer who'd ask whether any urgent family phone calls might be needed, and whether anything was pressing heavily on the individual's mind.

After the first or second day of induction, all of us new receptions were formed up in a phalanx outside Hardy House. Next these ex-military screws would teach us how to march as though we were on a parade ground. It was hilarious. Fifteen to twenty lanky, skinny, medium, short, fat, and round teenagers playing toy soldiers. I can still hear the orders being barked at us in a strange clipped and broken way:

"Party, 'shun!" which translates to "Party, attention."

Followed with, "By the left, q-u-ick march. 'Eft... 'ight... 'eft...' ight...'eft...'ight..."

I remember this was exactly the way it was pronounced, as though the screw was a staff sergeant leading his platoon off to battle. To this day, I can still march as well as any squaddie on Sandhurst's parade ground. This whole new experience was based on the military: having to call all screws "Sir," the forced circuit training in the gym, the squared-off bed-packs and inspections, the shining of shoes, and losing points and privileges for any infractions. It seemed to me every squaddie who left the forces received a letter asking, "Have you considered a career in the prison service?"

The most exciting addition to my life though was the presence of a full-size snooker table, which was a feature in each of the seven houses. Those who wished to could become good snooker players over the coming months and this would translate into becoming fantastic pool sharks after borstal. I've been a reasonably good pool player all my life and it's down to those initial years of playing snooker in Portland.

Since my time spent in Scrubs, I was a much more confident prisoner and my swagger had returned. The days of having my cigarettes stolen in the Lambeth holding cells were behind me and I could walk with my head high knowing anyone wanting to mess with me did so at their own peril. After a few inevitable altercations, I established myself as a capable fighter.

We were teenage boys with high levels of testosterone vying for our spot in the hierarchy. Just as it had been in Latchmere House, being called out to fight was a very public affair involving hours of lock-up knowing you were entering the circle of spectators in a gladiatorial fight for supremacy. I remember having at least one of these moments in the recess on the third floor of Hardy House before entering the borstal proper, possibly two. I came out victorious and thereby achieved my rank in the hierarchy as opposed to being a "sap" on the wing—the worst affront one could hurl at a fellow borstal boy.

Both the climate and environment of Portland were a completely new experience for me. Outside the stone building, a heavy, damp shroud of fog increased my sense of isolation, and I often couldn't see more than two yards beyond the windows. The nights were cold with blustery winds crashing off the huge building, seeming to challenge its very foundations, and changing direction at the slightest whim. I was too far from the breaking of waves I knew weren't far below to hear them but could always hear the incessant caw-cawing of seagulls that only abated at night.

After induction week, due to my age, I had to attend classes in the education block and, while I was there, managed to achieve a couple of O-levels and got reasonable marks in both maths and English. I was then allowed to leave school early and start a vocational training course working towards a City & Guilds in welding.

More influential than my traditional education and vocational training, however, was the personal education within my cell during lock-up. I was a voracious reader and would read three or four books per week. I also kept a notebook dedicated to words I was unfamiliar with. At the end of each week, I'd take a dictionary and write down the definitions of the words several times as a mnemonic. In this way I increased my vocabulary greatly. I would also write stories in my cell and have the education department's English teacher give me feedback on my writing. I now wish I'd continued in that pursuit, but another passion was about to enter my life, one that would consume me through to today.

I came across a book titled *The Rudiments and Theory of Music*. I opened the book and found pages and pages of esoteric symbols sat upon or between lines and decided in that moment I wanted to learn how to read music.

The orthodox route to take was to be given a recorder or similar beginners' instrument and be taught to read and play slowly but simultaneously by a teacher. I remember having two or three such lessons in Oak Farm School before I was expelled and then placed in care.

I painstakingly went through each chapter of this fabulous book and learnt what time values different note-heads represented, the relationship to pitch that each line and space of the musical stave denoted, and I learned about sharps, flats, and natural symbols and how they would change the pitch of a note. Key signatures, cadences, the cycle of fifths—I studied all of this but had no instrument to play or hear the sounds on. I somehow knew the time would come when I would want to put this knowledge to use. For as long as I could remember, I'd been obsessed with listening to music and in this moment a determination to become a performing musician grew within me. Little did I realise then this driver would become my eventual salvation.

Another aspect of my personal education came from the fictional books I was reading. There were many books around UK subculture doing the rounds that were absolute rubbish, but they contained many of the first references to drugs I encountered. Then there were some other, much more interesting books that are classics within their genres—Hunter S. Thompson's *Hell's Angels* and *The Great Shark Hunt*; Jack Kerouac's *On the Road*; Allen Ginsberg's *Howl*. I was embracing these counterculture books during my formative years. Each time I'd hear the name of another mysterious new drug, I'd research its classification and its effects in the *Encyclopaedia Britannica*. Looking back to my borstal days, two things become evident to me: I was determined to become a musician, and I was determined to become fucked up on drugs.

I also managed to get in some scrapes during these first few months. Saturday mornings were reserved for the governor's inspection followed by all prisoners having to clean, scrub and shine the floor of every landing and room, every toilet bowl, and each copper and brass pipe. Every recess in Portland borstal had such glowing brass and copper pipes you could easily see your reflection in them.

After breakfast each Saturday our cell doors were left open for a period so we could sweep and mop our floors. Once this was done, our doors would be banged up and we'd then need to fold bedding into a neat box-like bed-pack, shine our shoes, and generally have our cells dusted and ready for inspection. Then, visiting and inspecting one cell after another, the governor would try to find dust in the most unlikely places, criticize the shine of your shoes, or pull your bed pack apart mumbling what a shambles it was. Privileges were at risk if anything was out of place. Once the inspection was over, it would be time to clean the whole wing before lunch was served in the communal dining hall.

One Saturday my case officer made an unreasonable cleaning demand of me. A case officer was the screw who'd been allocated to write reports on an individual's progress and behaviour. This young screw who demanded I clean the snooker room floor with a green scouring pad was my case officer. I didn't like him, wasn't impressed with his reports on me thus far, and he seemed not many years older than me, which made taking orders from him difficult to bear. I told him I wouldn't do it, at which point he uttered the ultimate screw's threat:

"That's an order, Austin."

Oh bollocks, here we go, I thought. I knew, in the first place, I wasn't prepared to get down on my knees and scrub the floor and, in the second place, take orders from this little prick. There was only one place I was going: E-hall.

"Look, if you want it done so bad, do it yourself, 'cause I ain't," I assured him.

"Austin, I'm ordering you one last time..." He was loving it as we both knew I was going down the block, would miss my association, and would probably lose some remission if I didn't comply. *Fuck it,* I thought—*I don't give a shit.*

"I told you, I ain't doing it and, while I'm at it, you're a little prick. Go on, fuck off." With this parting shot I walked back up the stairs to my cell and slammed the door behind me.

Next morning, I was given the charge sheet and led to E-Hall where two screws were waiting at the open door of the building. I was handed a bed pack and told to run. The two screws ran with me, screaming all the way to intimidate me until I reached the cell with the open door. I flew into the cell, the door was slammed behind me, the sound of the screws' footsteps diminished, and I was left in silence.

That's the singular thing I recall most from my visits to E-Hall, how quiet it always was. There were screws' houses on the other side of the wall—I knew that because myself and some other prisoners had recently been on a detail creosoting their garden fences, and occasionally I'd hear an ice cream van's jingle and the sound of children's voices.

Children's voices! If there was one sound that could draw a multitude of emotions from within me, it was that of children's voices. The sound would sometimes leave me with a beaming smile across my face and at others with tears streaming down it, especially when I'd been slung into solitary confinement. There were many occasions when I was in any one of the different cells in that block, so many, in fact, that I could never remember which was which. I recall one Christmas I was sent down there.

I've no recollection of what my crime had been. I recall the governor walking along the cells, asking how each prisoner was behaving and then giving them an amnesty and allowing them back up on the wing. As stated, it was usually so quiet in E-Hall you could hear a pin drop, so I heard every echoing word spoken by the governor and the screws. This was looking good. I heard them approach ever closer and release more of my companions. Then they were outside my door, keys jangling in the lock. The door opened and there he stood: my nemesis.

"How's Austin been behaving then?" he asked the screws, eyeing me up and down with scepticism.

Even the block screws must have been infected with some festive spirit because they responded with, "He's been conforming, Governor, yes."

"Well, one more week ought to do it, then."

He turned and walked away, and the door was closed on any chance I'd had of Christmas back on the wing.

My first response was anger. Anger at the governor and the system. The screws had given it their best shot to have me freed, as they knew the real me—we'd share banter each time I was sent to their domain, and they knew I was an okay kid who was angry at the system that had placed me in borstal and angry at a life outside that kept seeing me nicked. They'd seen kids like me repeatedly for as long as they'd been in the service.

After the last of the prisoners was freed, the governor left the block, and I heard the door slam behind him. The screws on duty returned to their office and silence once again descended on E-Hall. I felt sick I'd been excluded from the Christmas amnesty. I stood on the heating pipe that ran across the back wall of the cell and gripped the cold metal bars of the window so I could watch the snow softly falling in the yard beyond. Children were laughing on the other side of the wall, playing in the snow, excited it was Christmas time. The huge wooden trestles used for sawing firewood were covered in snow, as was the railway sleeper laid across them. During the daytime us prisoners would be out in that yard, one on each end of a huge saw. One boy pulled his end of the saw while the other allowed it to move away from him, the other would pull his end, and so on. Then it was chopped into pieces with an axe by a trustee prisoner. This was firewood for the elderly, and I had enjoyed the physical exertion.

Tears began to roll down my face. "Fuck off, self-pity!" I wanted to scream but the tears continued, my nose began to run, and the silent scream was all through me—that terribly loud scream that was often close to the surface but could not be voiced for so many reasons.

I find it amazing how resilient I was when I scan back to those years. I was fifteen years old, and the inchoate scream was there inside me, yes, but it was never there for an extended period. I had a fantastic facility for suppressing all the shit that came my way. I'm not implying that was a healthy option. As will be seen, when the suppressed shit rose to the surface it usually had devastating consequences. But I developed some powerful coping mechanisms during these formative years.

Once this stint in the block was over, I returned to the welding workshop and tried to concentrate on learning skills as I was trying to prepare for a career in the real world, one that would see me break away from the cycle of crime, courts, and prison.

I attended the training workshop each day and I remember enjoying my time there. It felt to me what it was—the beginning of a transition from boy to man: I was no longer in school and was working. The course was entitled Fabrication Welding, which involved not only learning welding but also the attendant engineering skills necessary for such a vocation. Many of these skills have stood me in good stead over the years and helped me earn a living so my time spent there wasn't wasted. I completed the course and attained the certificate after another month or so.

* * *

The metallic rattle of keys and bolts followed by the borstal's huge double gates creaking open rang like a sweet melody as I stepped towards freedom. The gates opened further and the warmth of the morning sun bathed me in its bright wash.

That's the last time I'll ever hear the sound of those keys, I told myself with smug satisfaction, then crossed the road to greet my mother and younger sister, Camilla.

I dropped my bag to the floor, took my sister in my arms and gave her a strong hug.

"Christ, am I happy to see you," I said, kissing her cheek, "and glad to put that place behind me."

"Hi, Mum. Good to see you."

I pulled my mother close and wrapped her in my arms, pecked her cheek, and asked how the journey had been.

"It was fine. We started early so were halfway here before the traffic was bad. How are you? You look as though they've been feeding you well."

I threw my bag into the back of the car while Camilla climbed in the opposite side then I faced the sun and stood for several moments before climbing in. With my eyes closed I breathed deeply of this fresh, slightly cold morning air…free air. It felt wonderful and all I wanted was for us to put distance between me and the borstal.

Without casting a glance back at the stone walls or wooden gates, I jumped into the car.

"Let's get out of here," I said, and my mother pulled away.

The journey home was filled with optimism and assurances to both of them that I'd straighten myself out and wouldn't get in trouble again. But soon events would occur that would ensure I'd continue with a criminal lifestyle for another twenty years. Events that were unforeseen by me and that were much bigger and much stranger than any of us could have imagined.

For now, however, I was free and there was a completely new energy in Totland Close and all over the UK. It was called punk rock.

I'd been listening to this new music in the record room of Nelson House where inmates could have vinyl records sent in or brought on visits.

Our favourites were, *Borstal Breakout* by Sham 69 and *Gotta Getaway* by Stiff Little Fingers—perfect for all of us angry incarcerated young men. I'd also been listening to the Sex Pistols, The Clash, Angelic Upstarts, Buzzcocks, Patti Smith, Iggy Pop and the Stooges, and a whole gang of other bands falling into this rebellious, highly charged 'Fuck the System' genre. Fuck the system is what we were all about and punk came along at exactly the right moment for us.

For some, their teenage years were Bill Hayley "Rockin' Round the Clock" with his Comets or Elvis Presley gyrating his hips to salivating teenage girls; for others it was Sonny and Cher or the Mamas and the Papas or the Doors' Jim Morrison teasing crowds with his onstage "Did ya see it?" antics. My mum was crazy over Johnny Ray in her day. For my generation and, even more so for my delinquent criminal fraternity, the nihilism of punk rock came at exactly the right time. The spitting, the rage, the ripped clothes, the safety-pin piercings, and the curled lip of Sid Vicious. This rebellious new subculture was the product of those times with their meteoric and simultaneous rise of Thatcherism and unemployment, the looming troubles with trades unions, and the new forms of state-sponsored violence that attended these historic events.

Would my life have turned out differently in the absence of punk? I doubt it: I was on a collision course towards the life I was destined for. Destined by the fuckups of my father, the care homes, and learnt behaviour from my contemporaries.

The punk scene was anarchic and fun, sure, but it wasn't giving me or my messed-up friends the kind of teenage kicks we were after. It wasn't anarchic *enough* for us. We'd hang out on Chelsea's King's Road with other punks and dress up in home-made bondage trousers, spit, get hammered, and generally be a nuisance but what we most wanted was to drive cars like the guys a few years older than ourselves. So, stealing cars was next on our agenda.

With hindsight, I don't know how we weren't killed or seriously hurt, or how we didn't maim any members of the public. Me and my reprobate Farnborough mates learnt to drive by nicking cars and crashing them until the crashes became less and less frequent and the cars less and less wrecked.

Around this point my mother suggested I go and spend some time with my godmother in London who I hadn't seen for a long time. We both knew I'd soon be banged up again if I remained in Farnborough. She was always coming up with new ideas to change my errant ways, but my father's legacy fucked it up every time.

6

London Calling
(The Clash)

A couple of days later I was standing outside Willesden Green tube station with a suitcase awaiting the arrival of my Godmother, Angie. It was late summer, and I was pleased to be away from Farnborough and its constant mayhem, pleased to be in the bustle of London, which still had a slight feeling of home each time I returned. I was sixteen years old, and I wasn't in borstal, which was plenty to feel good about.

My mother had told me Angie was a fashion photographer, and I'd soon discover that she was of Irish descent, loved to party and get high, she was gay, and she had a crooked kind of smile with something whacky going on with her front teeth.

The car pulled up and I got a glimpse of her smile and a huge pair of dark glasses. I threw my suitcase on to the back seat then she jumped out and gave me a huge hug, which felt absolutely genuine.

"Oh—my—God! Look at you!" she exclaimed. "Wow, you've grown so much! We're gonna have such great times together," she said enthusiastically as we pulled out into the traffic. She said we were going to visit Toni in West Hampstead.

"You remember Toni, right?"

Oh yes, I remembered Toni—a goddess.

Angie pulled the car into the kerb outside Toni's flat and shut down the engine. She jumped out and led the way up the entrance stairs of a terraced red brick building with three or four floors, and gleaming, white-painted windows—Toni was evidently doing well for herself. Angie pressed the intercom buzzer and shortly Toni's voice responded then the door opened.

We entered the flat and the voice called us into the kitchen. Toni was standing on a kitchen chair changing the ceiling light bulb.

"Hi," she said to Ange, then to me, "Hi. Wow, you've grown up!"

She was gorgeous and I was smitten immediately. She was twice my age but looked to be in her mid-twenties. She wasn't so tall and had dead straight blonde hair cut in a bob. I offered to help and changed the light bulb for her, then she led the way to the lounge and offered us drinks.

We sat down and I took in my surroundings. There was music playing on the stereo and I'd imagine it was Stevie Wonder—his *Talking Book* or *Inner Visions* album are the most likely candidates. I was introduced to a lot of music by Angie and Toni during this period, the beginning of my education into real music, not the punk music I'd been listening to for the past year or so. Toni returned with the drinks, sat down, and asked me what I'd been up to, though I guessed she already had a good idea from conversations with Angie.

"Shit, getting into lots of trouble, I guess," I responded. "Care homes, borstal, stealing cars, police…" My voice tapered off and I fell silent. I realised I had nothing positive to say.

"So," Angie said. "We've been planning a visit to your father's in Norfolk. We'll leave tomorrow. You all good with that?"

I agreed it sounded fine with me. I'd seen my father sporadically since my mother had separated from him and knew he was usually living in different parts of London with friends. However, he'd recently moved to Norfolk to be closer to his ailing parents.

The following day, Angie and I got up and grabbed something to eat then drove to Toni's. When we arrived, she was giving her daughter, Deana, instructions on how to survive for a week on her own. Deana was a year or two older than me and we'd shared a kiss in a field at my father's place near Alton last time I'd seen her. We'd been around twelve years old then, shortly before I was placed in care. She was a bright girl with a pretty face and slim frame but, unlike her mother, wore her straight blonde hair all the way down her back in a ponytail.

Toni jumped into the front passenger seat and Angie pulled away heading towards Finchley Road then north out of London. I remember the weather was sunny and bright—it was late summer/early autumn, and the car windows were all wound down. Music was playing on the stereo, Angie and Toni were sharing spliffs all the while and the car wove through the London traffic until we left it behind and hit the motorway.

My father lived in Downham Market, a small town not far from King's Lynn, and within a couple of hours we arrived at a remote house in the countryside outside the town. Angie pulled into the driveway and honked the horn a few times to announce our arrival. The three of us jumped out of the car and in a moment my father had walked out from around the back of the house.

I don't remember how I felt about my father at that time; whether I loathed him, whether I was still terrified of him, or whether I was indifferent. I'd guess I thought because he was my father I should have some kind of respect for him. Perhaps I felt this could be a new beginning for our relationship now that I was older.

"Hey, perfect timing," my father said. "I only recently got back from town. Here, let me help with those bags…"

He smiled at me and grabbed the holdall I'd just pulled from the boot.

"Here, follow me, and mind the steps."

Leading the way, he retraced his footsteps and we all followed then entered the house into a large kitchen. He placed my bag onto a long bench and gestured for Angie and Tony to place theirs in the same place.

There was an open wine bottle on the kitchen table and my father pulled some glasses from a sideboard then filled them with the ruby liquid, handing us each a glass.

"To friendship," he toasted, and we all clinked glasses.

Although my memories of my father were tainted by the domestic violence he'd doled out to my mother, my siblings, and me in Clapham, I do remember he was always the good host when in the company of his friends. I feel he was well liked by many of his friends up until the point he'd move onto drinking spirits...this would change him into someone else. For the moment, though, he seemed an amiable guy having a couple of glasses of red.

"I'll show you around."

It was a huge house. Not so tidy nor messy, but lived in. My father, Nick, or Nicholas to the three of us, gave us a guided tour of the ground and first floors, showing us our sleeping places, and then the garden that was more like a field it was so large.

And we were introduced to some dogs—a trio of Irish Wolfhounds and a pair of Belgian Shepherds. My father always had dogs around and they were often Wolfhounds or Salukis, although many other breeds too.

We were all tired after the drive from London so, after a few more glasses of red wine, we had an early night. Angie and Toni went to their respective rooms and I joined my father in his room. There was a double bed and a single, so we said our goodnights and I slept in the single.

The next morning, we headed for Downham Market and wandered around the town for a few hours, dipping into antique shops, looking at paintings and ornaments, and all kinds of stuff that I found interesting but wouldn't be interested in buying myself; I was a tough and dangerous sixteen-year-old punk rocker sneering at such pretentious crap.

We had a drink in one of the pubs in the market square and then went back to Nicholas' house to get washed up before going out for an evening meal and more beers. Throughout the past couple of days and all of that day I'd been steadily becoming more and more attracted to Toni. In my experience, when one is a teenager, older women are tremendously appealing. Perhaps this is due to their being more experienced in matters of sexuality, or perhaps it's something more Oedipal and Freudian than

that. Regardless, I was falling for this stunning thirty-six-year-old woman whose daughter was a year older than my sixteen years.

I feel I need to explore the dynamics of this relationship between myself, Toni, Angie, and my father, and their development so I can maybe have a greater understanding of what eventually transpired between us and how it affected us all. The next couple of days' events would influence my life for the next twenty years and would leave permanent scars on the four of us with far-reaching consequences.

The following morning, I was up early, and I entered the kitchen to find Toni at the cooker with her back to me.

I silently approached her and wrapped my arms around her waist from behind and nuzzled my lips into her neck. I'm not certain today but she may have heard me approach.

"Christian, what're you doing?" she said, and the sixteen-year-old practical virgin declared his love. Very corny. I should probably add at this point that Angie and Toni had been lovers perhaps ten years previously but were now friends; apparently, after a gay fling, Toni had decided she preferred men, much to Angie's disappointment. The world this naïve young Christian had entered was fraught with all kinds of weird interconnectivities and new experiences, but they would all add to the fucked-up-ness that would guide my star for decades to come. Fuckups bestowed upon me by those who were supposed to be my carers and role models.

At sixteen years old, I remember, I felt I was an adult. I'm certain many of us do at that age. I had a set of dubious principals I lived by and had proved I could stand my ground when challenged by those who were considered tough in the world of care homes, borstals, and prisons. I wouldn't take any shit from the police or prison officers who were sent to control me, and I felt strong enough to deal with whatever life threw at me. The truth, however, is that I was still a child. The tough kid who could fight off any attacker in the playground or the prison wing or exercise yard was a scared kid who had never received the love that is tacitly promised in the social contract between parents and children.

I continued to make it clear to Toni how attractive I found her and it became a kind of flirtatious joke between us. The next couple of days were pretty relaxed. We were blessed with warm summer weather and spent the time walking the dogs—or running around the garden with them in my case; riding the horse that belonged to my father's neighbour; and my being given a driving lesson by Nicholas in his car on the privacy of his own land. This was less of the *Drive It Like You Stole It* school of motoring. Perhaps I was leaning towards forgiveness around my father's violence towards me and my mother at this point; he appeared to be treating me more as a father ought to treat a son.

The last day of our visit arrived, and we were due to head back to London the following morning. A goodbye meal and drinks at the local pub were in order. We drove to the pub and ordered food and drinks, and I probably chose some music on the pub jukebox or perhaps we played some pool. We had a few beers together and then Nicholas drove the three of us back to his house.

We all said our goodnights and Angie and Toni went to their room. My father and I went upstairs to our shared room, and I climbed into my single bed and said goodnight to him and began to drift off to sleep.

"Christian, come and get into bed with me," I heard from my father across the room. At this point I was no longer the tough borstal boy punk rocker. This was my father demanding something of me and immediately I was once again that young boy in the Clapham council flat.

I did as he demanded and climbed into his bed. I laid my head on the pillow to go to sleep and then felt his hand touch my skin. I froze and was suddenly wide awake, alarm bells shattering my mind. I didn't know how to respond to this sudden intrusion. I couldn't shout to alert anybody because he had total power over me—a power that went back years, a power that was deeply ingrained in that scared child cowering in the corner and being beaten with a dog lead in a second-floor flat. I was there again. I was that scared small boy again.

"Get on your knees," he ordered, and I did exactly as I was told, as I had always done; compliant as ever. But then it dawned on me what was about to happen: my father was about to take me from behind. He actually wanted to have anal sex with his sixteen-year-old son. I was on his bed on my knees and this was going to hurt.

For the first time in my life, I said to my father, "No!"

There was no way I was gonna get fucked by anyone, not even by my sick, fucked-up, gay-but-married-with-children, domestically abusive father. No!

I was trapped between a rock and a hard place and there was only one solution my slightly drunk, trapped, and confused teenage brain could come up with. Only one way to avoid the physical agony and eternal ignominy of what my father was suggesting.

"No, let's do it the other way," I said to him.

You see, after avoiding and surviving the sexual abuse doled out in the care homes, I was still too tough to be the victim. By placing myself in a role of protagonist, I somehow saved myself, probably from eventual suicide or even worse dysfunctions than those to which I succumbed in the ensuing years.

I try not to dwell on the events of that evening forty years ago. I've asked myself so many questions over the years. But have I found any actual answers? No, I'd say not. I don't know anyone else who's had a similar experience but, then again, who talks about such shit? My drug counsellor in rehab knows I was sexually abused by my father. But, hey, hang on a minute, who abused who? I couldn't be completely honest with my drug counsellor so therefore his work was only half-complete. He could only truly help me if I was one hundred per cent honest; I was not ready to be that honest. It's taken another twenty years for me to be ego-less enough to be honest even to myself. What a head-fuck! Everyone knows the term "motherfucker" and many people use it...but how about "fatherfucker"? It's probably culturally far worse than "motherfucker" but is beyond the realms of the imagination. So way beyond the realms of the imagination that no one ever thought of or uttered it.

Instead of allowing him to penetrate me, I penetrated him: my flesh-and-blood father. Throughout the whole ordeal I pretended it was Toni

I was with, and I vividly recall talking about her to my father during the intercourse; my coping mechanism. I pretended it was Toni throughout so as to blot out the reality of what was happening. And I guess the sickest thing for me isn't what occurred that evening but that my father was twisted enough for either way to be fine with him.

Why am I prepared to share this awful story today? It has to do with the resilience of the human spirit...this human capacity to endure and find ways to deal with terrible situations that befall us. Time has taught me that by acknowledging such an event instead of denying it, by owning it and speaking it out loud, it's set me free.

I'm certain I wouldn't be alive today had I remained on my knees, and I believe that role reversal saved both my sanity and my life.

It also concerns survivability.

Not just my ability to survive such an outlandish experience but also the facility to arrive at an understanding I had no agency in the situation; the facility to not allow it to completely destroy me; to continue striving for development and growth; and possibly even reach a place where a fatalistic acceptance brings peace—it's been forty-five years now and I feel I'm almost there.

I've not revealed this insane secret to many of my partners or friends. It's not something one discusses over a pizza, or while sharing popcorn during the cinema trailers.

The few people who I have confided in can't believe I haven't committed suicide years ago. Today, I say the same words to each of them:

"You can't commit suicide when you have children."

7

Hurt

(Johnny Cash)

Back in Farnborough I returned to hanging out in 'The Square' with friends who were just as dysfunctional as me. My reason for repeatedly returning was the importance of my 'reputation' as a tough guy. Both within the prison system and in the square I felt I was recognised as a 'somebody'—at least, that's how it felt to me back in the early eighties and this attitude would hold me in its cyclical grip for several more years to come. Retrospection is a wonderful thing to possess but I needed to survive more trauma before I was able to achieve such awareness.

Life reverted to sniffing glue, getting drunk, listening to screaming punk rock, stealing cars, and waiting for my next borstal sentence. There was a vitriolic anger and rage burning through my veins and I couldn't destroy myself quickly enough.

It didn't take long for these desires to become reality, and I was soon a fugitive due to multiple car thefts heavy with my fingerprints. This ensured I was a target for any copper who spotted me. I didn't give a fuck, and this would continuously be my downfall.

I was walking through the estate when a copper spotted me and gave chase. The one thing I remember about this guy is he was a decent copper.

That fact would have meant little to me back then as I was in the heyday of my delinquency and criminality so viewed coppers as the enemy. It's only as time has progressed and I've re-evaluated what I stood for then and stand for now that I remember he was a decent guy.

This policeman would not quit chasing me; he must've been a marathon runner or an athlete, and eventually I could run no more and stopped, gasping from exertion,

"Look, Christian, I'm going to have to arrest you. You know that, don't you?"

"I'm not coming with you and that's it. Fuck off and pretend you never saw me, okay?" I was bent over with my hands on my knees, gulping deep breaths, waiting for the blood in my veins to slow.

"You know I can't do that. Just come with me to the station and we'll sort this out. They'll release you afterwards, I'm certain."

"They won't release me. They'll send me back to borstal and I ain't going back so I'm walking now. Just leave me alone."

I turned to leave, and he placed his hand on my shoulder.

"Touch me again and I'll punch you," I warned him and turned to walk away again.

I felt his hand on my shoulder again. We'd been directly facing one another, and I was turning to my left away from him to leave. He grabbed my right shoulder, which meant the punch I swung at him travelled 180 degrees before connecting. I was no stranger to fighting and had learned through necessity how to throw a good punch. This one broke his jaw.

"I warned you to leave me alone," I said to him as I resumed my walk away from him.

I broke into a run so as to escape this guy and any of his colleagues who would soon appear and made it to a friend's house. From here I made my plans to escape Farnborough.

* * *

My mother had always been a law-abiding, hard-working woman and, despite the fact we lived in what criminologists call a socially disorganised neighbourhood, she had never been complicit in any of my crimes.

However, on this occasion she knew I'd be locked up for another year or more, so she changed her tune. Maybe she'd finally realised that what the authorities considered "best for Christian" didn't seem best for Christian at all. Things kept getting worse and I was being locked up for longer and longer periods with little evidence of successful rehabilitation.

She called Angie and explained there was a policeman who'd been assaulted and a highly wanted Godson and wondered whether she would welcome him back to North West London where he was a lot less wanted. Angie agreed and once again I was headed for Willesden Green. I landed there with my bags and the following day Angie received a call from my mother. The police had knocked on her door, she'd been unable to lie, and had given the police Angie's address.

Angie and I grabbed any evidence of my presence from her flat, jumped in the car then drove to Toni's place in West Hampstead. She dropped me off then went home to answer the expected knock on the door from the police.

Fate seemed to be on my side. I was now living in a flat with an older woman who I totally had the hots for, and her seventeen-year-old daughter who was equally attractive.

We hung out together a lot, Angie, Toni, and I. We ate in central London restaurants, spent many evenings dancing at J. Arthur's nightclub in Chelsea's World's End or Les Elites on Finchley Road not far from Toni's place. For me, at sixteen years old, it was a wonderful education.

I found a job at a mechanic's workshop on Cricklewood Broadway welding Jensen Interceptors, Jaguars, and other cars and slowly began to earn enough to not only pay Toni rent money but also to pay my way when we all went out together. Angie wasn't super successful. Her line of work as a fashion photographer was intermittent and I remember her girlfriend, Linda, used to supplement the household income with prostitution. It's only now while writing these words I'm forced to re-evaluate my preconceptions of some of the people I thought were cool as I was growing up and see how reprehensible their behaviour was. Angie used to pimp Linda out when she was skint and would occasionally beat her.

I'm left wondering where my mother fit in with all these people. The more I consider it, the more I'm left thinking they were my father's friends rather than my mother's. I'm not suggesting I know my mother so well I think she'd never associate with these people. They simply don't seem to fit with her style.

Things were going okay. One good thing to come from this London experience was I was a long way from my Farnborough cohort and its criminal proclivities. I hadn't considered breaking the law once since I'd moved to London. Living in the flat with Toni and Deana was easy. I guess Toni had no complaints. I was tidy, I was nothing but nice to her because I had such strong feelings towards her, and Deana was usually either at work or out with her boyfriend.

New Year was approaching. There'd been a party at Toni's, and I'd gone to bed once everyone left. I was awoken by the sound of the door opening and a figure in the dark climbing into bed with me. I realised it was Toni, but I was half asleep.

"Wow, I must be dreaming," I said.

"Well, you can carry on dreaming if you want," Toni said, implying she'd return to her own bed in the next room.

"No," I responded and raised the covers to allow her into my bed. She climbed in beside me and the next couple of hours were everything I'd been dreaming of.

We continued cuddling for some time afterwards before Toni whispered she had to return to her own room. She climbed out of my bed and disappeared with soft footsteps. I wish now I could see the smile I had on my face as I fell back to sleep.

I discovered what Toni did for a living due to a slip of the tongue made by Linda. She'd revealed Toni worked in a massage parlour on Kentish Town Road. At sixteen years of age this didn't freak me out as I was naïve and didn't have a clear understanding of the things that occurred behind their doors. I also happily believed Toni's "I only do massages." Like many men before me, I heard and believed exactly what served me best.

Our nocturnal encounters continued for several weeks, and I was falling deeper and deeper into Toni's beautiful brown eyes with each night of passion.

On my seventeenth birthday, the four of us shared a meal in a fancy restaurant in West Hampstead. A guitarist walked around the tables singing classic songs and we got through a few bottles of red wine. We then moved on to Les Elites where Toni said she wanted to discuss our relationship.

"Listen, Christian, I think we need to cool things down for a bit," Toni informed me once Angie and Linda were on the dancefloor.

"I can't take the risk of Deana discovering what's been going on between us. It would destroy my relationship with my own daughter. I'm certain she doesn't suspect anything at the moment but it's becoming complicated, and I can't shake the feeling she'll find out."

She took my hand in hers and said, "I've spoken with Angie, and she's agreed you can move into her spare room this week. I'm really sorry, but this is how it has to be. You'll be okay and we can just be friends like before."

What a wonderful birthday present, I thought while holding back the warm tears I felt threatening to spill. I forced them back, determined not to break down in front of this woman I felt so deeply in love with.

A few days later, I moved to Angie's flat. Over the following weeks it became evident Toni had meant every word she'd said. It was over. I was heartbroken and couldn't think straight. One evening I was walking the streets close to Angie's not knowing how to cope with the shit and the pain scrambling around my mind, unable to process anything, unable to deal with my scattered emotions.

I bought a packet of paracetamol and necked the lot, swilled down with some beer. I was aimlessly wandering the streets around Kilburn High Road and was wondering how long it would take me to die. I'd had enough of grownups fucking me over with their selfish agendas.

I don't for a moment think Toni was the sole reason I decided to take my own life. I think Toni had been an incredible distraction since the incest with my father but, now that distraction, that bolstering of happiness and the good feelings her attentions had provided me with were gone, I had to deal with some real feelings. And I didn't like those feelings. This was in early 1980 when there were no mobile phones. Angie couldn't contact me, Toni was determined to not see me and I was feeling completely unwanted. I began to wonder how long it takes to die from a paracetamol overdose. I had an idea—I'd phone a hospital and ask a nurse or doctor how long it would take.

I found a phone box, looked through the book and found a hospital phone number. I threw in a few coins then dialled the number.

"Hello. How can I help?" asked a lady with a strong Caribbean accent.

"Err…Hi there. Listen, I've taken an overdose of paracetamol tablets, and I want to know how long it will take to die."

"Aww, darlin', it'll slowly destroy your liver. It'll take days and will be so painful. Where are you?" That good woman on the other end of the phone saved my life. Obviously, I've no idea how things would have panned out had I not gone to a hospital.

"Darlin', where are you? Tell me the address of that phone box and I'll have a taxi come and collect you and bring you here to the hospital. Alright? Can you do that?"

So, it would take days of pain. I hadn't planned on that. I'd guessed after three or four hours I'd be dead and that would be the end of me.

"Yes, I can do that," I replied, and I gave this lady the address that was written inside the phone box. I waited outside and after a few minutes a black cab pulled up and I got in. True to her word this angelic lady came out to meet the cab and paid the driver. She was a big round middle-aged black woman with a colourful scarf wrapped around her head holding her hair in place. The cabbie drove away, and she took me to the A&E department and handed me over to a nurse. The nurse led me to a room where my stomach was pumped, and I saw what was left of the tablets in a plastic bowl filled with fluid from my stomach.

I was asked if I had any relatives, so I gave them Angie's number. I was taken to one of the floors above and was given a bed to climb into. I was exhausted from the stomach pumping, and I drifted off to sleep.

After an hour or two, Angie walked in. I'll never forget how she looked. She was in a huge floor-length fur coat, and she'd aged thirty years—she looked haggard. I don't remember the words we shared but I think she was smart enough to realise this wasn't just about Toni.

8

Solitary Confinement (The Members)

I was back in jail. Ashford young offenders' institution on the outskirts of London. A couple of policemen in a patrol car had randomly pulled me on a London street late one rainy evening as I was walking back to Angie's flat. I was beyond caring so gave my real name. They placed me under arrest for punching a policeman several months previously and a catalogue of driving offences, and I'd been placed on remand. I'd felt a pleasant relief to have been forcibly removed from the trauma around Toni and Angie.

I'd only been here a week and already found myself back in trouble.

"Oi, get your head back in!"

"Fuck off, ya muppet!

"Hey, next door," I screamed from my window, "they're spinning cells."

In prisoner parlance this meant the screws were carrying out an organised search for contraband. I'd been warned by the guy next-door to me and it was my duty to pass the warning along the line of cells to my right as I faced the window—those that hadn't been searched yet. I'd managed to get my head out of the window to warn my neighbour and this prison officer demanded I pull my head back in and desist. No chance.

"Get your head back in!" he screamed at me again.

"Fuck off!" was my instant rejoinder. "Oi, next door! They're spinning cells!" I continued to scream to my deaf neighbour. Perhaps the next cell was empty, I didn't know.

It wasn't long before the screws unlocked my door and began to spin my cell for any contraband I might have. While these two screws were searching through my possessions, another couple showed up saying I had to accompany them to the block.

"What for?"

"You've been nicked for swearing abuse at an officer from your window."

"Yeah, okay, but why am I going down the block now and not in the morning when I'm given the charge sheet?" I asked.

"The Governor wants you down there now," the screw responded.

Bollocks, that meant I didn't have time to organise and stash some tobacco, papers, and matches so I would be without anything to smoke. They knew that. Bastards. Must've been the word "muppet." Nobody likes being called a muppet.

I could do nothing other than comply, so I followed them as they led the way to solitary confinement. We arrived, a cell door was opened, I entered, and the door slammed behind me. I knew it was going to be mind-numbingly boring, so I called the screw back, "Guv'nor?"

"What d'ya want, Austin?"

"Can I have a book and a couple of letters…and a pen?"

"Yeah, I'll bring them shortly," he replied. He might or he might not. It all depended on how long he'd been in the game and how sadistic he was. This one turned out to be okay—I shortly had the items I'd requested. I wrote a few lines to my mother and both my sisters who were at home with her; my brother was at a residential school for the handicapped in Henley-on-Thames.

I finished the letter, wrote another to a friend then read the book until dinnertime. When this arrived, the door was opened and I was handed a plastic plate of food, some plastic cutlery, and a plastic mug of tea. Prison food—think school dinners or hospital food but a little less palatable. I ate the food and read some more until I felt tired enough to sleep. I had an appointment with the prison governor in the morning and wanted it to be over with. As always, I fell asleep within moments and slept well.

The morning arrived and I was handed my breakfast along with a charge sheet. I read the charge against me while eating my breakfast and sipping my tea:

"On such a date at such a time inmate Austin did address Officer X in a denigrating manner, namely saying: 'Fuck off, you muppet!'"

The cell door was unlocked once again, and my plates were collected. I was able to have a wash and clean my teeth before being locked back in my cell to await the Governor's adjudication, as such a prison courtroom experience was known. I went to the window and looked outside while I was waiting but there wasn't too much to see—grey buildings spattered with barred windows, and walls topped with sharp razor wire. I bored of the view quickly and laid on my bed waiting for the doors to open.

After another forty minutes I could hear approaching keys, and my door was unlocked.

"Austin. Adjudication," the screw said. I got up and he led the way to the adjudication room. I entered once he'd opened the door and was shown a line on the floor at which I placed my toes. I stood facing a desk a couple of metres ahead of me, and two officers were before me. Their faces were inches from mine and they each stood at forty-five degrees to me. This always felt ridiculous at every adjudication I had the pleasure of attending.

It didn't take long to find me guilty. The governor sentenced me to seven days' solitary confinement, and I was led back to the cell, my home for the next seven days. The door was slammed, and I was alone again.

I was feeling pissed off, to be honest. I'd already had my freedom taken away when I was whisked off the streets in Central London. Now I was getting lots of shit from the screws and governor of this prison. *Fuck you! Fuck all of you!* sang through my mind. I was still thinking of Toni a lot, of Angie, my recent life in London, my upcoming sentence, my father, and the bullshit he'd put me through. Why did life have to be so *shit*? Why was my life so shit? Fucking adults, that's why…lots of adults all trying to control me, all giving me shit. Well, fuck 'em all!

It had already struck me while eating my dinner the previous evening how pristine the cell looked. Obviously, there'd been a recent new coat of paint and there was no sign of any graffiti. It occurred to me that was what was missing so I began to write. I wrote on the walls, the books, and the mattress. I wrote on everything that could be written on and stayed awake until dawn perfecting my art. Mostly, I wrote a mix of angry lyrics from punk songs and some of my favourite poetry—a crazy mix of Yeats, Larkin, Jim Morrison, Lynton Kwesi Johnson, Ian Dury, and John Cooper Clark. I wish today I could once again see what I spent the night working on.

I also wrote in four-inch letters on the mattress "The Governor is a Cunt," and I meant it. They were all Cunts, but he represented the pinnacle of all Cunts and therefore took the brunt of my frustration.

When I heard the screws change shift in the morning. I was still wide awake and buzzing from the anarchic "I-Don't-Give-A-Fuck" night I'd experienced.

Fuck you all, I thought, do your worst to me because, whatever it is, I'll survive it as I'm stronger than all of you.

The morning shift screw opened my door so I could 'slop out' and immediately slammed it shut again. Great, this was a good start for the mood I found myself in—I was totally wired, I'd got his attention and he'd now be reporting what he'd seen to his colleagues, his Senior Officer (S.O.) and his Principal Officer (P.O.). The governor would be notified.

Sure enough, the screw came back twenty minutes later with some friends and they allowed me to slop out, gave me some breakfast and a new charge sheet. The charge this time was "Criminal Damage to Government Property." They confiscated the books and pen then slammed the door behind me. I smiled to myself as I heard their footsteps disappear. I had a strange sense of achievement as I ate the breakfast and drank the plastic mug full of tea. Once again, I awaited the sound of keys to alert me it was time for my adjudication.

I stood before the prison governor stone-faced with my hands behind my back and listened to the words being read out by the charging officer. He explained he'd opened my cell door that morning and had been confronted with a black and white artwork of dubious quality where there ought to have been only white walls; how the books I'd had in the cell were likewise graffitied; and how little remorse inmate Austin had expressed regarding the criminal damage. He also pointed out that I had written all over the mattress cover and, at this point—adding an element of comedy—two more prison officers entered the adjudication room each holding one end of the defiled mattress.

Here it was, an ode to the governor from inmate Austin's perspective. He must surely be impressed by my attention to detail. Each letter had been painstakingly drawn with a precision that only comes with a whole night's maniacal determination.

"I see," the governor said. "Well then, you'll understand why I'm sentencing you to a further twenty-one days' solitary confinement taking your total punishment up to twenty-eight days. Take the prisoner away."

I could have added to the proceedings by screaming and shouting at the governor, but I was feeling a calm satisfaction due to his having seen my work firsthand. To this day, I can still visualise the wording on that mattress, each letter identical in height and width. I'd spent a long time over each letter and ensured it was as neat as possible. The fact the mattress was brought into the room was more than I could have hoped for.

Now that I'd successfully ruined one of their cells and been sentenced to an extensive period in solitary, the screws led me to a new cell. Within this room was a concrete table set into the wall, a concrete stool set into the floor, and a bed with six-inch legs…also robustly fixed to the floor. This bed didn't have any springs because these might be removed and used as a weapon, instead it had flat metal slats. These slats criss-crossed one another resulting in four-inch squares regularly formed across the whole frame. I'd never usually make a point of studying the way a bed had been designed. However, this bed's frame was visible to Ashford's solitary confinement prisoners throughout each day as the mattress was removed in the morning and returned in the evening. The system didn't allow inmates on punishment to have a lie-in in the morning nor to take a nap during any part of the rest of the day. It was either lie on the metal frame of the bed, sit on the concrete stool, stand on the heating pipe to gaze from the window, or pace up and down the five by four metre floor.

I'd rotate all four of these options over the next few days while varying their order. The novelty of each only lasted a while before it was time to move onto the next option. I was allowed no books due to my graffiti exploits.

How long is a day? Now, at the tender age of sixty years, I realise a day can have many different lengths depending on circumstances. Time can be used as punishment upon one who is impatient. But time can also be a wonderful companion in prison and, if the requisite state of mind is achieved, the judge, jailer, or governor no longer has power over the prisoner—the power structure is inverted in the prisoner's favour. Once the jailer realises a prisoner considers the opening of his door an intrusion on his meditations, solitary confinement is no longer a punishment. Whenever the door was opened it would be for the delivery of food or for a vicar to daily measure the temperature of my soul.

The first day of my solitude was spent rotating the four options I've listed. Day two found me adding an additional exercise to this list. I had my toiletries in my cell with me—toothbrush, toothpaste, soap, and shampoo—and the utter absence of anything interesting to do led me to discover how intriguing my bottle of shampoo could be. It was a clear bottle; I can see it now in my mind's eye.

It was clear and the shampoo was a toxic-looking viscous orange. The bottle wasn't full. I'd say only an inch or so of the shampoo had been used, which meant the bottle contained an inch of air. I'd turn the bottle upside down and watch as the bubbles slowly rose from the bottom to the top. Large bubbles of air next to many tiny bubbles of air, all travelling at different rates with some merging into others to form larger bubbles than they had been. There was a universe of bubbles in this shampoo bottle, and I spent hours studying them. My own impromptu lava lamp.

I find it strange to think of today because the experience was months before I began messing with hallucinogens. But this was trippy—hours and hours of watching galaxies and nebulae formed from bubbles. Then, I'd lay down on the metal frame of the bed—which never lasted long as it was so uncomfortable—or gaze out of the window towards the wings where other inmates had a greater degree of freedom. There was a chapel I could see out of that window. Sitting on the concrete stool was part of the bubble-gazing experience.

I was shaken from my hallucinogenic reverie when a set of keys rattled outside the door then turned in the lock. The prison chaplain walked in and greeted me. He'd initially come and introduced himself on my first day of solitary as one of his duties was to do the rounds in the block and offer his ministry to us sinners. I've no idea how successful he was in adding new members to his flock. Judging from some of the "vulnerables" on normal location back on the wings, I'd imagine he gained a fair few every week. A lot of the inmates in Ashford were first timers; they'd never had the education in care homes I'd had and were shit scared. Just the kind of people a man of the cloth might convert.

"Good afternoon, Christian, how are you doing today?" he asked me.

"I'm good, thanks," I responded, thinking the less I said, the quicker he'd leave me alone.

"I'm happy to hear that. Is there anything I can do for you?"

I'm sure the guy was fine but, to be honest, I had no interest in his Jesus, *The Cross and the Switchblade* book every prison vicar had ever tried to give me, nor his offer to say prayers for my loved ones.

"I'm fine," I told him. "I like it down here away from all the fuckwits, Father. Sorry, I meant away from the err, the err…"

But he was fine; he knew we weren't angels.

"So long as you're alright. I'll be leaving you then and I'll see you again tomorrow."

As he began to leave something occurred to me.

"Hang on, Father."

He halted before leaving the cell. "Yes?" he asked me.

"They've taken all my books away and left me with nothing. There's one book I can still have, right? That I'm entitled to? I can have the Bible?"

"Of course, my son. Shall I bring you one tomorrow?"

Thank fuck for that, I thought to myself, *I'm going crazy in here without anything to read.*

"Yes, please."

The chaplain left my cell and locked the door behind him and my Groundhog Day continued until my dinner was brought to me. The Bible was on my mind now. I'd been taken to church a few times in Clapham when I was six or seven years old. I don't know why because my parents never showed any leanings towards the church. Perhaps it was to give me a small taster in case I had an urge to become a cardinal later in life as opposed to the criminal I turned out to be.

The following afternoon, the chaplain arrived and, true to his word, he had the Good Book with him.

"I hope this brings you some solace during these challenging times."

"Thank you," I said as I took the weighty tome from his hands, and I sincerely meant it. I assured him I was fine again today, and he left to continue his rounds.

I sat down on the concrete stool and weighed the book in my hands before opening it. I felt happy I'd fucked the system in a small way by receiving a book when they'd banned books from my solitary existence. I also remember a sense of wonder around the knowledge I was about to read the thing. As we all have, I'd heard segments of it being read out during church services in Clapham, Winchester, and St. Edwards school so was familiar with several of the most popular stories and parables. But to sit down and read it myself felt like an incredible undertaking. I opened the book's cover and began reading:

"In the beginning God created the Heaven and the Earth. And the Earth was without form, and void; and darkness was on the face of the deep. And the Spirit of God moved upon the face of the waters. And God said: Let there be light. And there was light."

A short while later, the keys turned in the door lock and I was handed my dinner on the plastic plate with the plastic utensils and plastic mug of tea. I didn't notice the jailer at all. I ate the food and drank the tea and continued with my reading. The keys jangled once more, and I was handed my mattress. I laid it on the metal bed frame and went back to reading until I was too tired to continue then went to bed. In the morning, I slopped out, washed, cleaned my teeth, and then ate my breakfast. Once I'd eaten it, I continued reading. I was hooked and this pattern continued for days and days.

I found both Genesis and Exodus interesting stories and a nice introduction although the first hurdle in reading the Good Book is becoming acclimatised to its archaic style. The same is, of course, true of Dostoevsky, Hugo, Dickens, Milton, and Hardy. The section where someone begat someone and that someone begat someone else and they, in their turn, begat another, *ad infinitum,* drove me a bit nuts. I discovered God was a wrathful God and I found the story of Sodom and Gomorrah's retribution most satisfying. There was Ruth and Job and Saul and many other familiar characters I'd previously heard mention of in church sermons. I remember little of it sitting here writing forty years later, but I do remember how much I enjoyed the Old Testament with its fire and brimstone. There were armies and there was slaughter and it read like an adventure story, albeit one with lots of tedious interludes. I don't suppose I ever would have finished reading it were I not banged up in solitary with no other books permitted.

"Austin, you've a visit," said the voice of a screw I'd not noticed opening the door. I returned to the reality of my five by four metre cell, stood up and asked, "How do I look, guv'nor?"

"Stop taking the piss, Austin, and follow me."

The screws knew me pretty well after my being in the block for a fortnight already and I'd built a rapport with some of them. It was mostly staffed by the same screws so there was a regular rotation of familiar faces. I followed this one through the usual ceremony of unlocking and locking about fifteen doors to get to the visit room.

My mother and my two sisters, Camilla and Serena, had driven the twenty-five miles to visit me. They weren't at all surprised to discover I was in solitary again.

"What have you done this time?" my mother asked as soon as I sat down at the table. "The officer said you're in solitary confinement and can't have any of the stuff we've brought for you."

They were as upset as I was that I couldn't benefit from the goodies they'd brought for me, including the tobacco as they were all smokers. The visit lasted only thirty minutes, so they asked what I'd been up to, how I'd got in trouble yet again.

"I called a screw a muppet and they gave me seven days' solitary. So then I graffitied the cell they put me in, and the mattress, and anything else I could write on and the governor gave me another twenty-one days. Now I'm not allowed any books but the chaplain gave me a bible to read…I reckon I have enough time to read the whole thing."

They cracked up laughing at this gem.

"You'll be joining a religious cult when you're released then?" Camilla quipped.

She told me who else had been nicked on the GLC estate and what they'd been nicked for as she still hung around Totland Close so was up to date with the latest news. Serena was a few years older than Camilla and didn't hang out with the same people we did. It wasn't long before a screw announced, "Five minutes to finish," so we said our goodbyes and they hit me with the usual "Stay out of trouble" and "Don't make it any worse than it already is" lines.

"Sure," I said, giving them all hugs.

"Thanks for coming. Take care, I'll see you soon."

Then they were gone. I was led back through the maze of corridors and returned to my cell to discover the sun shining brightly through the window. Sunbeams in the shape of the window were slowly crawling across the wall of my cell. I was gutted I couldn't leave with my family and also that I wasn't allowed the provisions they'd brought for me.

I dwelt on the memories of seeing my family for a short time while staring from the window, picturing them leaving the prison gates and climbing into the car to return to the family home, the place I'd been excluded from by the courts—and, let's face it, by myself. But was I to blame? Was this all my fault? This might seem the perfect time for a soliloquy, but it was actually time to throw the mask back on, lock all emotions down, and deny there was any problem.

Besides, I still had the Good Book. I continued reading, turning page after page after page. Such thin pages, too. I remembered the times we'd use Bible pages as cigarette papers in Winton House in Winchester when we were desperate to smoke.

I was somewhere around the Book of Jonah at this point, with his refusal to become a prophet until being coerced by God's punishment of living three days inside a "great fish."

The days were long and even having reading material didn't completely dispel the ennui. I'd take breaks from the Bible to gaze from my window or take a nap on the metal bed frame. The shampoo bottle was now only used for washing hair. The prison chaplain still showed his face every day and some days we'd have discussions over the latest section of the Bible I'd read. Like most prison chaplains, he was okay. He had his faith and was trying to do his best in a bad situation, much like a drug counsellor facing a ninety per cent failure rate. Sometimes I enjoyed our chats and other times I'd feel he was too dogmatic and I'd cut the conversation short by being deliberately abrupt or sullen to encourage his departure. I'd rather be alone than have someone trying to convert me.

These periods I spent in solitary confinement were priceless as they taught me how to enjoy my own company; how to sit with my own thoughts and be comfortable. It's taken me decades to come to achieve that. Often around this time, when not incarcerated, I'd be desperate to leave the house, wherever I was living, London or Farnborough. I'd be desperate to hit the streets because I couldn't stand being alone. I hadn't learned how to appreciate solitude and enjoy being without society. When in prison, however, being confined to the block was often a welcome break from the intense energy and nonstop stress of being on the prison wings with its ever-present danger. Twenty-eight days, however, was a bit too long without contact with a friendly face, a fellow inmate, a scally who I got on with.

I finished the Old Testament, then began the New Testament. I found the change in tone hard to take to the point of it being annoying. I still read all of it, but I remember my enjoyment waned a lot because I found it sycophantic and much more dogmatic. It was more about following the scriptures and adhering to the words Jesus spoke. Don't get me wrong, there were still some fantastic anecdotes and parables in the books of Matthew, Mark, Luke, and John, but they didn't feel as valid to me as those in the Old Testament. This was disappointing and tarnished the remaining days of my solitary.

I finished reading the whole Bible with only a day or two of my punishment left. I was then escorted back to a cell on normal location, among my friends once again. It was a different cell than the one I'd previously occupied and my friends all donated tobacco, cigarette papers, a lighter, and some snacks so I could "enjoy" being back in general prison population. A few weeks later I appeared in Crown Court and was sentenced to another six months to two years in borstal, dependent on my behaviour.

9

Enjoy Yourself (It's Later Than You Think) (The Specials)

Silos filled with potatoes was where the farm manager started me off: I had to sift through them and eliminate those with any rot. He would have been a civilian worker as Mr. Bridger in the welding workshop had been. Proper screws didn't do this kind of work. Civvie workers were generally less strict and were more likely to be amenable to the occasional bribe. This was true throughout the prison estate during my years of incarceration. To them, it was a job rather than a career with prospects of promotion.

I wasn't on the farm very long before a position became available in the gardening department. Once again, it was stressed what a privilege it was to be working outside the borstal walls.

I followed my new boss, another civvie worker named Mr. Cummings, as he led me to my new place of work. He was a little shorter than me with a head only half populated with thin grey hair while his chin was buried behind a thick grey beard. He walked with a slight limp, so I had to slow my pace in order to stay with him.

We walked south from the farm, parallel with the edge of the cliffs, until we came to the gardens area. We continued walking another short distance and I was introduced to the prison officers' bowling green.

If you're not familiar with an English bowling green, it's a square area of well-tended grass that can be found in many cities, towns, and villages in the UK. Portland was no exception, and my new occupation was keeper of the bowling green so the staff could play bowls on summer evenings and weekends.

Mr. Cummings introduced me to the tools of my new trade. There was a wide rake that he explained was for pulling up the old grass roots before mowing began. He gave me a demonstration by starting in one corner and dragging the thing behind him, first one way then the other. Everything had to be just so, and the eventual stripes were to be diagonal so everything preceding also had to be. Next, he introduced me to my new best friend: a Webb Witch cylinder lawn mower, a manual machine because a motorized mower might drip oil or fuel onto the grass.

Once my training was complete, I set about the task of managing all the items required for optimum bowling green maintenance: the large rake, the mower, a huge yard-broom that had been created by screwing three yard-broom heads onto a long piece of wood with a T-handle attached and, finally, a monstrous cast-iron roller with a barrel a metre in diameter, which seemed to weigh about half a ton. I ought to have been beaming with satisfaction at this point, but I wasn't. I pretty soon decided it was a crap job, and I told Mr. Cummings so.

"It's a privilege to work outside the borstal," he insisted.

"Well, I think it's crap. Can I get a job change?"

"When's your EDR?" he asked, this being my Expected Date of Release.

"December," I told him.

"Well, there you go," he said with a smile, "that's when you can have a job change." This was in May 1981 (I remember because the Sheena Easton song "9 to 5" wouldn't leave my head all the while I was mowing).

"That's fucking hilarious, Mr. Cummings," I told him.

He spent a few moments adjusting the blades of the mower and then walked away leaving me with my seven-month contract. I returned to pushing the mower and the bloody thing kept getting jammed; it had been fine before he'd adjusted the blades.

That same day or the next, Mr. Cummings returned and found me sat on the grass instead of working. It was a nice sunny day.

"What you playing at, Austin?" he asked me.

"I'm having a fag, guv'nor," I informed him.

"Well, you can smoke all you like after work. Get back to it."

I remember he adjusted the blades one more time before he walked away to continue with his other duties. I placed my hands back on the handle of the mower and began pushing it again. After a couple of paces, it jammed, and my momentum caused my upper body to jerk onto the handle. It did the same thing with the same result after another few paces.

You know that thing where something irritating keeps occurring and you snap? I do, and I did that sunny afternoon.

"Fuck this shit!"

I'd had enough. I pushed the handle down so the blades were off the grass and it would roll easily and pushed the mower towards the South West Coast Path.

There was a low wall about waist-height, so I stopped and lifted the mower over the wall, then climbed it myself. I was now on the path. There was another waist-height wall then the drop of the cliffs to a small beach below. It was a descent of perhaps a couple of hundred feet. My heart began to beat with adrenalin as the enormity of my intention filled my whole being.

I bent down and disconnected the green bucket that collected the grass when mowing. I look down and noticed a small path running laterally halfway down the cliff. There were no people on it. I raised the green metal box above my head and threw it down and out towards the beach below. The beach was further out than it looked. The box plummeted down through the air and first hit the ground a third of the way down. It kept falling and tumbling until it came to a halt at the bottom.

My heart was beating like crazy. This was a fantastic feeling. "Fuck 'em all," I said to myself. "Fuck their bowling green, fuck their gardens, fuck this privilege bullshit." I was reclaiming some control, and it felt incredibly good.

I next got a good grip on the actual lawn mower, surprised by its weight. Again, I raised it in the air and launched it out and down towards the beach. "Ha-ha! Yes, get the fuck out of my life!" I sang out loud.

The mower was several times heavier than its green box so landed on the cliff even sooner than its counterpart. A couple of pieces broke off then it was in the air again, tumbling down closer and closer to the beach, crashing, and smashing to pieces. Oh, joy of joys…what an amazing feeling. There was no spare mower I knew of and, even had there been, they'd never entrust it to me. There was such a satisfaction in the knowledge I had put that job behind me, despite Mr. Cummings's assurance my next job change wouldn't be until December. I hadn't felt that happy in some time and was beaming from ear to ear. I took a final look at the scene below and returned to sit by the bowling green to wait for and face the music.

A short while later, sitting in the blazing sunshine and enjoying a cigarette, I saw Mr. Cummings approaching.

"Austin, what you doing now? Why aren't you working?" he asked.

"I can't work, guv'nor. I ain't got a lawn mower."

"What?" he asked. "What do you mean you don't have a lawn mower? What've you done with it? Where've you hidden it?"

"I haven't hidden it. I threw it off the cliff," I happily informed him.

"Don't be daft. Where is it?" He was looking all around in search of the missing lawn mower.

"I did, I threw it off the cliff. Look, come 'ere, I'll show you…" and I led him over to the wall and scrambled over it.

"Look, down there. See all those bits? There's yer lawn mower."

Mr. Cummings stood staring down at the now destroyed mower, speechless.

I remember having to shake him out of his incredulity, saying, "Come on, are we going down the block, or what?"

We both walked back towards the borstal together and entered through the main gates. He escorted me across the huge yard past the admin block towards E-Hall. I couldn't care less what would happen to me. I was completely satisfied I'd shown them they had no power over me. *Job change in December, my arse*, I thought.

We reached E-Hall and there was a reception party waiting for me—word had travelled fast from the gatehouse. Mr. Pratt was there and ginger Mr. Thompson. They both knew me from my last whack and now this one—probably a total of three years at that point. I'd meet Mr. Thompson again later when I was promoted to adult prisons. They were both reasonable screws as far as I was concerned, not vicious bastards as some could be.

Mr. Pratt handed me my bed pack, and they didn't even bother making me run too fast on this occasion—I think they both realised I'd pay a heavy price for this stunt, and they were right.

When I saw the governor the next day, he was livid. He informed me the lawn mower was worth £750 and insisted I could have killed someone.

"No, sir, I checked no one was on the path before I threw the lawn mower."

It fell on deaf ears. This guy was pissed off.

"This is far too serious for me to adjudicate, Austin, so I am passing it on to the Board of Visitors and you shall remain in the custody of E-Hall until such a time as they next visit. Take him away."

Back to my cell. Back to the meditation and re-living various aspects of my life, disappearing from my surroundings for hours at a time with a smile on my face, only returning for mealtimes. I wasn't in prison—I was back in London with Angie and Toni, with Deana, with my Farnborough posse.

I still had the circuit training in the mornings and bowls of cold water to wash with afterwards, the silence only broken when a new prisoner ran to his cell with his bed-pack or received a kick-in for getting too gobby or was violently served some "liquid cosh" for an act of violence (slang for a syringe full of Largactil, a psychotropic drug used to tranquilise the unruly).

I'd also read books. There was a limited selection of books in E-Hall, probably only eight or nine, and I found it a strange coincidence two of them were *Gone with the Wind* and a Vivien Leigh biography. I read them both as they were the best of a bad bunch. I was in the deep South with Scarlet O'Hara and Rhett Butler, the Hamiltons, and Mammy and all the other help. It was a great read, though not something I'd have chosen outside solitary confinement.

The day of my execution finally arrived, and I was hauled in front of the Board of Visitors, a middle-aged trinity of scowling faces come to sentence the Antichrist.

The charges and details were read out and it didn't take them long to find me guilty. I was asked to leave the room while they deliberated my sentence. After a brief wait, I was invited back in.

"We sentence you to the loss of twelve weeks' remission. You may go."

Three months had been added on to the time I had left to serve. It was only a shitty lawn mower. Three whole months.

It was agreed I'd already spent enough time in solitary on remand, so I was allowed back on normal location in Grenville House where I received a hero's welcome from many of the other cons. The lawn mower stunt had earned me some kudos.

And while I'd been in E-Hall a good friend of mine, Jem Hammick, had arrived in the borstal and been placed in Nelson House. I had some tobacco sent to him through the cleaners (these guys smuggle contraband in borstals and prisons because they were out on the landings all day). I sent messages to friends I knew in Nelson House to look out for him and ensure he wasn't bullied. Life returned pretty much to normal.

I applied to do another City & Guilds course, this one in capstan lathe setting and turning, and I was accepted. It entailed learning how to use micrometers and Vernier scales, and the reading of technical drawings, which was my forte due to my CSE in technical drawing. I was trained on lathes and milling machines for the next few months, which I enjoyed. It taught me many skills that I still employ to this day.

The marching everywhere continued, and the weekend parade ground roll calls; the altercations and fights in the recess, either with old enemies or with new receptions trying to establish themselves in the hierarchy; the arguments with the screws; and the inevitable stints in solitary. I'd see Jem in the gym or on the parade ground sometimes and we'd catch up on news from home, or I'd hand him some tobacco. He was slightly built and could easily have become a victim. Another thing with Jem Hammick was he was a nice guy, and I never knew him to be disliked. In borstal and prison though, nice equals weak.

"How are you settling in?" I asked.

"I'm okay. They're putting me on full-time education. The guys on the wing seem okay. As for the rest of it, you know how it is: march here, march there, 'Party 'shun!', all that bollocks."

We both laughed loudly at this.

"Well, any problems with anyone, just let me know, okay? I'll make sure you're alright. Although I'm up for release in a couple of months. Can't wait to get the hell out of here."

"You and me both."

10

Is There Anybody Out There?
(Pink Floyd)

I was released from borstal and returned to my stomping ground, an error I repeated over and over without learning. It was so dumb, like pissing on an electric fence and wondering where the shock was coming from yet continuing to piss. I was back with the old crew with their dyed spiky hair and ripped clothes, their snarls and safety pins.

My sister, Camilla, had "normalised" into society by this time and was working in the Tesco "Bake and Bite" in Queensmead, a precinct in the town centre. She was spending less time in The Square and was concentrating more on earning money.

I applied to a programme in Guildford, which would enable me to continue my training in engineering, working towards becoming a lathe turner and tool-cutter. Sitting here today, I'm pleased that didn't come to pass and realise, with the advantage of hindsight, that I was nowhere near ready to settle into "normal" life.

I stuck out the training for a while but getting up early and commuting to Guildford each day wasn't for me. Dysfunction's call was too strong, so I resumed trying to numb my life by getting high on solvents around Totland Close with my equally dysfunctional friends. Mostly this involved sniffing glue but occasionally myself and my friends would inhale Tippex thinners or shoe conditioner. This had the effect of causing blackouts and a dreamlike state where the individual could still function but would have little memory of the experience afterwards. I'd head for Queen Elizabeth Park so I wouldn't be seen and couldn't cause any trouble yet I'd still wake up in a police cell.

Any functional human being reading this will have little comprehension of this desire to opt out, not only from society, but from life, from consciousness. I was searching for oblivion as it truly felt a better place than my reality. I'd pushed the trauma of my life deep down within my psyche but, in rehab parlance, it was "coming out sideways." And, once I discovered a vehicle to transport me to oblivion, I bought the long-distance ticket.

This ticket, ironically, came via my younger sister trying to help me.

"I don't know why you hang out with all those idiot friends of yours sniffing glue all the time. You're supposed to have a brain." My sister had no way of knowing what had occurred between me and our father so didn't realise the lengths I'd go to pursue stupefaction. "Why don't you just smoke weed like Bob and Ellen?" she continued.

"Err, okay," I responded, pricking up my ears. I'd read about a cornucopia of drugs during my borstal time and was now being offered access to the portal. "How do I find Bob and Ellen?" I asked.

"They live in Ballantyne Road," she said and told me their door number.

I thanked her and said I'd go and check them out. I didn't go to their house immediately but a couple of days later I was stood at their front door awaiting an answer.

A tall guy with a big smile opened the door and greeted me with, "Hey, man?" The next thing I noticed after his smile was his long blond curly hair hanging either side of his face in ringlets. He was wearing blue jeans and a checkered shirt.

"Yeah, hi, man. Are you Bob? My sister, Camilla, said I ought to come round and introduce myself…um, maybe hang out with you guys a bit."

Bob's grin became even broader, he opened the door, and I entered.

"Sure. Camilla's cool. Come in, come in ... What's your name, man?"

"Christian," I told him, and he took my hand and gave it a firm shake.

I walked through the door and Bob closed it behind me. I followed him into the room straight ahead. Thick smoke filled the room and there were hangings and posters on the wall. Strange music was playing on a record deck, and the atmosphere was like nothing I'd experienced previously. A younger-looking guy with similar features to Bob and crooked teeth pulled a huge bottle from his lips and blew an enormous cloud of smoke up to the ceiling. He also had long hair falling below his shoulders. Also in the room was an old school friend of mine named Alison and another woman I didn't know who I assumed was Ellen.

"Guys, this is Camilla's brother, Christian. He's gonna hang out with us for a bit. Christian, this is Ellen, and this is Alison…"

"Yeah, we know each other from school," I responded giving her a smile. She returned it, nodding her head and quietly saying, "Hi."

"And this is my younger brother, Andy," said Bob. Andy extended his hand, shook mine, and gave me a wonky-toothed smile. I instantly liked this genuine grin. Andy would soon become one of my best friends.

I sat down next to Alison, and Andy asked if I wanted a "bong." I correctly assumed he meant the huge, pickled onion jar filled with water and a long pipe coming from its wide cork stopper.

"Sure, why not?" I told him. This was, after all, why I'd come to visit—to switch my disgusting glue-sniffing habit for some civilised smoking of cannabis.

Andy took a large pinch of what looked like tobacco from a magazine on the table and packed it into a small round bowl that he attached to the top of the bong.

"You ever had one of these before?" Andy asked me.

"No, never," I responded honestly, "only spliffs."

"Okay," he said passing me the big jar, "You put your finger over this hole in the top of the cork, yeah?"

I took the jar and followed his instruction. It was heavy as it stood about ten inches tall and was three-quarters full of yellowing water. With the bong balanced on my lap I took the pipe in my mouth. Andy swung his long hair back over one shoulder and prepared to light the bong for me. He told me to place my finger over a hole called the "shotgun," then said, "Inhale when I tell you then, once the jar is full of smoke, take your finger off the shotgun and take all the smoke into your lungs, okay?"

I nodded my head with the pipe between my lips ready to go. Andy flicked the lighter into life and I did exactly as he said. The smoke from the bowl began to swirl within the chamber of the jar and I kept inhaling. I could feel the smoke entering my lungs. I could taste the hash as well as the tobacco, then Andy told me to take my finger off the shotgun. All the remaining smoke in the chamber filled my lungs, and I desperately tried to retain it, but my lungs were not used to this and within seconds, I was coughing and spluttering like a man recovering from drowning. My lungs and throat felt as though they were on fire.

I realise today what I felt next wasn't simply the rush of the hashish but also a rush from the instant ingestion of such a huge quantity of tobacco. My head span round and round from an overload of nicotine and THC.

After several moments, I could breathe more easily and the spinning within my skull had slowed a little. Bob slapped me on the back. He was crying tears of laughter while rocking back and forth. Andy found it equally funny. I gradually regained my composure and joined in with their laughter, coughing and holding my chest intermittently. I began to feel great with a similar feeling I'd get when smoking spliffs with Angie and Toni but more pronounced because a bong is way more intense. I also felt as though I'd successfully passed an initiation without embarrassing myself. Bob now took the bong from me and reloaded it, passing it to Ellen and lighting the bowl for her.

Ellen also had blonde hair. She had a round face with bright blue eyes and was wearing clothing that I'd now say were in a hippie style—a sheepskin waistcoat over a light blouse with a long flowing tie-dyed skirt.

I would soon learn she and Bob had been together for three years and that Andy and Alison were also in a relationship.

Both my musical education and my sampling of drugs began in that room and continued for the next year. I was introduced to a lot of psychedelic music by Pink Floyd, Soft Machine, Led Zeppelin, Genesis, Crosby, Stills, Nash and Young, and a lot of contemporary music such as Japan, Talk Talk, Peter Gabriel, King Crimson, and Steve Hillage. The posters around Bob and Ellen's living room were the archetypal hippie-era posters you'd find in every self-respecting hippie household in the late seventies/early eighties period: Roger Dean images from the Yes album covers.

The thing my sister didn't realise when she'd directed me to Bob and Ellen's front door was they weren't just dope smokers. They were experimenting with every drug available. This was something one didn't advertise either then or now so my sister holds no blame for introducing me to a world I'd been seeking since leaving borstal; my research around the many different types of drug and attendant paraphernalia was to be centred on that house over the coming months.

I was still getting into trouble with the police at this time, stealing cars and fencing stolen goods. Moreover, the house in Ballantyne Road would be raided by the drug squad occasionally so it didn't take the police too long to figure out that Christian was entering the world of drug-taking. My probation officer at the time, Christine Giles, asked me if I was getting involved in drugs and wanted to help me, but I was not interested.

Just as my father had back in Clapham, Bob and Ellen would occasionally borrow money from the gas meter's cash box. This cash would always be returned, and we learned how to replace the wired lead seals that showed the gas meter hadn't been tampered with. We also discovered a fantastic new use for the cash box and stashed the drugs within it. The police would never think to look inside it and it was a delightful feeling getting one over on the drug squad this way. Once a search was complete, we'd retrieve the drugs and continue with their consumption.

Beginning with cannabis, I progressed quickly to amphetamines, LSD, and magic mushrooms. I had some of the most fantastic trips of my life in that living room with a psychedelic soundtrack swirling around me. Strange and surreal days blended into weeks of nothing other than chemicals, music, and nonstop bong-smoking. It was funded by my illicit dealings in drugs and stolen goods in Totland Close, which was just five minutes away. I drank alcohol only occasionally, usually while waiting for a customer in the Prince Louis pub; chemicals and weed had become my drugs of choice.

Following a predictable progression, the needle came next. I was intent on destroying my life and snorting speed, eating acid blotters, or scouring fields for psilocybe mushrooms weren't going to destroy me quickly enough.

One afternoon an old friend named Jamie showed up at the door. We'd been at junior school together before I'd been placed in care homes. Jamie's family home was practically next to the school, and I'd often spent time with him after school was over. I'd lost touch with him as we'd been sent to different secondary schools. He hadn't changed much and still had the same round face, flat nose, and scarred chin I remembered—these last two medals from a fight in the junior school playground. He wore his dark hair long as was common in those times and would constantly flick the long fringe from his deep brown eyes while speaking.

"Hey, Christian, long time no see. How you been?"

"Yeah, I'm good…just trying to stay outta prison."

"Good luck with that around here," he quipped flashing a grin at me.

He pulled off his coat and sat down next to me then reached into his shirt pocket.

"I got some heroin for sale if any of you are interested?"

It quickly became evident to me this wasn't the first time Bob and Ellen had encountered the drug as they were immediately keen. Andy wasn't fazed either and said he'd buy a bit. I also nodded my assent. Why the hell not?

I'd read enough books featuring heroin while I was in borstal so knew this was the top of the pyramid when it came to Class A drugs.

It was the only drug I hadn't yet tried, and I was keen to discover how it felt and why it was listed so high in the UK's classification of drugs.

Jamie pulled a set of digital scales from his coat pocket and weighed out five ten-pound deals of the light brown powder. Each deal was placed in a folded square of paper, carefully wrapped then handed to each of us. Money was passed to him in return, and he then fetched a dessert spoon from the kitchen and set about preparing a "hit." He placed the correct amounts of smack, water, and citrus acid into the spoon and held a lighter beneath it until the liquid began to boil. At this point, he removed the flame and set the spoon down. Next, he dropped a swab of cotton wool into the spoon as a filter and sucked the light brown liquid up into a 1ml. syringe. He held the syringe upright and flicked it a couple of times to send any air to the top then pushed the plunger until the air had been expelled and a tiny drop of brown fluid spurted from the needle. I was watching all this with fascination. I'd been injecting speed for some time that was also cooked up in a spoon, but this was the first time I'd witnessed smack being prepared. I hadn't realised it needed another chemical to break it down.

Jamie pulled his belt from his trousers and looped it around his bicep. He fed the leather end through the buckle and pulled it tight. Gripping the leather end between his teeth to keep it taut he began to open and close his fist. This action quickly caused the veins in his lower arm to bulge. He carefully chose a vein, pressed the tip of the needle against it and pushed the skin for an instant. The needle broke through the skin and Jamie pulled back the plunger. Thin, wispy ribbons of bright red blood merged with the light brown liquid. He released the belt from his teeth and slowly pushed the plunger all the way home, filling his vein with smack.

I'm curious at how I'm feeling while writing such a voyeuristic account of a process I completed thousands of times over a period of nearly twenty years. I'm happy to report it doesn't leave me salivating with a yearning for smack; neither does it repel me. It's simply a ritual my dysfunctional self of many years ago performed that served its purpose then. I'm a different person today, one who no longer feels the need to seek oblivion.

* * *

I met Heather through Jamie. He brought me to her house to score smack. There was a protocol around bringing strangers to a drug dealer's place, but Jamie had told Heather on the phone he'd known me since junior school.

Jamie and I stood at the doorstep waiting for an answer to his knock. A young girl opened the door, probably around ten or eleven years old. She knew Jamie so walked away from the door back into the house and Jamie and I entered.

We passed through the dining room then crossed into the lounge through some curtains that had replaced the door to find a middle-aged guy sitting on some throw cushions.

"Hi Jamie," he said, gesturing towards the sofa for us to be seated.

"Hey, Johnny. This is an old friend of mine, Christian."

"Pleasure to meet you." John greeted me with a smile and held out his hand. I shook it then joined Jamie on the sofa while Johnny returned his focus to the spliff he was rolling.

The curtains were closed even though it was gone noon. I scanned my eyes around the room. The walls and ceiling were covered in large egg-trays to improve the acoustics and prevent noise bleed. These had been sprayed a deep blue colour and the lighting in the room produced a pleasant, moody atmosphere.

Music was playing on the record player that contained strong expletives with some great guitar riffs: Marianne Faithful's *Why'd Ya Do What You Did?*

Beneath the stereo units lay one of the largest collections of vinyl records I'd ever seen. Bob, Ellen, and Andy were really into their records, but this took album collections to another level. My musical education went from school to university in this room over the next several months. Johnny was an *aficionado* of music from the '60's and '70's and would soon introduce me to some of the best albums I'd ever come across.

A woman silently entered the room through the curtains. She had long blonde hair and was, I'd say, in her mid-thirties and about five-and-a-half feet tall. She came further into the room and gracefully lowered herself on the throw cushions beside Johnny. She moved with slow and deliberate movements, which I found mesmerising.

"Hey Jamie, how you doing? How's Adam?" Adam was Jamie's brother.

She gave me a smile and offered her hand. "Hello, I'm Heather, nice to meet you."

"Hi, Heather. Christian. Likewise, I like this place. Nicely done out."

"Thanks," she said, "that's mostly down to Johnny here. He's the artist."

"What can I do you?" Heather asked Jamie.

"Can I get five grammes?"

"Sure," Heather said. She lifted herself back up and left the room.

The remaining three of us shared Johnny's spliff and, when Marianne finished on the record player, Johnny put on *The Low Spark of High-Heeled Boys* by Traffic from the early seventies, an album I came to love.

Heather returned with the smack, Jamie handed over some crinkled notes and we both left. We returned to Bob and Ellen's where we all smoked the smack on silver foil this time. I would alternate between this method, known as *Chasing the Dragon*, and injecting for many weeks before settling on solely injecting. Jamie assured me it wouldn't be long before I could phone Heather myself to go to score smack from her directly. This proved to be the case. I began to score for me, Bob, Ellen, Andy, and others, and to sell a little more each time and thereby pay for my own smack.

I began spending more time at Heather's with Jamie, getting high on smack and also being introduced to lots of new music by Johnny.

There was always a lot of traffic in and out of the house. At all times of the day visitors would knock on the front door to score smack or Charlie, or drugs in pill form, or the green prescription liquid methadone, popular when no smack was available and withdrawal symptoms loomed. There were often one or two people locked in the bathroom banging up (slang for injecting). It wasn't unusual to see a girl drop her jeans in a room full of people and inject herself in the groin because she had no other veins left. The groin was always the go-to vein when all others had collapsed from overuse. I became accustomed to many things far from the norm during this apprenticeship—it was a crazy scene. Heather's house epitomized an early eighties drug den, and it attracted all kinds of misfits from Farnborough's underbelly. The visitors weren't solely drug-takers. I remember many of Farnborough's tough guys, who were mostly beer-drinkers, spending afternoons in the house during the summer months. There was a good atmosphere and music would be pumping out from the open windows.

Within a few months Johnny disappeared from the scene. I'm not sure whether he was in prison or whether he was in a different town—he was just not around. Not long after his absence, I began sharing more than Heather's stash and ended up in her bed. From that moment on, I no longer needed to pay for my own smack.

Being with Heather was dangerous because my intake was increasing. Despite using smack a lot during those days, I had no sense I was dependent on the drug. My use was becoming a daily occurrence, and I was no longer chasing the dragon at all. Injecting had taken over. I was also spending more and more time at Heather's house and less time with Bob and Ellen, Andy, and Alison. Slowly I was being sucked into this world of hardcore heroin users, and Heather ensured I didn't need to search for it anymore.

I returned to the house one sunny afternoon to find a driving instructor's car parked outside. I'd seen it before when the house had been busy and remembered it belonged to a guy named Adrian. In fact, it belonged to his father who ran a driving school. I walked into the house and up the stairs to Heather's bedroom and found the door was locked. I was certain I'd heard more than one voice inside before I turned the handle. Adrian wasn't just injecting with Heather in there.

Heather's eldest son, Darren, had an air rifle in pieces by the bottom of the stairs, near the kitchen door, so I picked up the long barrel section by its thin end. The other end was rectangular and weighty.

I stepped outside the house, walked over to the driving instructor's car, and shouted up at the bedroom window.

"Adrian, get your arse out here."

Looking back today, I know I should have walked away. But I'd become dependent on the scene, on Heather, and on the heroin. Instead of being angry at Heather who had chosen to take another guy to her bed, I was angry at Adrian.

"Last chance, Adrian. I'm gonna trash the fucking car!"

I saw the curtains twitch but there was no sign of anybody coming outside to face my fury.

I smashed one of the car's headlights with the rifle barrel, the explosion of glass extremely satisfying.

"Come on out or I'm gonna keep trashing the car."

There was still no sign of Adrian, and I guess that's not surprising. Were the roles reversed, I don't think I'd have come outside to face me either.

I smashed the second headlight, which was just as satisfying as the first. Then the windscreen, while still shouting at Adrian to come outside. The glass exploded everywhere, inside the car, all over the bonnet, and onto the street. I knew one of the neighbours would have called the police by now, so I had to satisfy myself with trashing a couple of the side windows and getting the hell out of there.

The next day I returned to the house.

"I don't know why you had to overreact like that," Heather said, immediately trying to place the burden of guilt on to me. "Adrian and I were just banging up but, when he heard how angry you were, he was scared and asked me not to open the door."

"Yeah, sure, Heather. You just keep telling yourself that. I know what was going on and nothing you say will change my mind."

"Adrian's father has reported you to the police so now you'll be nicked for smashing the car up and you'll be locked up again. How very clever of you." Her voice was scathing.

"I won't be nicked for it 'cause you're going to pass on to Adrian *and* his father that if I am, I'll come looking for them both."

I turned and left, slamming the front door behind me. I never was questioned by the police so I guess it may well have been the most expensive afternoon of sex Adrian ever had.

Heather and I didn't stay together for long after that incident. The relationship—if it could be called that—had lasted around four months.

It ended badly, following a similar pattern to the end of my relationship with Toni. Heather said goodbye, I was banished from her house, and the reliance I felt on her once again found me trying to end my shitty life. I was fucked up on heroin and had been dumped by another woman I was certain I loved. I'd learned from my last suicide attempt paracetamol was no way to kill oneself. As an injecting drug user, however, I now knew exactly how to end it all—air. An injection of air. I knew that would kill anyone.

My recollection of this second attempt on my own life is crystal clear. I remember my eyes were blurred with tears. My life was so fucked up. *Why the hell does it have to be so painful?* I asked myself. I was inside one of the stairwells in Totland Close, it seemed fitting for my dead body to be found on the cold concrete half-landing of my old stomping ground. The place where so many of my memories had been lived out.

I drew the needle towards my vein, my left hand to the crook of my right elbow. My vision was blurred from the warm tears etching tracks down my face.

This was it—instant death this time. No going back. No burden on the hospital. No stomach pump. I heard footsteps coming up the steps, but I really couldn't care less. I pushed the needle until it punctured my skin.

The couple who had been coming up the stairs stepped on to the half-landing and saw me crouched down, injecting myself. I heard the man speak to his wife, his girlfriend: "We have to get out of this fucking place!" before they continued up the next flight of stairs.

Neither of them was to know they were witnessing a fellow human being ending his life. To them I was just another Totland junkie banging up smack in a stairwell.

I pushed the plunger and I remember hearing the air bubbles racing up my vein. I waited to die. "How will I know I'm dead?" I wondered. I guessed I would swoon into blackness, the void. But there was nothing. I was still conscious in the stairwell. I repeated the action and injected another syringe full of air into my vein. Same thing. I heard the bubbles travelling through the vein, but I was still alive. I was evidently not meant to die that evening.

I stood upright, wiped my eyes dry and headed back down the stairs the way I'd come. I walked into the square of Totland Close and looked up at the clear sky above. I was alive, my life was still shit, but the desire to die had left my being so I slowly walked away from the square back to my mother's house and collapsed into my bed. Sleep was welcome and I awoke the next day still feeling heartbroken but glad I was alive.

Heather and I were separated and, just as it had with Toni, my heartbreak was cured by another spell in prison. I'd had some shoplifting and fencing charges pending in the magistrates' court and I was sentenced to six months in Winchester prison.

Writing this now, I am pleased to say that was my final attempt at taking my own life. Heather died three or four years ago and, when my friend told me the news, he commented a lot of Farnborough's mothers would have been happily singing on that day. I've no idea what demons Heather had been dealing with before I met her or how she had been fucked up in her own time.

Today I listen to a lot of Dr. Gabor Maté's lectures and talks on YouTube. Maté is a Canadian physician, addiction expert, and public speaker. I have an awful lot of respect for him and his ideas around childhood trauma, addiction, and recovery. Some of his work was conducted on the Lower East Side of Vancouver, the district with the highest number of injecting drug users in the world. He says that every single female drug user he has dealt with over the years was a victim of sexual abuse. Every one. I cannot second-guess the problems that led Heather to become Farnborough's most prolific heroin dealer, but I wouldn't be surprised if there was a history of sexual abuse. She was on the same self-destructive trajectory as all of those who bought her product but was lucky that she outlived many of them. I'd guess she was in her early seventies when she died, which confirms the adage "the only problem with heroin is no heroin." She'd learned early on to ensure she always had a constant supply.

I'd been sentenced to six months' imprisonment for various offences and was sent to what was termed the "Doll's House," the young offenders wing at H.M.P. Winchester. It didn't take long before I was brought to the governor's attention for causing trouble on the landings and, once again, I found myself stood before him in an adjudication.

"What's the charge?" he asked the screw.

"Disobeying an order, governor," the screw informed him.

"Okay, Austin, I can see from your record you're going to pose a control problem for my officers so I'm going to 'star you up.' Tomorrow you'll be transferred to the men's prison next door where you will complete your sentence. I'd be pleased if you could keep your head down and we see as little of each other as possible. Do you understand?"

"Yes, sir," I responded, secretly pleased I'd be escaping the doll's house. This was in the spring of 1982, so at nineteen years old, I was being transferred to the adult prison where prisoners were over twenty-one years old.

The next morning a screw came and collected me from my cell, and I was led through a series of gates out of the young offenders' block and into the main prison. I was taken to B-wing and led to a cell on the lower floor.

"You'll be working in the kitchens," the screw told me. I learned this lower floor of B-wing was dedicated solely to kitchen inmates, the biggest advantage being a single cell. It was fantastic news. I'd guess the doll's house governor had spoken with the main prison governor and I'd been given the position as a means of trying to help me integrate. Kitchen jobs in prison are a genuine privilege, and it would soon become evident why.

The first day or two involved the usual induction process. I met the prison chaplain, the welfare officer, was instructed on the prison's rules, and was told I'd be the butcher's assistant in the kitchens. This was a great job and had all kinds of perks attached to it. I soon discovered I could sell sugar and coffee to inmates up on the wings. I also had access to the fridge that held the cheese and the cold meats, so these items also found their way up the stairs in exchange for tobacco, cash, or hash. This was in 1982, and heroin wasn't yet common within the prison estate.

During the day my duties included helping the butcher (also an inmate) carry halves of pigs or quarters of cows from delivery trucks in the yard to the freezer. He taught me how to bone some of the meat, so I'd assist with that while he was busy with other more refined butchering duties. I'd also have to prepare the butters and some of the special diets' dishes. It was a good job to have landed, and the perks were incredible.

We all had access to the best food and could help ourselves to pretty much anything throughout the day. It was forty years ago but I remember the twenty inmates down there formed a reasonably happy family. Mr. Frost was the kitchen manager. He was an enormous man and he wasn't averse to having a joke. One day he picked me up and placed me in one of the huge kettles filled with water that were used for cooking different vegetables, soups, and stews. It wasn't the oppressive atmosphere normally associated with prison labour. It was summertime and the daily hour in the exercise yard was balmy and enjoyable. I have fond memories of my time spent there.

It sounds a contradiction in terms, prison time being enjoyable, but life doesn't simply stop. We formed friendships, we could get high on weed in the evenings once the screw had locked the doors and departed. There would still be a night screw doing the occasional walkabout on the landing but, if we wanted an early warning system, we'd sprinkle sugar on the floor outside our cell doors and be alerted by the crunching beneath any screws' shoes. There were occasional fights, sure, but that's to be expected in a male environment, especially one filled with criminals and violent offenders.

When it came time to serve the food, it was all hands on deck. Every inmate in the kitchen had to serve because there were hundreds of prisoners coming through the servery area. They would come through one wing at a time, hundreds of men then, finally, the Rule 43 prisoners, escorted by screws in front and behind. Rule 43 prisoners are those on protection. Men who wouldn't last more than a few minutes living amongst the general population. There were many different reasons for this—some were rapists, some were child molesters, some had murdered women or old people in particularly nasty ways and other inmates wanted to hurt them for their crimes. Some had asked for protection because they had debts they couldn't pay and weren't able to defend themselves.

There were different punishments meted out to such prisoners if they were discovered in the general population, depending on their crimes. The most hated of these were the child molesters and rapists and, if discovered on the wings, they'd potentially have their face cut open with a razor (perhaps two razor blades melted into the end of a toothbrush, a particularly nasty and effective weapon). Another common punishment was a kettle full of boiling water with half a bag of sugar added to it. This would melt the victim's skin from their face. These punishments were horrific, and occasionally it would transpire the victim had been innocent.

On the flip side, there was a disgusting practice among the "nonces" —prison slang for rapists and child molesters—of the sharing of their depositions amongst each other. Depositions is the collective term for prosecution and defence papers, doctors' examination reports and the like. The idea of these types of prisoners sharing these documents for their own self-gratification is reprehensible and beyond belief. I'd heard of this practice from different people several times over the years.

Around this time a woman had been raped and murdered while walking her dogs in the Aldershot area. It felt more personal to me as I'd read of it in Farnborough's local paper. The guy who committed the crime had been sentenced and I'd serve him his food each day. An anger would well up in me each time I saw him approach and I glared at him as I slammed mashed potato on to his metal food tray. I'd like to have smashed him around the head with his tray, to be perfectly honest.

I was told the governor wanted to see me. I'd see him in the kitchen regularly because one of his duties as governor was to taste a sample of the lunchtime meal. He was in Mr. Frost's office and had the sample of food before him when I walked over.

"Ah, Austin," he greeted me. "Do you like your job in the kitchen?"

"Yes, sir," I answered. It was true—I had a profitable racketeering scam going on that kept me in all the luxuries I desired.

"Well, perhaps you might desist from intimidating some of the Rule 43 prisoners. What do you think? There are plenty of prisoners who'd happily take your job."

"Yes, sir. I know that. I'll follow your advice, sir."

"Good. Mr. Frost, perhaps you could see to it Austin serves from the back of the servery in future?"

It wasn't long after the incident with the nonce that I was moved into the bakery to work. There was less black-market trading for me in the bread business, which was unfortunate. But I was nearing the end of the four months I'd had to serve. I also remember working in the wash-up area as I counted down the days to my release.

The wash-up area was situated in what was once the "drop-room" in the days of capital punishment. It felt strange knowing the bodies of men sentenced to death had dropped through what was now a ceiling and swung about waiting to be pronounced dead. They'd then be cut down and buried on unconsecrated ground within the prison.

My release date came and, once again, I collected my possessions and was spat out of the prison's gates and onto the streets of Winchester.

"See you in a few weeks, Austin," the prison officers cheerfully called as I walked away. I didn't bother responding, just continued down the hill from the prison towards the city centre with my few possessions.

Freedom! Not only freedom but the inexpressible feeling of freedom that comes with being released from a cage that, unless you've been caged for months on end, you could never truly understand. Months of looking up at what Oscar Wilde referred to as "that little tent of blue" in his *Ballad of Reading Gaol*, of being surrounded by twenty-foot walls designed to keep a man within the prison perimeter.

I'd read this *Ballad of Reading Gaol* several times through my prison years, and my favourite and most apposite stanzas are these:

Each narrow cell in which we dwell
Is a foul and dark latrine,
And the fetid breath of living Death
Chokes up each grated screen,
And all, but Lust, is turned to dust
In Humanity's machine.

Oscar Wilde, 19 May 1897

"All but Lust." So very true. Lust is all we were left with. Homosexuality was an option but not one that seemed common in prisons I spent time in—at least not openly. I did hear over the years it was more prevalent in lifer prisons, but those guys had to consider they were behind bars for fifteen years or more, not just months. For me, being celibate for a few months or even a year or two wasn't going to change me; I'd simply await my release date.

I knew Winchester well from my days spent in Winton House and Ashborne Lodge, so I headed for the train station but stopped at a pub *en route*. I hadn't drunk a beer in four months, and this was traditionally one of the first duties of a newly released prisoner. I ordered a pint of lager and bought a pack of "tailor-made" cigarettes from a machine on the wall—a pleasant change from the hand-rolled tobacco mostly smoked in prison—then found myself an outside table to sit at where I could absorb and relish these first tangible moments back in the real world. I alternated a sip from the chilled fresh beer and a long drag from the smoke, closing my eyes as I exhaled.

The sun was now higher in the sky, rising above the adjacent buildings and casting its glow over the beer garden, slowly warming my skin, something I'd not felt enough over the preceding months. I wanted to make the most of the feeling of soft grass beneath my feet, listening to the birds' chirping mingling with the sounds of passing traffic instead of slamming doors and sharp jangling keys. The taste of free air and of beer and smoke combined with a heady sense of raw excitement.

I finished the beer and bought another—resisting the urge to shout, "I'm free!" at the bartender—and lit another cigarette, enjoying the moment, a new moment where there were no expectations, where nobody knew me, and where I felt a sense of anonymity for the first time in months.

11

Let the Sunshine In
(The Fifth Dimension)

Car after car flashed past me without stopping, bright sunlight bouncing from their enamelled shells as they slid by. A forty-foot truck and trailer roared along behind them, and I had to shield my eyes from the dry cloud of dust swirling in its wake. I'd been stood on this same spot with my thumb out for twenty minutes since my last ride dropped me off.

Ahead of me was the main route towards Basingstoke, behind me a long post and rail fence with miles of green crops waving in the light breeze. I had a small backpack, a two-man tent, and a guitar. I couldn't walk any further because the road ahead was motorway and so forbidden to pedestrians. It was 1 June 1984, and I was hitching to my first Stonehenge festival. The air was heavy and lazy, I was covered in a patina of sweat, and my life was about to take a new and different direction.

Possibly the hundredth car to roll by me slowed, pulled on to the verge, and emitted a beep. Pulling the backpack onto my shoulder and grabbing the guitar and tent bag, I ran to the driver's window. A smiley guy with blond hair was grabbing stuff from the passenger seat and slinging it onto the back seats ready for me to jump in.

"Hey, where you headed?" he asked.

"Stonehenge, if you're headed that way?"

"Sure am. Driving right past it, then all the way to Exeter. Jump in."

I opened the rear door, threw my gear inside then climbed in the front. The hot leather of the seat burned my legs as I sat down, and the car pulled away.

"Hey, my name's Scott," said my new driver, stretching his right hand across to me.

We shook hands then he pulled away into the traffic. I guessed he was around ten years older than me and was dressed casually with a suit jacket but had a good build. *Probably no stranger to the gym*, I thought.

"You're visiting the monument?"

"Christian. Thanks for the lift," I responded, shaking his hand in return. "I was starting to roast out there. Yeah, kind of, but I'm mainly going for the festival being held there."

"There's a festival there? I didn't know."

"Well, to be completely honest, I only know about it coz my friend was there last year and hasn't shut up about it for twelve months." We both laughed at this as I continued, "His wild stories have made me wanna check it out. What're you doing in Exeter?"

"Oh, I'm speaking at a conference there tomorrow, at the University," he said. "I do research around farming practices in third world countries. It's really boring unless it's your subject."

We both laughed again. This guy seemed cool.

"You're a musician?"

"Let's say I'm trying to be."

"I used to play trumpet but then—without really noticing—one day I no longer did. I suppose too much responsibility landed in my lap. Oh yeah, and the wife and kids leave me with less time. Much less."

Scott smiled at his own words, and I sensed no blame or regret; he sounded happy with the way things were. We soon arrived at the junction I needed, and excitement filled me as I spotted the monument with a splash of colourful marquees and vehicles scattered close by.

"Hey, this'll do me. Thanks for the lift." I pulled my "tat" from the back seat, said goodbye, and Scott pulled away.

I was about to step into the most pivotal and transformational moment of my life. The subculture I would experience at Stonehenge was like nothing I'd ever encountered and, along with my experiences of absconding from care homes, would change and strengthen my character enormously. It's no exaggeration to say these experiences saved me from the early death that befell so many of my contemporaries, and the probability of my being sentenced to life imprisonment. I picked up my backpack, guitar, and tent then walked along the road towards this new future.

As I neared the festival site, I saw it resembled a settlement of tents, marquees, coaches, small- to large-sized vans and trucks, all painted in bright colours with curtains in the windows and metal chimneys jutting out from their roofs. I'd never seen anything like it.

Placing my backpack on the ground and laying the guitar against it, I sat on the dry grass and rolled a spliff. I wanted to acclimatise myself to this new world and experience it slowly, to take in each moment and sight. Bob had been right: this would open my eyes to things completely outside my range of experience. I lit the twisted end of the spliff and scanned these strange surroundings.

My dealings with hippies up to that point of my life had been limited. Bob, Ellen, and Andy identified as hippies although Alison would never have done so—she was more of an early Goth. Some of the guys who showed up at Heather's also looked like hippies, and perhaps a few other people around Farnborough but not to this extent. There were plenty of punk-looking types in the field too but most of the people living in these vehicles fit my stereotype of hippies.

The next day, more people arrived, and the site began to grow. This continued each day and soon my focus revolved around an area consisting of friends from my own stomping ground—Farnborough, Camberley, and Yateley. Keith Lovett was there, as was Jem Hammick, Claire, Sonia, Richard Burbidge, Hellan, Sheridan, Lisa Bowen, and many others. Andy Clubbs turned up with his brother, Dave, and together we built an innovative bender (a tent made from ash poles and a tarpaulin similar to an inverted basket).

Over the next week this settlement became a small town. Stages were set up, as were medical tents, small shops, a multitude of food concessions, bars and scrumpy stalls, and innumerable small camps where performers and artists were welcome. The green field I initially arrived at soon became a sprawling colourful carpet of tents, marquees, benders, and live-in vehicles. I'm really not surprised this world became my own over the next couple of decades. It felt wonderfully new and exciting to me, and I was completely in awe of this alternative scene I'd stumbled upon.

I quickly integrated myself into this community and soon felt at home. Many encampments displayed pricelists of different types of hash, LSD, and many other substances. It was incredible. Every few yards were boards on display with prices announcing:

"Red Leb, Thai-sticks, Malawi grass, Red Seal" and a whole bunch of other smokables.

"Smiley Mushrooms, Red Hearts, Windowpanes, Blue, Black, and Purple Microdots" and other types of LSD.

"Speed" and "Cocaine" priced per line or per gramme.

The opportunity to earn money soon presented itself when other less canny festivalgoers asked if I could source drugs for them. I quickly became a small-time dealer and also began consuming the acid tabs myself each day. One day I might drop one tab, the next maybe two. The thing with acid is a tolerance is gradually built up—meaning I needed a larger dose for the same effect each time—so over the course of the four weeks I was at the festival, my consumption increased daily from one to two or three or more for the same effect. Along with acid, I was also dabbling in buying speed, hash, and cocaine for others—again, enabling me to consume what I wanted without having to spend my own cash.

The festival was a police no-go zone. I'm uncertain of the reaction they'd have been met with had they walked on site in their uniforms, but they evidently weren't willing to give it a shot. I wasn't so stupid as to believe there were no undercover police blending in around the site but uniformed coppers? None. At least, not at that point.

The sun slowly lowered in the west casting long shadows. Keith, Jem, and I were wandering around this town that felt like our own dipping in and out of different experiences—a hot knife here, a line of coke or speed there, a chillum every time we heard the cry of "Half a mix." Every few yards we travelled along the main drag one source of music would blur with another then the same process would repeat over and over—so many encampments playing their own music, either through car stereos or on musical instruments.

I glimpsed many different smiling, talking, singing faces in the glow of all the fires we passed. These were built to keep warm and gather around at each encampment using wood from the nearby forest or pallets and timber brought to site on return trips from different hometowns. The delicious smell of wood smoke carried across the site and hovered a short distance above the tops of the multitude of dwellings. We arrived back at our own camp and entered the bender.

I found an empty space and sat on the carpeted floor. I was feeling the acid coursing through my veins. Everything seemed funny and wondrous in equal measure. My friends' voices, and my own, played tricks with my hearing, either running ahead at faster speeds or slowing like someone placing their finger on a record's turntable. Colours and music blended together and washed over me in waves. A bong was being passed around, so I took it and inhaled until its chamber filled with smoke. I released the shotgun and felt the smoke's bite hit deep. I felt amazing, floating so completely high on the different chemicals pulsing through my system. Speed, nicotine, acid, opium, hash, cider, all vying for supremacy within my mashed brain. This was the normal of my 1984 period and, although many of these listed drugs are considered detrimental, not all were. My experiences with psychedelics—i.e., acid, psilocybe, fly agaric, and to a lesser extent, cannabis—changed my perspective and my world view to the extent that I'd never think "normally" again. These types of drugs opened avenues in my mind that I feel converted my whole way of thinking. Such changes didn't occur immediately, but these encounters contributed over the ensuing years to my breaking away from the violent dog eat dog world I'd inhabited up until that point. I feel they increased my empathy until I slowly turned my back on the activities I'd learned were the norm from my teenage experiences. They also helped me conclude I never wanted to lead a life that was mainstream.

As the sun hovered in the mid-morning sky the following day, I walked through this magical village towards its main entrance then crossed the road to visit the Stonehenge monument, joining the throng of regular tourists in asking the same questions: *Why was this even built? How did our ancestors manage to transport these enormous menhirs from such far-flung locations as the Preseli Hills in South West Wales? What kinds of ceremonies had been enacted here over the millennia? What force had toppled some headstones while leaving their pillars upright?*

The English Heritage leaflet and the many information boards scattered around all failed to give satisfactory answers and seemed mostly conjecture backed up by spurious archaeological data, so my questions remained unanswered.

I turned and slowly left the standing stones then headed back towards the festival, nodding and smiling at occasional hippies I encountered, sharing a tacit rapport with them. The sight from the road filled me with the same awe it had since the middle of June: a sea of around 30,000 people awash with colour; long buses scattered here and there among the smaller vehicles; tents, benders, and marquees; and innumerable multi-coloured flags flapping in the gusting breeze.

I crossed the road and entered site from the main entrance then walked in the direction of my camp when I heard a voice call from nearby.

"Hey, man, you got any room for a tattoo?"

The speaker was sporting a dusty maroon beret, a faded blue denim jacket, and a large, happy grin. There was a few days' stubble scratching across his chin and he was squinting into the sun with one hand above his eyes to reduce the glare. I walked closer and found him sitting at a small campfire with a blackened kettle, a few mugs, various pots, and a huge chrome bong made from large hexagonal nuts gradually decreasing in size from bottom to top.

"I see you have some tattoos. I wanna test my equipment…hoping you'll be my guinea pig. They call me Tattoo Pete, or Bom Shanka Pete. What d'ya say?"

"Hi, man. Christian," I replied, offering my hand. "Why not?"

He pulled a camp chair closer to the fire and bade me sit then handed me a box filled with sheets of small transfers, different images on each.

"Here, choose something you like while I set up the gun."

Another seminal moment in my life, this one bringing me both a new friend and my all-time favourite tattoo.

Pete finished setting up the tattoo gun and attached its two crocodile clips to the terminals of a twelve-volt car battery. The gun instantly jumped to life with a bright whirring noise, and I could see the needle flashing rapidly from its end. Pete next set up a small table and placed jars of different coloured inks and a box of tissues on it.

"You wanna smoke? Opium and black? It's medicinal."

"Of course." I laughed. I'd always had a good tolerance for pain, but the prospect of this pain killer was welcome—it would agitate the acid still in my bloodstream and lift me a little higher.

The bong had a long flexible pipe that I placed in my mouth, then Pete lit the mix inside the bowl. I drew on the pipe and was quickly bathed in clouds of thick smoke.

I chose a picture of a large yellow sun rising above two clumps of magic mushrooms—one clump of psilocybes and another of fly agaric (the common red mushroom covered in white spots). This held a significance for me then and still does today because the smiley mushroom tabs I'd been consuming for weeks had a similar image on each: that of a fly agaric mushroom with a pair of eyes and a huge grin on its wide stem.

Tattoo Pete placed the transfer on my upper left arm then peeled it off. He next followed the image left there with the tattoo gun and I felt the heat of the needle burning like a hot wire being drawn across my skin. He followed the image's outline in black ink first then used coloured ink to infill the yellows, reds, browns, and greens of the sun, the grass, and the mushrooms. After thirty minutes, my tattoo was complete. Pete cleaned the image of blood and coloured ink and finished with a smear of Vaseline, a swab of lint, then a bandage, and an instruction to keep the tattoo clean.

* * *

A day or two later, I was lying on my stomach in the summer sunshine and heat, surrounded by a few friends, when I saw a sight that both amazed me and filled me with trepidation. I wasn't in fear for myself but, rather, for the future of this fantastic wonderland I'd been a part of for weeks.

Taking a walk around the site were three high-ranking members of Wiltshire's constabulary. I couldn't believe it. These coppers had walked through the whole site, witnessing every hash, speed, cocaine, and acid "For Sale" sign *en route*. To me, this stank of future trouble and my hunch was to prove correct. I believe to this day that walkabout contributed more than anything to what occurred the following year.

12

All the Young Dudes
(David Bowie)

Securing the rope with a tight knot, we finished hanging a water butt filled with red diesel from the ceiling of the coach then fed a thin hose from its mouth down through a hole in the floor. The fuel pump was fucked so gravity was the only way to feed the engine. At the back end, the coach's ceiling was covered with sheets of plywood and a large tarpaulin because Adrian was rebuilding the roof to render it watertight again. This was fairly typical of travellers' vehicles during the 1980s, moving from one festival or site to another with repairs half complete. As we pulled out of the field leaving the Silver Moon festival behind us, we joined the convoy heading west, the diesel container heavily swinging above Adrian's left shoulder as he drove.

The convoy snaked its way along country roads past Alston and down to the main roundabout on Penrith's ring road. Several police cars had stopped all other traffic from using the roundabout to allow the convoy to enter the A66. This was one of the craziest convoys I'd travelled with up to this point, and the Cumbria police force wished to escort it out of their county so it would become another force's problem. Farther into the journey, service stations were blocked along the route so vehicles couldn't refuel and the police picked off many travellers as a result of this ploy. Buses, trucks, vans, and cars filled with hippies straddled all three lanes of the A1 motorway, many only capable of speeds around forty miles per hour. I remember the whole scene being chaotic although the weather was fine and dry and I was absolutely enjoying the adventure.

The greater part of the convoy made it to Nostell Priory, close to the city of Wakefield. This was the home of the Oswald family and there was to be a three-day festival showcasing bands such as Steeleye Span, Lindisfarne, Van Morrison, The Damned, and Doctor and the Medics.

We arrived a couple of days before the festival's start date and the atmosphere was chilled, not busy. I spent the day performing various duties around the café—tying guy ropes, sledge-hammering long metal pins deep into the ground, chopping vegetables, whatever needed doing. This alternative site was situated alongside the main festival and was dedicated to us travellers. My friends and I had erected our small marquee and prepared the same café we'd worked at the Silver Moon festival. Once set up, I made a huge tobacco and hash mix and began rolling spliff after spliff, each of which would eventually be sold for a pound each. While I was busy rolling the spliffs, the rest of our crew cooked large pots of food to tempt hungry punters with.

My evenings were spent checking out the rest of the site and hanging out with Bom Shanka Pete and other friends I'd met since arriving at Stonehenge two months beforehand. Phil the Beer was there, as was One-Armed Pete (a previous army medic with only one arm and a Leyland FG named Ygor's Revenge), PD, Roger the Dodger, Alex (or 'Bump,' as he was known), Gyp, John the Greek, and many others whose names are beyond the scope of my memory today.

Also among our group were a couple of geese named Boris and Doris. These two characters waddled freely around site scavenging whatever food they could from the many traders' concessions. They were also the head of a promotional company named Boris and Doris Productions. I'd previously seen this moniker on posters advertising musical events.

I dropped some acid on the second evening after our arrival and became transfixed by a shirtless guy breathing fire. Large balls of red, yellow, and orange flame exploded from his upturned mouth and lit the night sky, each ball dimming the image of the floodlit priory in the background.

He noticed me staring at his performance with burning eyes and mouth agape.

"Wanna try?" he asked with a beaming grin. He had some kind of accent, maybe French. Another huge ball of flame spewed from his mouth.

"Is it easy?" I responded to his question.

"Sure is. I can teach you in five minutes."

It's an incredible and exciting memory today. My tripped-out mind was torn between the fundamental fear of fire and the excitement of being able to mimic this living fire-breathing dragon within five minutes. I decided to go with the dragon. He quickly taught me how to expel white spirits from my mouth in a powerful spray while holding a burning faggot a couple of feet from my face. He told me to draw my head back as I spat out the spray and, *voilà,* I too was breathing fire beside him. My new friend was a Frenchman named Etienne with a tanned brown body and dreadlocked hair tied into a topknot on the crown of his head. We sat down on the dry grass together and I drew a spliff from my pocket.

"Where you from, man?" I asked him as I lit the spliff from the burning faggot.

"Lyon, in France," he replied, "although I've been in the UK for a couple of years now." It showed in his spoken English. While heavily accented, it was way better than my basic French.

We finished the spliff, extinguished the faggot, and I invited him to our small encampment and introduced him to the gang.

The festival appeared to be going really well although—unbeknown to me—there were problems brewing within the organization. I didn't spend much time in the main festival and simply hung around the traveller's field with my new family. I do recall hearing the music from the main stage throughout the afternoons and evenings, particularly the set played by The Damned.

On Sunday, the final day of the festival, while the remaining bands were playing on the main stage, I heard the tale of the festival's problems through the site grapevine. Whether this was the true story or not I'll never know as rumours abound and Chinese whispers become 'facts' as quick as a flash. Word was there hadn't been sufficient promotion of the event, which subsequently manifested into a poor turnout and few ticket sales—instead of the anticipated 30,000 punters, a mere 2,000 turned up. This resulted in the event organiser absconding with the takings before paying the catering staff, stewards, and security guards. They'd be paid no wages.

A collection box circulated among the traders and dealers on our site and around £800 was handed to the caterers as payment for their equipment: bain-maries, hotplates, industrial cookers, and a large marquee. The marquee was promptly dismantled and the equipment loaded onto trucks.

The following day, the police showed up demanding the return of the catering equipment. There was a meeting between the travellers and the police, and an agreement was reached: the equipment would be returned and the police would escort the convoy from the county of Yorkshire so we would, yet again, become a thorn in the side of a different police force. The catering paraphernalia and marquee were returned and preparations to leave commenced across site. Several vehicles were in various states of repair, including Adrian's coach. I also recall Gyp's bus had no wheels attached and was sat on large wooden blocks.

I spent the Sunday evening in a round yellow-and-red-striped marquee where some bands were playing. The place was packed, and I was sat in the audience with friends. One of these was Etienne, and he declared he'd lost a page of acid, perhaps as many as eighty tabs, so a bunch of us scoured the immediate area but came up empty-handed. This meant the loss of a significant amount of capital, which spoiled the mood a little. I needed to visit the toilet so left the marquee and, while returning to our spot, I noticed something white lying on the ground amongst the straw and the grass. I bent down and realised it was Etienne's page of acid. I happily handed the page to him, and he promptly tore off a few tabs and handed them to me as my reward. I accepted the proffered gift and swallowed them. The remainder of the evening was soon lost in a blurred haze.

I do recall the following morning, however. Sitting in Adrian's coach, I'd watched the night turn to day and was drinking a cup of tea when someone entered the bus and said hundreds of police were swarming towards the site. Looking out through the window and up towards the priory, I discerned two or three phalanxes of black-clad policemen with Transit vans leading each.

This was an early hour of the morning, so most people were sleeping. A shout went up that was soon echoed by many others, and it didn't take long for everybody on site to converge on the yellow-and-red-striped marquee.

The women and children made their way inside while the men formed a protective shield around the entrance awaiting the arrival of the large force of police. We were soon surrounded by hundreds of them looking extremely menacing in visored helmets, riot shields, and batons. Many of our men were tooled up with sticks, billhooks, and axes, and the tension felt like an electrically charged fence between us. One misjudged move from either side had the potential to descend into an angry and violent melee.

The black sea of policemen parted as the most senior police officer on site made his way through and stood before his men. He wore the three silver pips of a Chief Inspector on the epaulettes of his white shirt, a flat cap with a fancy crest above its shining black peak and, raising a megaphone to his lips, uttered possibly the funniest words I've ever heard.

"I'd like to speak to Boris."

The moment of tangible threat, of these two bodies in ominous confrontation, instantly changed to a duality of uproarious laughter and utter confusion. Laughter from the traveller group because everybody knew Boris was a white goose with a yellow beak, confusion from the policemen because they had no comprehension as to why their prey had suddenly switched from protective fear to deep and almost painful belly laughter.

Despite many travellers clutching weapons in their hands, violence would have been offered by very few—it was more a display of tribal protection. Most of these people identified as peace-loving hippies, and the only real risk of violence came from Thatcher's militia.

All the men were escorted to a cluster of waiting police vans. I was the last to be loaded onto my van and was sat opposite a guy who'd perhaps offered some resistance because his hands were 'cuffed behind his back. Once the rear doors were closed, he asked me to pull out his wallet from his inside jacket pocket. This I did. He asked me to open it and place the tab of acid within it onto his tongue. This I also did, proffering a hallucinogenic Eucharist to the faithful. I admired the guy's temerity—off to the dungeons but happily dropping a tab with a guaranteed eight- to ten-hour trip.

The van pulled away from Nostell Priory's grounds and we were ferried to Leeds Bridewell. I know now that there were circa 250 men arrested and deposited in different police stations across the county of Yorkshire. Unbeknown to all of us, while everybody was surrounded by the larger portion of policemen, others were trashing vehicle interiors, smashing windows of vehicles, and pulling out wiring, afterwards claiming to be searching for guns. I also heard Gyp's bus was dragged from its blocks and around the field by a large tow truck, destroying its underside and exhaust pipes. The rumour mill and some alternative media outlets suggest Yorkshire's police chief claimed he was "powerless to act against the convoy." Once the Whore of Babylon—Margaret Thatcher—heard this, she hit the roof and demanded action.

Once in Leeds Bridewell, I was herded into a thirty-man cell with many others, where mayhem prevailed. CCTV cameras were ripped from their mountings and the men began pulling out chillums and pipes and wasted no time in getting high. This may sound incredible today, getting high in a police station, but it must be borne in mind we had been flung into a fleet of police vans *en masse* with no searches taking place beforehand, as might usually be the case. There was little control possible at that point because, unusually for the police, they were dealing with many prisoners with a common bond, a sense of unity. It wasn't until we were taken out individually and asked for our details—names, addresses, dates of birth, etc.—and then ferried to smaller police stations that any real control was possible.

I ended up in Pudsey police station and was interviewed by the police. Despite my denial of any wrongdoing, I was charged with "internal possession of both cannabis and LSD," a spurious charge that rather galled me. I'd never been caught in possession of drugs and this was a source of pride for me, so to be fitted up in this way left me with a sense of betrayal. This was the most common charge among all those arrested and, when speaking with solicitors, we all gained the same response: "This is from the top." Regardless of the solicitors' views on our way of life, I sensed they weren't happy with the government's response. The following day, I was remanded in custody by Leeds magistrates' court.

Armley prison sits on top of a hill in the city of Leeds. Just as in the police station, these screws had never faced a large group of people with such a common bond. Confronted with 250 travellers with a completely strange and different look about them really freaked them out. I witnessed an uneasiness in the screws I'd never experienced in a prison reception before. We were processed in groups of two or three and it was comical. Everybody gave real names and addresses, dates of birth, etc., but the occupation question elicited some fantastic answers. There were many jugglers, clowns, trapeze artists, and unicyclists. The screws were thrown into confusion, and I enjoyed witnessing their discomfort. It was the same on the wings over the next couple of weeks. We got away with a lot more backchat than was usual.

I was a long way from home, as many of us were. Our names were handed out on visits and subsequent visits were arranged. A lovely hippie chick I'd never seen before showed up and kissed me to pass me an eighth of hash from her mouth. A wonderful sense of community and solidarity prevailed, one that I've rarely experienced since.

After a week in Armley prison, I was delivered to Leeds magistrates' court once again. I recall being held in a single cell while awaiting the call to go upstairs and face the magistrates. I began to sing and was told by the duty policemen to desist from singing. I ignored their demand. Three policemen approached my cell, unlocked the door, and entered to give me a quick beating. This wasn't unusual in those days pre-CCTV cameras in custody suites. One policeman gave me a final kick and punch then left the cell and locked the barred door.

Eventually, my cell door was once again unlocked and, angered and bruised by this police brutality, I was led up the stairs to the courtroom. I was asked to plead, and I pleaded not guilty to the spurious charges. I was remanded in Armley for another week and gradually it dawned on me, along with most others, this cycle would repeat until a plea of guilty was entered. On my next magistrates' appearance, I pleaded guilty, was given a £25 fine for each false charge, and walked out into the sunshine a free man.

13

I Fought the Law
(The Clash)

The UK government proclaimed in early 1985 the Stonehenge Free Festival would not take place that year. A High Court injunction had been obtained prohibiting its occurrence. Depending on who you listened to, this was due to its becoming too big for police to manage—the government and Wiltshire County Council's stance—or it was the festival's twelfth consecutive year, which would render it eligible for a Queen's Charter, a rumour stating that any village fete or festival held on the same spot for twelve consecutive years subsequently becomes a people's right. It was probably more because some fucking idiot agreed to allow three policemen to walk around the police "No-Go Zone" at the previous year's festival.

I and many others didn't spend too much time researching either of these premises but instead determined to go ahead with the festival planning and to hell with that Whore of Babylon, Margaret Thatcher, Michael Heseltine, the rest of the UK government, and their militia. Before long, the mantra, "Go for It" was being uttered from every traveller's lips and was emblazoned on every traveller's bus. The festival would go ahead.

* * *

We were waiting in Jan's flat on Perring Avenue in Farnborough. Fitz had gone out to find a suitable vehicle to ferry the six of us and all our belongings to the pre-Stonehenge festival rendezvous, Savernake Forest on the outskirts of the beautiful market town of Marlborough.

We were listening to tunes, drinking, getting high on hash, maybe smoking a bit of heroin on silver foil, all excited we were heading to another Stonehenge festival.

"Here he is!" someone shouted at the window. "He's got a Transit. Quick, grab your gear. Let's go."

A mad dash out of Jan's flat and down the stairs. Everyone bundled their tents, sleeping bags, backpacks, and themselves into the Ford Transit then we were on the road. I pulled some bottles of beer from my bag, Steve McCarthy rolled a spliff or two, the stereo was blasting music. Fuck yeah, a mobile party all the way to Marlborough. We were all praying we wouldn't get stopped by the police.

Fitz was driving and laughing his head off, high as a kite.

"Yeah man! There was a long row of these at the rental company on Victoria Road. They all had the keys hanging in the ignition," he informed us. "Fucking doughnuts! Ha-ha! I jumped in and drove it away—don't think anyone even noticed!"

Police communications weren't as efficient back in the '80s as local police forces weren't nationalized until 1987. It was dumb. So, while the police in Hampshire might be looking for this stolen Ford Transit, we were having a party. The moment we crossed into Surrey County, we would be in the clear.

We made it to Savernake Forest without incident. The Transit van's registration number was recorded by the police as we entered the forest but, as I've said, the lack of a national communication grid worked in our favour. I'm certain within a day or two, word would have reached the guardians of the gate a stolen Ford Transit had slipped through their net. The police would be confident they'd arrest the thieves on their way out and retrieve the vehicle.

Theoretically, the police did have this covered but the reality was another story. Half the vans in the forest were also Ford Transits.

I began asking Transit van owners whether they might need spare parts. I sold the drivers' door to a girl whose own sported a big dent and she also bought the alternator. Both back doors were quickly taken off and sold, then the starter motor, next the complete exhaust assembly. After a few days the van was sat on bricks instead of wheels and soon after that the axles were sold too. It seemed every Transit owner on site was happy to take advantage of my half-price brand-new spare parts bonanza.

A few of us were sleeping in the van at the time and all kinds of drug-taking was occurring: glue-sniffing, chasing heroin, necking Valium, snorting speed. I mean, Christ, we were the most fucked-up coterie from the London overspill known as the GLC estate and Totland Close. Fitz was there, Jem Hammick, Steve McCarthy, Jason Tegg, Little Peewee (all five of whom are no longer with us today, wasted and dead after many years' drug abuse). Jan survived as she wisely left Farnborough shortly after these events.

The ceiling of the van was covered in graffiti, written with the soot from a candle flame. I can see it to this day…the names of my dead-and-gone friends written in smudged black all over that pristine white ceiling. Writing these words today brings the Les Miserable song to mind, "Empty Chairs at Empty Tables" —a different revolution, sure, but one we believed in just as vehemently. (Due to copyright law, I'm not able to quote from the song but a quick internet search will provide the lyrics.)

Over the next week or so I combined selling LSD, cocaine, and hash with trading Ford Transit engine and body parts. Finally, when there was nothing left of the Transit but a shell, we contacted a local scrap dealer who came and paid cash for it. It was lifted onto the back of a flatbed and driven away while we laughed at the thought of the police watching aghast as it left the site.

My heroin habit wasn't raging at this point. I was dabbling in it but wasn't at the stage where I'd suffer withdrawals without it, so the majority of the money made from the Transit was spent on cocaine.

14

Itinerant Child

(Ian Dury)

June 1 arrived and most people were prepared for the drive to Stonehenge. Around midday all roadworthy vehicles were ready to go. Many police across the road watched this assembly, counting vehicles and travellers, relaying the intelligence on to their commanders via walkie-talkies. They must have been incredibly hot in their thick black uniforms and helmets. They'd be even hotter once they all crammed into the many police vans and followed us for hours in the direction of Salisbury.

I'd jumped in my friend Jill's bus along with more friends I'd spent the previous year's festival with—Keith, Claire, Sonya, Richard. The guys I'd driven down with were in various other vehicles waiting to leave. Jill sat in the driver's seat waiting for the vehicles in front to set off. It didn't happen quickly—hippies have a reputation for being behind the beat, as a musician might say.

I was stood on the threshold of the Bedford's nearside door that was situated where a passenger seat would usually be. The door was open and tied in place, so I was hanging out and holding onto a handrail attached to the door opening's side. This was a fantastic position from which to witness the day's events. Looking ahead and behind me, I could see all the vehicles lined up waiting to go. Many travellers were sat on the roofs of some of the buses, or sat on tarpaulins on roof racks or, like me, hanging out of open doorways.

Flagpoles made from ash branches were lashed onto the front and rear ends of buses, coaches, trucks, vans, and even cars—a vivid splash of fabric fluttering atop each one: Peace, CND, Greenpeace, Anarchy, Che Guevara, Tibetan, Confederate rebel. A collection of assorted ideas all springing from the same foundation, that of the travelling festival community, a cohesive community striving for freedom of movement and fighting the oppression of Thatcher's policies and increasingly restrictive laws. Most of the people gathered at the forest entrance that day had been with me at Stonehenge the year before. Many had been at Molesworth when Michael Heseltine and his camouflaged troops had evicted the camp. Many had earned their wings under the harsh conditions of the Greenham Common women's camp, protesting against the US' deployment of cruise missiles. We had all tasted the oppression of Thatcher and her militia's baton in one way or another. To these people, me included, this day was a form of standing up for one's beliefs…as well as being a reckoning.

The lead vehicles began to move. We were situated behind the Rasta bus, a cream-coloured bus emblazoned with the red, yellow, and green stripes of the Rastafarian flag. Vehicles in front of us began revving engines and the convoy slowly breathed life. A hazy smog pervaded the balmy air around the forest entrance, the harsh bite of diesel fumes filled my nostrils, and adrenalin filled my veins as this collective beast came to life. More vehicles began to move, evident from the whooping of voices and the long blasts of horns. As the Rasta bus pulled forward, Jill dropped the Bedford's clutch, and we too shifted forwards…slowly to begin with but with increasing momentum. Each vehicle's engine and horn blast added to the cacophony of whoops and screams as more and more trucks, buses, coaches, double-deckers, cars, and vans joined the exodus from the forest's mouth onto the road to Salisbury. The moment we'd all gathered for and awaited this past week had arrived. We were heading for Stonehenge—only twenty-five miles away but it may as well have been on the moon.

One of the most enduring memories I have of this convoy journey was a couple of miles after we'd left the forest and hit the countryside with its wide-open fields. I hung from the bus doorway and looked back. The view reminded me of the way I'd draw a road as a child: ranging over a few hills but having a different start and end point on each hill with the hills decreasing in size the farther away they were. Only this road was filled with colourful vehicles flying flags with happy hippies clinging onto their roofs. The most dominant sound, however, was the constant buzzing of the police helicopter overhead tracking our every move.

The onlookers we passed were mostly on-side, it seemed, and hadn't been infected by the negative media attention we'd recently garnered. They stood in their doorways gleefully waving at us—old couples, young, children in arms, a tableau of smiling faces who appeared pleased to see our carnivalesque convoy. These would be the last friendly faces we'd see.

Shipton Bellinger is a small village in Wiltshire, and it was in this area the police had decided to spring their trap and stop the convoy. At a tight turn in the road into the village of Cholderton, just before a petrol station, the council had dumped around forty tons of gravel in the road to prevent further passage. Immediately in front of these mounds of gravel was a parked police Transit van and many riot-clad police lying in wait for our arrival.

Smelly Kevin—another of those fantastic traveller pseudonyms—had been nominated as the front vehicle and was therefore expected to ram any police vehicle that stood between us and the Stonehenge monument. He was driving a yellow British Telecom 7.5-tonne truck and dutifully rammed it into the parked police van. There was no chance of shifting the van, breaking through the cordon, or promoting the revolutionary charge towards the festival site but he did his best. He rammed the police van with enough force to be seen to have done his duty while ensuring he didn't incur any serious injury—an expedient balancing act.

Within moments the riot-clad police were running along the line of vehicles, smashing batons into bodywork, angrily screaming at their occupants. They allowed no time for the shocked hippies to respond before smashing windscreens and side windows. Travellers were dragged from vehicles by their hair or their dreadlocks. Simultaneously, the rear end of the convoy received similar treatment—windows smashed, and individuals violently arrested despite having committed no crime. Male, female, young, middle-aged, or old—it didn't matter. The Whore of Babylon's militia had been unleashed, and they were pumped full of adrenaline, scared, and wild. The media hype around us folk devils was unleashed and moral panic prevailed.

With the virtue of hindsight and clarity today, I'm left wondering what these officers were warned to expect.

Rumours have surfaced over the years. Testimony from soldiers stationed at nearby Bulford Camp who have stated they were briefed and told they may have to become involved in preventing the convoy from reaching Salisbury Plain. Many of our antagonists wore black boiler suits with no epaulettes or numbers on show, this guaranteeing impunity. Whatever the case, nobody will ever know exactly who took part in this operation. Was it solely policemen gathered from several forces? Was it an amalgam of policemen and local military forces disguised beneath the anonymity of black boiler suits?

I saw none of this initial clash between travellers and Thatcher's control forces. I've read much about it since then and have spoken to many friends who were there at the initial fracas. I did, however, hear the metallic trashing of vehicle bodywork, the smashing of windows, the screaming of my companions being dragged from their seats, and the warnings of those running towards us attempting to escape the wrath of the many batons.

The convoy had been halted in its tracks on a single-lane road in rural Wiltshire. No one could move forwards or backwards due to neighbouring vehicles. Looking forwards, there was an impenetrable wooded area on the left-hand side and on the right side stood a post-and-rail fence interspersed with occasional small trees. We were between a rock and a hard place; stay here and have your vehicle destroyed by these crazed policemen or try to get to the pasture on our right, the only direction of escape. Very quickly, many men and women grabbed machetes, axes, bowsaws, or handsaws…

anything that could breach the barrier between the vehicles and the lush green pasture only metres away. The chaotic sounds of smashing glass and screaming voices were coming closer and closer, which lent more urgency to the task.

I was sawing, smashing, kicking, breaking my way through the fence… desperately trying to create a large enough entrance for Jill's bus to make it through. Gradually, headway was made. One, then two, then three vehicles drove through into the field beyond then more followed through the same openings. Some managed to enter the field unscathed but many lost some skirting as they traversed the border between the road and the tree line. Once beyond this line, the surface of the field wasn't too rough.

I don't remember how Jill's Bedford fared because I was inside the vehicle. What I do remember, however, is how these many vehicles resembled a Wild West wagon train driving round and round in circles to prevent a police incursion. As they continued circling, they were joined by more and more successful vehicles until we had a fair-sized contingent in the pasture; enough to forestall a charge from the militia and sufficient numbers to take a breather and consider our options.

The police didn't appear interested in storming our peaceful retreat yet, so those of us who'd been lucky enough to escape the police violence managed some respite. A reconnaissance party was sent out to evaluate our possible escape routes and returned stating the field next door was a crop field and beyond that was an escarpment—no escape in that direction, then. The only way out was through the police lines and that wasn't happening.

The police appeared content to have contained us for the moment. There were now hundreds of travellers trapped in a field determined to start a party despite the incumbent government's intentions to the contrary.

We were surrounded and weren't going anywhere, so the drugs came out—the mushrooms, the LSD, the cocaine, the pipes, the chillums, each to his own.

"Half a mix?" reverberated across the field. The party we'd all been looking forward to now commenced. Speakers pumped out The Enid,

Here & Now, Hawkwind, Ten Years After, Jethro Tull, Led Zeppelin, Pink Floyd. A flood of sound from the many different vehicles.

I spent my time hopping from one spot to another, never too much time with one group. Playing guitar, singing, joking around. I have to reiterate, it was fantastic for me because I didn't have a home to lose, nor children or a partner to worry about. I was a twenty-two-year-old who didn't give a damn. I mean, I wasn't even fuckin' *me*—I had a stolen driving licence in my back pocket and simply needed to pray it would serve its purpose.

The stand-off lasted into the balmy, dry, and sun-drenched evening. There were many parleys with the police at the scene of Smelly Kevin's collision with the police van. Neither side was prepared to cede ground though, and the approaching sunset meant someone in government (Margaret Thatcher or Michael Heseltine) had to decide on a course of action. Their choice became clear when the movements and attitudes of the police along the road fell into straight, organized lines.

As often happens in cases of moral panic, the media had been colluding with the government in demonising the hippie-traveller folk. Just as at Nostell Priory outside Wakefield where there'd been a similar mass arrest the previous summer, there was an attempt at justification citing reports of guns buried in the woods alongside the Stonehenge '84 festival site, and of dangerous travellers ready to take on the police with axes and machetes—a veritable gang of voracious brigands awaiting the collapse of society instigated by themselves so they could rape and eat England's innocent children.

All these travellers need axes and machetes on board their vehicles to cut and split firewood for their wood-burners, whether living in benders, buses, or trucks. They are necessary tools of survival, and this practical function is usually absent in the tabloid newspapers' reportage. This demonization would continue and reach fever-pitch in the coming days. In fairness, the broadsheets gave more measured accounts than the tabloid press and the TV reporters who witnessed events firsthand that afternoon performed with honesty, compassion, and integrity. Unlike the hundreds of policemen on the field that day.

The order to smash the convoy was given. The police's capacity for violence had been made clear the moment they began trashing vehicle windscreens and dragging travellers out by the hair hours ago and now they were steadily marching towards us. The threat had remained during the lull, undiminished by much hope of help. The promise of its fulfilment, signalled by lines of police forming along the road, was felt by all within the field.

Most travellers were either now on foot in the field or had jumped back into the vehicles they'd driven from Savernake Forest. I and the other occupants of Jill's bus had reassembled. The black boilersuit-clad militia were steadily advancing with truncheons and riot shields in hand determined to destroy people's homes. There was no escape, nowhere to flee, only a beanfield at the edge of this field and an escarpment beyond that. This beanfield, however wasn't like the pasture we'd spent the afternoon in, it was deeply furrowed and not fit for driving on. Regardless, once drivers witnessed police chasing and lashing out at other vehicle, arbitrarily smashing windows, they were forced to drive onto the uneven ground. Side-skirtings were ripped from their fixings and were left where they fell. The vehicles fleeing the crazed cops began to crisscross the field with no room to manoeuvre. Vehicles almost crashed into one another and, when this did occur, whichever vehicle stopped to allow the other to pass was quickly surrounded by groups of policemen. The side windows would be smashed with truncheons, flint rocks from the field would be hurled through windscreens. Police equipped with fire extinguishers hurled these through windows and windscreens. Adults, teenagers, children, and babies were sprayed with hundreds of tiny nuggets of flying glass.

The Earl of Cardigan was present on the field that day. A member of the British aristocracy, his family has owned Savernake Forest for generations. He'd decided to accompany the travellers' convoy on a motorbike with a friend. This enabled him to travel incognito. In his own words:

"Police rushed out on foot, from behind their barricades. Clutching drawn truncheons and riot shields, they ran round to the driver's door of each vehicle, slamming their truncheons into the bodywork to make a deafening noise, and shouting at every driver, 'get out, get out, hand over your keys, get out.' He states the police's instructions to 'get out!' and the smashing of vehicles often happened simultaneously, giving travellers no time to react before police used riot sticks to break the vehicles' windscreens. Cardigan described seeing a very pregnant woman being 'repeatedly clubbed on the head' by police. He also saw police with hammers smashing up the dashboards of several of the now-abandoned motor-coach homes."

The Earl would eventually be an important witness in a subsequent court case investigating the legality of the police behaviour that day.

I could never do the same justice to the awful events on the beanfield that the jarring urgency of film cameras can (there are plenty of Battle of the Beanfield documentaries available on YouTube)…nor the words of ITN journalist, Kim Sabido:

"What we've witnessed in the last half hour here has been surely some of the most brutal action by the police forces in Britain for a long time. Whatever the causes, the end product seemed to be just hitting out wildly by the police. Young women with babies in their arms were hit as well.

"At one stage one of the cameramen from Fleet Street was arrested for being on this site. We were pushed and shoved to one side but the worst of it all was that the people in those coaches who were trying to escape from the police were just grabbed. Their windows were smashed and they themselves were just beaten, sometimes senselessly, on the floor. And this is not over yet. They intend to carry on with their campaign around here for another day yet but whether they'll survive after what's happened at the hands of the police today, we'll have to see. Kim Sabido, ITN." (Sabido then falls into an exasperated silence as a look of sadness washes over his face.)

The police had now caused nearly all vehicles in the beanfield to halt, had apprehended those vehicle's occupants and were hauling them off to the roadside to be processed. However, the Rasta bus was still mobile and was filled with a group of whooping travellers possessed with a determination not to stop.

This Rasta Bus was a Bedford Panorama twin steer, colloquially known as a "Chinese six" due to its twin steering axles and single rear axle—six wheels in total, hence its nickname. A magnificent coach and the same type as that used in the Michael Caine film *The Italian Job* and the Beatles' *Magical Mystery Tour*. I saw several of these buses on various sites, but they're now as rare as rocking horse shit—museum pieces.

The Rasta bus became strong in traveller folklore for many subsequent years. The police couldn't trash the windscreen because it didn't have one—it had been replaced with a sheet of steel mesh (most often used for concrete reinforcement in the construction sector). This vehicle was designed to keep the police out. There are photos of its final moments to be found on Google Images ("Rasta Bus Battle of the Beanfield"). As the last bus to stop and consequently the one that pissed the police off most, it attracted around fifty officers. Like locusts, they swarmed all over it, clambering through side windows and trying to climb in through the windscreen because the doors were sealed closed. It seemed every policeman left on that field was determined to be included in this final seizure.

I wasn't witness to this because I was on Jill's bus. She was proud of her bus and although she'd joined the melee trying to flee the police batons, she wasn't prepared to have her bus destroyed nor to floor it towards human beings. So she stopped the bus when the policemen waved their batons threatening to smash windows if the door wasn't opened. The front side door was tied closed but, after some fumbling, I managed to untie it and slid it open.

"Out!" screamed several policemen. "Get out and down on the ground."

I could feel their fear and adrenalin and knew from experience how much those wooden truncheons hurt. It felt to me that these policemen had all been told to expect violent resistance from us all. The way they acted that day was as though we really did have the guns the media had lied about…or even the "unlit petrol bombs." This fear made them scared and nervous, therefore highly dangerous.

Once we were all out of the bus, we were led away back towards the road and were marched past the smashed buses and trucks that had taken the first onslaught several hours ago.

Upon witnessing several travellers carried from the field on stretchers, I was pleased I'd kept my mouth shut and not resisted arrest. One guy on a stretcher had a broken jaw with a bandage circling his entire head to keep it immobile, others were sat in ambulances being treated by first responders.

We were led to a long queue of subdued travellers, many sporting bruises and bloodied faces. This queue of sixty or seventy people was waiting to be loaded on to the many coaches dedicated to our removal while many more had already been ferried away.

My turn to board came so I climbed the steps. I settled into a seat and slowly the bus filled with weary, vanquished travellers. Children had been taken from parents and placed into temporary care while mothers were taken away and locked in police stations, having committed no crime. All travellers' dogs were rounded up and many were put down on police orders—beloved family pets never seen again.

The coach stopped at different police stations, dropping off small groups of its weary cargo, then finally arrived at my destination. I was held at Kingston police station, near Portsmouth. One thousand policemen had arrested five hundred and fifty travellers and most police stations in the South of England were at capacity.

We were all processed that evening—"name, address, date of birth?" The same questions I'd faced many times over the years. I gave the details I'd memorized from the dodgy driving licence and was led to a cell where I laid on the mattress on the hard concrete bed, closed my eyes and soon fell asleep. I was completely shattered and glad to put the day behind me. I wouldn't discover until weeks later how much the events of that day would affect me and my future.

Monday morning came and we were all charged with "Unlawful Assembly," then released on bail to appear at a court somewhere a few weeks hence My false identity had held up and I was free…for now.

15

Sympathy for the Devil (Rolling Stones)

I returned to Farnborough like a moth to its inevitable flame of demise and, after a couple of days, stole a car to join my friends who were now gathered at Westbury's White Horse hill. Three of my friends jumped in with me as they were intrigued by my stories of the freedoms to be found within the travelling community. We left Farnborough and drove along the A30. I was full of Valium and was recklessly swigging from a whiskey bottle while driving. As we approached a lay-by on our side of the road, we spotted a long flatbed lorry with some canvas tarpaulins strapped to the front of its bed. These would be perfect for constructing a bender once we arrived on site. I pulled the car into the lay-by and stopped behind the lorry. There was no sign of the lorry's driver, so we climbed out and quickly unstrapped the tarpaulins, grabbed one, then loaded it into the boot of the car.

Typically, a police car drove past just as we were ready to jump back in the car and continue our journey. It turned around and then slowly joined us in the lay-by. A few reluctant ropes were still hanging from the boot, and we were unable to hide them before the police car rolled to a stop. I was completely wasted at this point and had the bottle of whiskey in my hand, the Valium coursing through my veins. One of the policemen approached me and grabbed me by my clothing.

"You're under arrest on suspicion of theft," he told me, then read me my rights.

I tried to wrench away from his grip but was unsuccessful. He immediately pulled out his truncheon and smashed me on the top left side of my head. I felt the heavy crack of the hardwood truncheon on my skull then the warm flow of blood running down both sides of my head, face, and neck. I was later to discover this was an illegal act as police regulations state the truncheon should never be used above the neck. Searching the internet for "target areas" with a police truncheon or baton today, I find the same proscriptions for modern policing:

> I've trained over 200 police departments, comprising over ten thousand men. In every class, I ask the officers if they've ever seen a subject subdued with one blow to the head. None of them ever have. What you're doing when you hit a man in the head is first, creating a serious danger of death, and second, you're numbing the one part of the body that can stop him. If you use my method with one or two strikes and step back, he realises that the thing has gone against him, and the confrontation is over. But if you hit him in the head and put him into a state of shock where he is almost immune to pain, and now enraged beyond reason, the only thing left for you to do is beat him into the ground. This is why so many police brutality charges came about when batons were used the old-fashioned way.
>
> https://en.wikipedia.org/wiki/Baton_(law_enforcement)#Target_areas

After the crack to my skull, the policeman became both an aggressor to defend myself against, as well as a uniform representing everything I resented around the state's power held over me throughout my entire life. A symbol of that power as opposed to the human being within that skin. He became every copper who'd ever deprived me of my freedom; he became every copper who'd exerted excessive force upon me during arrests. And, probably most influentially at that moment, he became every copper who had beaten and bloodied my friends on the beanfield less than a month previously.

Despite being stunned, I answered the crack from his truncheon with a straight jab to his nose and a left hook that broke his jaw, and I saw blood pour down his face while his grip on my clothing relaxed. I fled across the green fields in the direction of a housing estate leaving my shocked friends behind.

My hazy memory today recalls encountering several passers-by, people who understandably recoiled with shock and horror. My face was streaming with blood, and I had to keep wiping it from my eyes. My clothing was covered in blood—both mine and the copper's—and soon I was running to the terrible fluctuating wail of numerous police sirens.

It didn't take them long to track me down. I was arrested and offered no resistance—I knew I'd properly fucked my life up this time and something inside me prevented me from sabotaging myself further.

Considering the sporadic police brutality that existed in those days, I recall no police beating once arriving at the station. I'm certain many of the policeman's friends had a strong desire to injure me but I'd imagine the custody sergeant realised this might swing the upcoming court case in my favour so enforced temperance. The wound on my head was given eight stitches by a duty doctor after which I was led to a cell where the Valium and alcohol did their work sending me into a deep sleep.

Next morning I appeared before a magistrates' court where I was once more remanded in custody and returned to Winchester prison. I was placed back on B-wing with other remand prisoners, and it felt as though I'd never been away. I was placed in a cell with a guy named Mick O'Brien who hailed from Ash Vale, a small village not far from my hometown. We were both receiving "good visits"—i.e., visits where items of food, drink, and beer were permitted to be handed in by visitors (one can of beer was allowed each evening because we were unconvicted prisoners) —which meant neither of us was dependent on the other.

Oddly enough, when I reminisce over this time spent on remand, it was one of the best prison periods I experienced. This wasn't solely due to the good visits. I feel it was because I'd changed inside, and I gravitated towards a less violent and less criminal fraternity. My experiences in the fields and on the convoy, with more hash and acid and mushrooms than alcohol, had softened me. This must sound ironic considering I was on remand for a violent act but that act was committed within a toxic fog of barbiturates and spirits, along with a combination of adrenalin and cortisol induced by the heavy weight of a hardwood baton.

I settled back into prison life. This involved trips to the gym, the prison cinema at weekends, board and card games played with Mick in the cell, association in the evenings and weekends, and the nonstop ploughing through book after book to escape reality.

Walking around the exercise yard for an hour each day, prisoners who'd spend their days reading through Archbold's (the leading practitioner's text for lawyers in England and Wales), and therefore knew everything there was to know, informed me I was, "Well and truly fucked, mate—you're gonna get a five-stretch."

The thought of receiving a five-year prison sentence was terrifying but I knew they were probably right. Even with a plea of self-defence, I could still easily be sentenced to three years. I knew I was capable of serving that much time but that would be another two years of my finite life spent in a prison cell and every day spent in jail is a day where real life is placed on hold…and death is a real risk.

I tried not to worry as I knew it would be months before my sentencing date. Firstly, the magistrates needed to commit the case to Crown Court due to their limited sentencing powers, and then I'd be on the Crown Court's waiting list for many months.

I was surrounded by some dangerous prisoners. One guy, along with his friend, had enticed a teenage girl to allow them to burgle her parents' house while they were away on holiday. Her motive for this was never revealed but, during the course of the burglary, they stabbed her to death.

Another prisoner was most likely going to be sectioned under the Mental Health Act for arson. He'd visited a friend in a tower block and upon not receiving a response from the friend's doorbell, set fire to the bin-store to "get him out of bed."

A couple of guys I became friends with were London gangsters who'd been involved with some drug dealers from Aldershot, close to my hometown. The Aldershot gang members had visited one of the London guy's houses to collect owed money. Only the gangster's wife was home, so these men had tied her to a chair and tortured her, stubbing cigarettes out on her skin. In response to this vicious attack, the two offended guys went to deal with these gang members. They headed straight to an Aldershot pub to find the torturers, one wielding a loaded shotgun and the other a chainsaw.

I remember reading their depositions and one witness related what had occurred:

"I was sitting by the door nursing my pint when I heard what I thought was a moped being started outside the door. Three men sitting at a table close to the rear entrance got up and left rather in a hurry. The next moment, a guy came running in carrying a shotgun and fired both barrels into the bar's ceiling while another followed him with a running chainsaw in his hand and attacked the wooden bar with it."

Yeah, I was in the company of some real characters.

Life on the wings continued as normal with the same routine day in and day out: gym, cinema, association, the jangle of keys in the cell door with an occasional "Austin, you have a visit," smoking spliffs, buying and selling hash. This was my prison life for six months over the winter of '85.

* * *

I'd messed up a letter I was writing to my partner. Letters were set at a standard length and were issued by prison officers weekly. One piece of A4 paper was the limit. I'd messed one up so had to ask for a "rewrite."

There are two critical features of prison life that might result in flash-points: screws messing with a prisoners' mail—incoming or outgoing—and visits; anything pertaining to family, partners, or friends.

I knocked on the office door that was situated downstairs on the first landing (Mick and I were on the fourth landing among the top tier of cells).

"Guv'nor, can I have a rewrite?" I asked the on-duty screw, explaining I'd messed up the letter I'd been issued with. I was a control problem, and this screw knew me well, so his response was half-expected.

"Come and see someone tomorrow morning," he said.

"Guv'nor, it's a really important letter. Tomorrow's Saturday so I need to post it this evening. It's about a visit and, if it doesn't get sent tomorrow, my visit will be delayed."

Short of saying please, my voice conveyed the urgency I felt.

"I told you—ask an officer in the morning," he replied and dismissed me.

"Ah, fuck off," I angrily told him.

"Get back to your cell, Austin. You're on report."

"Course I'm on report," I replied. "Do I look like a fucking idiot?"

I wasn't getting a rewrite, so I departed and headed upstairs back to my cell.

As per procedure, the following morning a screw unlocked the cell door and told me to follow him to the block—"The Governor wants to see you."

"What for?" I asked him, knowing full well why.

"Says here you told last night's on-duty officer to 'fuck off.'"

Mick and I had stayed up until around 4 a.m. as the early hours were the optimum time for smoking dope with impunity—it was rare for cell doors to be opened during the night shift. I felt too tired for this shit.

"Well, you can fuck off, too, then," I told the screw.

He complied but I knew it wouldn't be long before a return visit. I'd started a chain of events that I was now determined to see through to their conclusion.

As anticipated, the sound of jangling keys returned and this time it was a gym screw in a blue track suit who opened the door and told me the governor wanted to see me downstairs in the block.

"Listen," I told him, "if the governor wants to see me so bad, tell him to come up here and see me."

"Don't be ridiculous. This is your last chance, Austin."

I responded with another, "Fuck off."

The door slammed behind the gym screw and both Mick and I knew it was time to get out of bed and get dressed—this problem wasn't going away.

I had my pisspot ready and intended to throw it over the first screw who came through the door.

The sound of approaching footsteps could be discerned once again. Keys turned in the lock, the door opened, and the gym screw said, "Last chance, Austin."

"Fuck off," I told him.

"O'Brien, out!" he shouted. My brother in arms instantly complied, standing up and exiting the cell without a backwards glance. Incredible, whatever happened to solidarity? I was now alone in the cell.

"One last chance, Austin," said the gym screw.

"I told you, just fuck off."

He drew his head back and the door swung open to reveal a gang of screws outside my door. I held my pisspot firmly in my hand, ready for their assault. The front screw had a rectangular plastic riot shield before him as he ran into my cell. His intention was to push me up against the back wall so his fellow screws could add their force and pin me to the wall—textbook. I threw my bucket of piss at him, it splashed over his shield, back towards me, and then to the floor.

The next moment, I was thrown to the floor with my face in my own piss and three screws on top of me, all trying to get hold of both my wrists so they could restrain me with wristlocks. They quickly succeeded and stood me upright. Then, with one screw on either side of me, my wrists were locked into my armpits with my elbows held against each one's chest. This is an effective wristlock and the more one struggles, the tighter the grip becomes and the more stress it places on the wrists.

These two screws were then led by a third pulling on their uniforms to guide them towards the staircase, enabling them to concentrate on nothing other than retaining their grip. Another screw took up the rearguard in case I managed to break free.

With each step down the stairs, my pain increased, and I emitted a short cry of pain.

"Stop struggling."

"I'm not struggling, you're breaking my fucking wrists," I screamed between gritted teeth. It's a really painful grip when being walked along a flat surface much less being manhandled down four flights of stairs.

The whole prison had been locked down for this exercise, no other prisoner was out of their cell. Someone had decided my recalcitrance to leave the cell willingly couldn't be passed up as an opportunity for a training exercise. Once we achieved the ground floor, there was an alleyway formed by two lines of screws being given an exhibition on how to subdue and control a reluctant prisoner. The line of screws led all the way to the block where I was placed on the floor of a cell with my hands forced up my back. Next, all screws except the one holding my hands in place flew from the cell. Finally, the last screw jumped up, fled the cell, and the door was slammed closed behind him.

I jumped up and flew at the door, banging and kicking it while screaming expletives. The observation flap opened, and an anonymous screw told me shut the fuck up before I made things any worse—as if that were possible.

I was back in the hole again and thirty minutes later I was stood before the governor.

"Austin, why am I never surprised to see you brought before me? And what is it this time? Throwing abuse at my officers, demanding *I* come and see *you*, refusing a direct order, being the cause of an hour-long prison lockdown. All this because you weren't permitted a fresh letter?"

He exhaled in a long sigh, tapped his pen a few times on my charge sheet for effect, then shook his head saying, "I must say I'll be more than happy once you're sentenced and moved on to a serving prison. Seven days' solitary. Take him away."

I wasn't yet serving a sentence and was an unconvicted prisoner so there was little else he could do. I was locked back in the cell after adjudication and promptly switched to my solitary confinement default: my own form of meditation. Closing my eyes, drifting off and recalling the events of my troubled life, especially the happier moments. I was no longer in Winchester prison, I was back at Savernake Forest, Farnborough, London…anywhere but that stone cell.

The day I was to appear before the judge at Winchester Crown Court arrived, and I'd been told in advance judge Lewis McCreery would be presiding over my case. Typical, the worst judge of all. I really might be looking at a potential five-year sentence.

My cell door was opened, and I was led to an interview room to meet my barrister for the first time. She was a very attractive black woman seemingly only a few years older than me dressed in an off-white wig sporting curls at its front and sides with her own long straight black hair framing the sides of her face. A white bow tie, a skirt suit, and a huge black gown completed her attire. My solicitor had studiously compiled the paperwork for my defence and passed it on to this barrister whose task it was to represent me in the crown court.

My first question was, "What kind of mood is he in?" referring to Judge Lewis McCreery. Incredibly, the Universe appeared to be on my side.

"Your judge has been changed. There's a Hell's Angels New Forest murder case and Judge McCreery has chosen to take that case today. You've a different judge."

This was great news for me.

"Who have I got then?" I asked.

"Judge Starforth-Hill," she responded.

There is a God, I said to myself with immense relief. I had switched from being tried by the worst judge on Winchester's bench to purportedly the most lenient. As an example of his leniency, this judge was later pilloried by the national media in a case of attempted rape, indecent assault, and indecency with a child by the girl's eighteen-year-old babysitter. During this case Starforth-Hill stated the nine-year old girl was "no angel" and sentenced her babysitter to only four months' imprisonment.

"Okay," I said to my barrister, "let's go guilty today."

"Fine," was her reply. "I'll see you shortly."

She stood, wrapped her ribboned bundle of papers and left the room. I was escorted back to my cell where several other prisoners were also awaiting their appearances.

An hour later and the cell door was once again opened, my name was called, and I followed the jailer towards the doors leading to the courtroom's dock. This same screw stood beside me throughout the case as a precaution against any attempt to jump from the dock in an escape attempt or possibly to attack the judge.

I was greeted by the all-too-familiar wigged judge sat on his dais front centre stage with the large and colourful British crest above his head. The room was huge and walled with dark wood-panelling. Judge Starforth-Hill was winged by my defence barrister and that of the prosecution, also wearing a wig and gown. A court usher presided below the judge's dais and a stenographer sat on a lower table transcribing everything that was said for the court's records.

There followed the usual procedure of being asked to give my name, date of birth, and home address to which I responded, then came the prosecutor's opportunity to paint a picture of me that would garner the longest possible prison sentence. To my ears, the catalogue of car thefts, fraudulent use of chequebooks, and a serious assault on a police officer sounded worthy of such a sentence.

The prosecution finished his dark and nefarious painting of my character. Next came my barrister's opportunity to try to brighten this black picture in some way. She concentrated on the duality of my intelligence and aptitude versus the dysfunction that had led to my ten-year history of criminal behaviour. Leaning heavily on the significance of my being taken away from the family home at a very young age, she emphasised how children in these circumstances often spiral out of control for a number of years before finding employment, possibly a partner, and then gradually an easing away from a criminal lifestyle. She concluded her statement saying I was mortified by my actions and wished only for the chance to use my intelligence to become a productive member of society. I felt she did a sterling job of representing me.

I had no real way of gauging which way things were going at this point in the case, but the sheer relief of knowing judge McCreery was presiding over a different case in another courtroom nearby gave me consolation.

Finally, the moment came where I was permitted to speak for myself. This was my chance to shine. Other than a few occasions in the magistrates' court, I'd never spoken publicly and found the prospect daunting. As such, I'd spent the previous few weeks compiling a letter to the judge. My reasons for this were twofold: firstly, to show the judge I had the intelligence to formulate my own ideas and to write a letter as well as he could himself, and secondly, to tell my own version of events.

My barrister explained she had a letter from me in her possession that I wished he would read. He acceded to this request and the letter was passed from the hands of my barrister to the judge via the court usher. A weighted silence descended on the courtroom as he leafed through the four or five pages. I scrutinized the judge's face behind his glasses, watching for any inflection that might offer a glimpse into my fate. Other than the occasional raising of his eyebrows or a slight frown, his features gave away little. Finishing my letter, he indicated to the court usher it was time to retire and consider his verdict.

"Court rise."

All in the courtroom rose and Starforth-Hill retired into his chambers to consider my pleas and my fate.

Once he had disappeared, a low hubbub commenced within the room. Both the prosecutor and my barrister began a conversation interspersed with low laughter. The professional adversity they'd displayed throughout the case had vanished and, I guess, to them this was just another case among hundreds they represented each month.

After an interminable period, the door to the judge's chambers opened and the usher once again called for everyone to stand. I was instructed to remain standing.

Judge Starforth-Hill looked down on me from his elevated dais and proclaimed to the court, "It is true the arresting officer was over-enthusiastic in his duty striking the defendant on his head and this action elicited a reaction from the defendant. I will take this into account in my sentencing."

Once the judge's summing up was complete, I was awarded a total of thirty months in prison. Considering all I'd been told by the prison exercise yard lawyers, this sentence was an enormous relief. The six months I had already spent on remand would be deducted from this term so, after some quick mental arithmetic, I realised I'd be free in just over a year.

He had one final piece of advice for me.

"If I were you, young man," he said, peering over the top of his glasses ominously, "I would give serious consideration to the direction your life now takes. You have been sentenced for some grave offences here today. If you fail to heed my warning, you may find yourself standing before one of my colleagues at a future date being sentenced to life imprisonment."

Outside the courtroom I thanked my barrister profusely, she'd done a fantastic job representing me and her services would be paid for by Legal Aid along with those of the solicitors who'd prepared the initial case.

I was returned to my cell and felt a glow of happiness I'd been sentenced to only two-and-a-half years' imprisonment.

Once back in Winchester prison, I was placed on a new wing while awaiting allocation to the prison where I would serve the entirety of my sentence. Due to my being a control problem, I knew which prison this would be—Dartmoor, in the county of Devon. This was the prison with the worst reputation in the UK and the one place my mother had always said I would end up when I was a child repeatedly getting into trouble.

16

Changes
(David Bowie)

As soon as I was able, I sent my mother a letter saying "Mum, I made it! I'm in Dartmoor," along with the details of my sentence and my probable release date.

This was a prison built from granite in the early 1800s to house prisoners from the Napoleonic wars and one which has over the decades held some of Britain's most notorious offenders. Like Thatcher, an old whore of the establishment. There was never a more desolate prison built on the island of Britain.

I don't recall the journey from Winchester to Devon, I just recall we were a busload of prisoners consigned to months or years in that grim place.

After a week or so, I met some acquaintances from both my early care homes and from my recent remand stint in Winchester prison. No surprises there, really—we'd all been a pain in the arse to the Winchester prison screws and governor. They weren't on the same wing as me, but we were all given the job of hand-sewing mailbags. It wouldn't be long before a small gang of us held sway in one corner of the workshop and, once we'd established ourselves, we had it fairly easy. Our wages were paid relative to piecework, and we quickly figured out a scam paying the guy who tallied up the piecework so were assured better wages. We'd pay him in tobacco or hash, and he would then take a bag or two from other prisoners' piles of finished bags and add them to our piles, fiddling the books in our favour. And, once he was in our pocket, he was in our pocket for good.

As I did in every prison, I applied to go on to full-time education. My thirst for knowledge was strong, something I'd possessed since a small child and a passion my mother always encouraged and assisted with. My request was accepted and, instead of attending the mailbag shop, I was escorted to the education department each day. This education included creative writing classes and some maths or geography. However, my passion for music was stimulated by the head of the education department. His name was Stephen King, like the horror writer, and he was also a saxophonist. I never heard him play sax, but I got the impression he played to a professional standard. There was a piano in the entrance lobby of the education space and Stephen heard me play on this piano, just a few licks I'd picked up over the years. He could also play piano—much better than I could—and taught me some chords and showed me how to improvise over the chords. It wasn't so much a formal study of piano; he'd just show me a couple of tricks and allow me to sit there and play for an hour or two a day rather than attend lessons.

There was always a screw sat in this lobby in case there was trouble in class. One day I was sitting at the piano when a fresh screw replaced the one who'd been sat there all morning. He seemed not to notice me while he was chatting to the screw he was replacing. Once the first screw left, he came over and asked what I was doing.

"I'm practicing some arpeggios and improvisation," I replied, assuming he was genuinely interested.

"No, you're not" he responded and proceeded to close the piano lid on my fingers.

"What're you doing?" I asked him. "I'm allowed to play the piano. Ask Mr. King, he'll confirm it."

At that moment, Mr. King came out from his office.

"Everything okay?" he asked.

"This officer's telling me I'm not to play the piano and should be in class," I told him.

"It's fine," said Stephen. "He has my permission."

And that was the end of that. Joy of joys. This screw sat down on the chair not more than a few yards away from me, opened the book he'd brought with him to read and had to spend a couple of hours trying to read with the intrusion of my faltering blues solos. Small mercies, I know, but a satisfying memory.

My passion for music, both the piano in the education department and the guitar and blues harmonica I had in my cell, ultimately detracted from my honing any writing skills I may have had. I possibly could have become a full-time writer had I continued with the creative writing classes and the homework in my cell, but music was my first passion and, from this time forward, I would devote all my energies towards the ten thousand hours purported to be the required amount to achieve a professional level. I've no regrets around this as I'm certain this love of music enabled me to develop a vision of a future that eventually saved my life. My vision now was to become a performing musician.

There was a highly talented classical guitarist on my wing who helped me in this quest. For some reason I never understood, he was involved in smuggling heroin from India to Spain. I'd guess a quick return was his driver but, unluckily for him, his plane was diverted to Heathrow airport, which had a solid reputation for being the best (or worst, depending on your point of view) for catching drug smugglers. He explained this to me in his heavily accented English.

He would loan me sheet music and assist me whenever I struggled over complex sections of the score.

My first experience of playing saxophone also came from this period. There was a Dartmoor prison brass band. Someone mentioned it to me, and I decided to give it a shot. I landed in the practice room one evening and a music teacher showed up and began handing out brass instruments to the regular attendees.

I introduced myself and said I was interested in joining his band to learn how to sight read and play an instrument. I explained I'd studied music theory without an instrument before, and that I was okay on guitar and piano.

"Okay, you can start with this," he said to me and handed me a strange-looking instrument.

"What's this?" I asked.

"It's an E-flat bass," he replied. "A member of the tuba family."

I noticed a long box in the cupboard he'd taken the instruments from. This was the only item left.

"What's that?" I asked.

"It's a tenor saxophone," he told me. This sounded a lot more hip than an E-flat bass.

"Why can't I play that?"

"Because this is a brass band and the saxophone is a woodwind instrument," he happily enlightened this philistine.

I joined the rest of the musicians and was given a cursory explanation of how a beginner might start playing notes on the instrument I'd been given. Throughout the band's session I couldn't stop thinking about the saxophone lying there gathering dust.

At the end of the session, I wouldn't give up and once more suggested I learn saxophone. He repeated it didn't belong in a brass band.

"So, you're telling me there's an instrument in the bottom of that cupboard that might save someone's sorry arse from this life of crime and prison, and you're determined to leave it there? That's the most narrow-minded attitude I've ever come across. Someone could be learning to play that…me, for instance."

It was evident I had more of a yen for learning the saxophone than the instrument he'd chosen for me, and beyond my expectations, this man said, "Okay, I'll make a deal with you. You learn the E-flat bass in my band, and you can take the saxophone back to your cell and learn it there.

"So long as your neighbours can tolerate the racket."

He gave a snort of laughter at this quip, but I was overjoyed. A saxophone in my cell along with my guitar and harmonica. I could see myself onstage with a saxophone already, playing in a band, the audience screaming for more.

"You've got yourself a deal."

He showed me how to assemble the thing and then replaced it in its case. I picked up the instrument and returned to my wing feeling as though I'd drawn four aces in a poker game. As soon as the cell door was locked behind me, I took the instrument from its case and assembled it the way Mr. Brass Band had shown me and took a couple of tentative blows. After a few awful squeaks and squawks, I replaced it in its case excited that I would make many more honking sounds daily until I'd learn to tame the thing.

Sadly, this first saxophone experience was short-lived although I'd always remember it as the point where this instrument became a possible future choice for me.

I managed to keep hold of it for a few days and realised I would ultimately learn how to gain some control of the sound, but there was a shortage of staff one evening and it was announced there'd be no association. We were briefly unlocked to empty pisspots and use the toilet but were told we couldn't get any boiling water for hot drinks. I needed a wash and went to the landing below to get hot water from the urn and a screw was straight on me.

"Austin, what're you doing?"

"I need some hot water to have a wash," came my answer.

"You've been told no hot water so get back in your cell now. You're not getting hot water."

"Watch me." I cockily gave back and filled my washbowl with boiling water from the urn. It would be a brave screw who challenged a prisoner holding a container of boiling water in his hands, so he contented himself with "You're nicked" as he banged me up.

The following morning, I was stood before the governor in the adjudication room with a ginger-haired screw inches from my face. It was my old acquaintance, Mr. Thompson, from my days in Portland borstal several years previously. He could see a glint of recognition in my eye as I received my three days' solitary confinement from the governor and was hurried out of the room to begin this new sentence of meditative practice and exercise. I had a quick chat with Mr. Thompson as he'd always been okay with me.

"How you doing, Mr. Thompson? Long time, no see, hey?"

"Still up to your old tricks, Austin? I had a feeling we'd cross paths again."

"It's me last stretch, Mr. Thompson, honest," I said cheekily. We both knew that was unlikely. I was as much a part of the prison system by this point as were the bars and walls.

"Course it is," he replied. "You'll still be supporting me when I'm drawing my pension." We laughed together at this while both having a sense his words might prove prophetic. It felt good to banter with him as he was an okay screw among many bad eggs. Go to work, earn your wages with as little aggravation as possible, pay the bills, put some food on the family table, sleep, repeat. He was on permanent duty in the block during most of my stay in Dartmoor, so we saw a lot of each other.

* * *

My time in Dartmoor was coming to an end. Not only had I been a control problem within the system, spending a good portion of my sentence in solitary confinement, I'd also spent my normal cell-time industriously, vacillating between honing my musical skills on guitar, singing, piano, and harmonica, and reading everything I could get my hands on, both fiction and nonfiction. I'd plough through many books each week, flying from my confinement as each page was turned, only returning to the grim and harsh reality of prison life when the jangling of keys interrupted this diversion.

One day, I'd read books regarded as classics, my interest piqued by the fact they were still living on library shelves a hundred years after publication. *Why have these narratives stood the test of time?* I wondered.

Nine times out of ten, the end of the book would vindicate their place on those shelves. I'd become lost reading anything from Tolstoy, Pasternak, Solzhenitsyn, Chekov, or Dostoevsky to French authors Hugo, Dumas, Zola, Verne, or Camus. I pored through everything written by Thomas Hardy and Charles Dickens during my time there, I loved the darkness of their tales and their descriptions of times and customs from years past.

(As an interesting aside, for many years whenever policemen asked for my name, I'd often give them the *nom de guerre* Jack Dawkins, which is the real name of Charles Dickens's Artful Dodger. I was never questioned over it, which leads to the assumption not many policemen are that familiar with Dickens's works.)

Hugo's *The Last Days of a Condemned Man* became a favourite, as did Defoe's *A Journal of the Plague Year*, with its terrible description of life in England during the Black Death and its horrendous statistics climbing each day. I loved practically everything written by both Hemingway and Orwell. I've read and re-read *For Whom the Bell Tolls, A Farewell to Arms,* and *The Old Man and the Sea* many times.

The classic tales of confinement and escape have been longtime favourites of mine, each revisited in different cells in different prisons: *The Count of Monte Cristo, Les Miserables*, and *Papillon*, these all contributed to my own figurative escape from prison. I'd be digging a tunnel alongside Edmund Dantes, learning alongside him with L'Abbé Faria and then walking side by side with him as he exacted his revenge on the conspirators and, finally, with a happy sigh of relief, sharing in his forgiveness as I reached the end of the tale. I'd be floating on the sea beside Papillon as he left Devil's Island behind on a coracle made from coconuts and sackcloth.

I'd be by Jean Valjean's side as he is given a second chance by Monseigneur Bienvenu, as he helps Fantine, then rescues and adopts Cossette and eventually saves Marius. Such wonderful, well-written tales would turn my solitude to joy and instil in me a sense of hope for my own future, the possibility of similar salvation.

* * *

There was a significant difference between my intentions each time I regained my freedom compared to those of my prison companions, especially pertaining to drug use. My intention was to go straight, find a job, stay out of trouble, create a normal life for myself. Many of my friends on the exercise yard would say, "I can't wait to get out and have some heroin," while my response would invariably be, "Are you crazy? I can't wait to get out and have none."

This, I sincerely believe, is the reason I am writing my story today while those friends are now either buried in the ground, or they today sport the ruined teeth and gaunt visage of the walking dead along with a commensurate lack of ambition. I planned to go straight each time I left a prison's gates but returning to Farnborough pretty much guaranteed failure. I stubbornly placed myself before a tsunami of old behaviours every time I returned to Totland Close. I felt my reputation there was important. I felt I was somebody there when, in fact, the neighbourhood's attachment was my unchanging nemesis. With today's knowledge, I see this was self-sabotage, the Christian created in my father's image believing in the worthlessness instilled in him at a young age.

Prison and, by extension, the musicianship I learned within its walls saved my life. While the UK's towns and cities were flooded with heroin's nefarious scourge in the early- to mid-eighties, there was little of the brown or white powder available in UK prisons at that time, so little as to be hardly noticeable.

There is an irony in my early delinquency and subsequent care home/borstal/prison experiences providing me with some vitally important lessons my Farnborough cohort were deprived of. Namely, the lessons learned when absconding with friends and living in Bournemouth or Southampton or the Isle of Wight. Sleeping on train stations all night awaiting the morning train, stealing money from café cigarette or fruit machines, or food from shops. Evading the law and learning that survival is easy with the right amount of fearlessness and bravado. Learning that everything will be okay regardless of the place I woke up and what I had in my pockets.

These experiences gave me the tools I would later need to build a life in a city where I knew nobody.

Yet another advantage of imprisonment was the opportunity to get clean and be removed from Farnborough where the risk of death through overdose was elevated. My frequent removal from society prevented me from becoming a statistic on the register of births, deaths, and marriages. It also saved my veins from completely disappearing like most users' as they had long periods of not being stabbed with needles daily.

I find there is a convoluted irony in this. Whenever I'm asked, "Don't you regret all those years you wasted in prison?" my response is immediate: "Not at all. I wouldn't be the person I am today without having lived through those experiences. Instead, I'd probably have either been dead or tied down with a mortgage, a career (possibly frequenting the same office in the same building daily, five days a week, for years on end), and many other mainstream constraints. Whenever I've had to work, I've always chosen outdoor work, probably as a consequence of being locked inside for so long—regardless of the season or the weather I've gravitated towards construction, tree surgery, or the erection of marquees and stages at festivals. All these vocations also act as a workout for the body. This has enabled me to stay lithe and physically fit.

Once again, I returned to my stomping ground and the chaos and drugs that world was comprised of. An interesting aspect of this world and its secrecy is that, prior to becoming involved in it, one is not *au fait* with its inhabitants. What I mean by this is that you may have known Peter, Paul, and Joanne, for example, for a few years, but it's not until you become a badge-wearing member of this club that you become aware they *also* smoke weed, or do acid, or inject heroin—information one is not privy to until you become a member of their club.

There is an argument smoking cannabis is a gateway drug. I can only speak of my own experiences from the early eighties, and under those dated terms, I agree with this statement…for the reasons outlined above. Until one is accepted into the club, all its inner workings and its participants remain hidden. It's only after you become a trusted member you learn who else is consuming which types of drug. If you don't smoke cannabis, it is unlikely you will discover who is dropping acid and unlikely you'll be offered acid. If you don't smoke cannabis or drop acid, it's unlikely you'll be introduced to anyone who does speed or cocaine or heroin, or to anyone who injects drugs. For these reasons I'd say smoking cannabis can be a gateway into the world of drugs. As has been seen, my trajectory from smoking cannabis to injecting heroin while sampling every drug in-between occurred over a twelve-month period. I determined to tread this path early on and my penchant for self-destruction was a contributory factor.

17

Gimme Shelter
(Rolling Stones)

Sitting outside the Prince Louis pub one sunny day smoking fags and drinking a beer, one of the regulars offered me a job. I've no recollection of his name today. He only knew me vaguely and he knew I'd recently been released from prison.

"Why don't you come and work with me instead of sitting around waiting to get back into trouble? You're young and fit and could be regularly taking home hundreds of quid a week."

This was exactly what I'd planned upon my release but indolence and the weekly signing on for government money had slowly crept in and I was doing little other than his correct description: "waiting to get back into trouble."

"Okay, what time you want me to start?" I asked him.

"If you're right here at 7 o'clock tomorrow morning, you've got a job. Deal?"

"Deal," I replied, feeling pleased a job had fallen into my lap. *Perhaps you're ready for normal, Christian,* I told myself, which would soon prove unbridled optimism.

I was picked up in a works truck the following morning and driven to Slough where I joined a gang of men preparing a factory floor for the fresh concrete that was due in the early afternoon. I was taught how to tie steel mesh together with wire. The work was relatively easy and by lunchtime the task was complete. After we'd all eaten some food, the first concrete truck turned up with its revolving drum full of grey slop. I'd have to get used to this as I'd shovel a lot of concrete over the coming years. I now discovered why I'd been promised good money: the work was backbreaking. I was given a shovel and, along with the others in the gang, had to spread and shovel the concrete around as it was pumped from a long black rubber tube. I felt as though I wouldn't make it to the end of the day, but finally the floor was finished, and the rear lights of the last concrete truck exited the gates.

"Now, the pub," my new boss said. We found one a few hundred yards down the road and all piled in to drink a couple of pints.

This job lasted for a couple of months, and I had disposable income from a legal source for the first time in years. I was getting up early each day, was becoming exceptionally fit with the amount of shovelling the job entailed, and I was no longer hanging around with the wasters of Totland Close all day. Life was going really well…then I met Denise.

Denise was a speed-freak and, like me, she was a fuckup. She lived outside a town called Farnham—several miles from Farnborough—on a council estate similar to Prospect Estate where I'd grown up. We shared a craving for self-sabotage, which made it easy to combine forces in achieving this dubious ambition, and it wasn't long before we were both happily injecting speed several times a day. I kept my job for a while, but eventually my lifestyle made it inevitable my boss would sack me. He knew I was back up to my old tricks, so we went our separate ways and my good wages went with him. Yet again I'd opted for the path of inevitable ruin.

Living with Denise was fucking awful. To me, she looked normal, but I'd guess to anyone outside our drug circle she'd look like a drug user. This was because the majority of those surrounding us all fit the same description: pale, gaunt, undernourished, haunted, hunted, and haggard.

Speed, speed, and then more speed. On this drug you don't eat, you don't sleep, so you're awake for four or five days and nights in a row, pushing the limits of your body and mind. There were instances of neighbours burgling Denise's house and then us carrying out revenge burglaries. There was scant loyalty among the miscreants of her neighbourhood.

It wasn't long before Denise and I embarked on a journey to the Isle of Wight to spend some time with an uncle of hers. While there we soon became involved in using stolen credit cards to fund our speed habit and were eventually apprehended by the police in Devon after a two-hundred-mile crime wave involving a stolen car. Which brings me back to the beginning of this account and my escape from Newport's Magistrates' Court.

* * *

I was looking forward to emerging from the boot of the car and standing upright as I felt really cramped from laying in an embryonic position for an hour, and I was still filled with uncertainty around who might next open the boot.

I felt the ferry's engines slow then heard the sound of footsteps as passengers returned to their cars. The doors to my car opened, and I felt Cookie and Tony settle into the front seats then the doors slammed closed.

"You okay, mate?" Cookie asked me.

"Sure, man, where's my beer?" I joked.

"Okay, this is looking pretty good. Let's get the fuck outta here." Cookie turned over the engine and then, once the cars ahead began to move, he joined the queue rolling down the ramp and onto mainland England. I was off the island. I'd made it.

The car surged forward, and we were off, bumping over the ferry's ramps onto *terra firma* confirming the success of our mission. Lymington train station was only a five- or ten-minute drive away.

Cookie pulled the car into the train station car park. Feeling and hearing the sound of the tyres changing from the road's tarmac to gravel added to my excitement. This was the moment I'd been awaiting over the past week, verification I'd escaped my captors. My co-conspirators waited for several minutes until the coast was clear so no one would witness a man emerge from the boot of a car.

"Okay, Tony," he said. "Coast's clear." Tony opened the boot then I unfolded myself as I climbed out, happy to feel my feet land on the gravel car park. My legs felt like jelly, and I had to support my weight by gripping the edge of the car for a few moments.

Slowly the blood supply returned to my legs, and I was more able to stand. I handed some cash to Tony, and he entered the station to buy me a ticket and check train times. I wanted as little contact with people as possible considering my description was all over Television South's news broadcasts and would only head for the train minutes before it was due.

Tony returned with my ticket to Bristol and both he and Cookie climbed back into the car. I offered them some cash for their troubles, but they refused to take anything.

"No man, you're gonna need that cash," they said, "and, besides, it's nice to get one over on the police and the prison service. You take care and gissa call to let us know you've reached Bristol."

Honest crooks. Heartwarming.

Pre-computerization, television networks and police systems weren't nationalized. Each region of the UK had its own TV and news coverage, and each police force was based within the county it dealt with. This meant only Hampshire Constabulary was searching for me and only Television South was broadcasting news of my fugitive status and description. All I needed to do, therefore, was to remove myself to a different part of the country, which is why Bristol had sprung to mind. I had good friends and places to stay there.

Arriving in Bristol, I headed straight to the Stokes Croft area and found some of my traveller friends. It wasn't long before I landed in a squatted house in Denbigh Street where there was no need to worry about the door getting crashed by police searching for me…unless, of course, there was an early morning drug bust, which was unlikely.

Denise came and joined me, and we stayed in Bristol for around a week. After Christmas we both decided to go back to Hampshire, to a convoy park-up near Basingstoke. My old friend Jill from the beanfield was parked up there along with lots of other friends.

The ground was incredibly wet and huge sloppy puddles lay everywhere while around fifteen different vehicles parked either side of the lane, a wide enough gap between for vehicular movement. I stayed in a small caravan next to Jill's bus with an elegant old wood burner that made for a cozy, warm, and dry home.

There's always some vile, nasty person who will shop you to the authorities. I've my suspicions who it was but, with time being the ultimate equalizer, it no longer matters. The individual I'm certain informed on my whereabouts died a few years after these events, found alone in a room dead from a heroin overdose.

It was way past midnight, and I was asleep in my bed when I heard the caravan door creak open. The light of a torch came through the door followed by a voice I recognized:

"Christian, there are lots of policemen here and there's no escape so don't cause any trouble and come quietly, okay?"

It was an old adversary from Farnborough's police force. They'd sent someone who knew how to deal with me as we had a fairly long history, and because I was known to become violent rather than be arrested.

I could do nothing other than get dressed and fume at the fact I'd been "grassed up." I was handcuffed and brought outside the caravan. Many travellers slowly emerged from their homes now the police had ceased being silent. I was led to the waiting police van and the doors slammed shut behind me.

I was well and truly nicked again and en route back to the Isle of Wight prison I'd escaped from all because some nasty bastard had informed on me. Firstly, I felt angry with myself for being so stupid as to return to Hampshire rather than remain in Bristol and, secondly, I felt I'd let down and disappointed those who'd put themselves at risk in helping me escape the island.

I spent several more weeks on remand at HMP Camphill and then, after applying to be moved to a prison closer to home to facilitate easier visits, it was agreed I'd be transferred to HMP Winchester on the mainland. I was immediately shown into an office in reception where the governor was sat at a desk.

"I've agreed to this transfer, Austin, as I understand how difficult it is to get visits on the island. However, any of your old tricks and I won't hesitate having you sent straight back from whence you came, got it?"

This was said in a jovial kind of tone. We'd known one another for a number of years now and he realised I would be trouble. This was his way of asking me to keep it within the bounds of acceptability. There was never any real resentment between the pair of us. He was doing his job, and I was a dysfunctional delinquent in his charge awaiting trial at Winchester Crown Court.

I had an appearance at Aldershot magistrates court for some separate charges two weeks after arriving in Winchester prison and was escorted there with much security due to my recent escape. The police were taking no chances, keeping me handcuffed and securely locked in while travelling in police vans. My case was called by the court usher, and I was led up the concrete stairs into the magistrates' court dock. I was surprised to see my friend Mia and her sister sat in the courtroom's public gallery.

The case against me was dismissed but I was still awaiting trial at Winchester crown court for different charges so remained in custody. I was led back downstairs to my cell and, shortly after being locked in, the door opened again, and I was told I had a visitor. The jailer led me to a small visiting room, and I entered to find Mia sitting at a table.

A mutual friend had asked me to help her and her partner move into one of the Totland Close flats a couple of years previously. Since that first meeting, we'd become friends, and I'd always found her incredibly attractive. We'd been corresponding during most of this period I'd been imprisoned.

She had a slim build and pretty, elfin face with slightly wavy auburn hair falling to just below her shoulders. Her hazel eyes shifted from green to brown depending on the light and she was a head shorter than me.

"Hey, Mia, how you doing? What a lovely surprise! I hadn't expected you to come to the courtroom, much less visit me."

"I'm really good, thanks. You mentioned today's appearance in your last letter, so I thought I'd surprise you." She flashed a cheeky smile across the table at me. There was something there behind her eyes, but I tried not to place too much meaning on it. I knew she was in a serious relationship and that she had two children.

"Well, you certainly did that." I laughed. I was really pleased to be sat across the table from her and reached for her hand. I gently held it and felt its warmth as we chatted.

"So, how are you bearing up? How long before you're released, do you think?"

"Having today's charges dismissed makes a big difference. Thankfully, the prosecution couldn't provide enough evidence for a conviction. The remaining offences ain't too serious so…I reckon, fingers crossed, I'll be free in two or three months."

She relayed the latest news of what had been going on in The Square and what our mutual friends were up to—she was good friends with Jill, Sonia, Claire, and Richard who I'd been at Stonehenge '84 with.

The jailer came in and told us we had five minutes remaining, so we said our goodbyes and Mia handed me a piece of hash that I quickly stashed and thanked her for. As we stood up and hugged goodbye, she kissed me full on the lips. I was happily surprised by this as I'd guessed there was a mutual feeling between us. I had no idea then something was not right with her relationship with her partner, Lucas, and nor did I care—I wasn't so much a friend of Lucas's as I was Mia's…I didn't really know him.

The jailer escorted me back to my cell and I had a warm glow coursing through me.

Today I realise what an error of judgement Mia made that day. To become romantically involved with me at that stage of my journey was tantamount to buying a ticket to hell. That kiss was the first step towards her own eventual demise, and I so wish events had turned out other than the way they did.

Several weeks later, I appeared at Winchester Crown Court and the judge concluded I'd served enough time on remand, even with the added "escape from custody" charge. I was free to walk from the court room and feel the heat beating down from a blue sky with my slate wiped clean.

18

Whipping Post
(Frank Zappa)

I returned to Totland Close. This time I was determined to find a job and stay clear of the heroin, so I began labouring on the new Princesmead shopping centre project. My task was to fix metal brick-ties to the steel frame of the building, ensuring the brickies (bricklayers) didn't catch up with me. I had a Hilti-type gun that screwed fixings through the holes in the L-shaped brick-ties. There was a real knack to using the gun and I became good at this job—so good, in fact, on the two occasions I was fired, they asked me back with an offer of more money. Nobody else was as fast or efficient as me.

I began hanging out with Mia's sister, Leslie, during the evenings after work. She lived in a flat in Totland Close. I really wanted to make a go of it this time, really wanted to keep the job and earn a regular wage, stay out of trouble, keep away from hard drugs and prison. I also wanted Leslie's sister and both Leslie and I knew this.

I spent the majority of my days outside working hours in Leslie's kitchen. It was early spring, and the weather was fine. I'd play guitar and sing, we'd share spliffs, discuss a hundred different topics—Leslie was intelligent and well educated—or cook food for the kids and ourselves.

Before long, Mia and I began an affair behind her boyfriend's back with many of our meetings or Mia's pretexts a collaboration with her older sister; it really was a strange situation.

There was a huge positive though: I was no longer hanging out with my usual crowd of fuckwits and smackheads, and I was clean. To increase my chances—as well as due to a promise I'd made Mia—I continued getting up and going to work on the Princesmead job every day. As often happened whenever I found gainful employment, I was enjoying the physical activity and the camaraderie that is always to be found on a construction site.

I continued with my newfound diligence, working hard each day drilling the wall-ties to the skeletal steel frame of this new shopping centre, watching it grow as it was wrapped in brick walls. The money was good, I was paying Leslie for my keep and my sole vices at this point were brandy, tobacco and weed. The construction site was only a couple of miles from home, so I was cycling each day and didn't have any fuel costs. Everything was going well. I should've realised things were about to get messy again. And this was due to the conniving witch I was living with: Mia's sister, Leslie.

Mia showed up at Leslie's flat one afternoon and I sensed her anxiety before she uttered a word.

"Lucas knows about us," she told me. "I've no idea how. Maybe we were seen together by one of his friends. He says he's moving out and going to live with his parents in Wiltshire and will collect the children at weekends."

I'd promised Mia I'd turn over a new leaf because I wanted us to be together. I'd agreed to give up heroin and I'd been clean for two months. We'd been falling more and more deeply in love and had no real plans or ideas on how this would eventually pan out—we were just living for each day while also realising it was a fool's paradise.

After a few weeks of this separation, Mia became completely torn and confused. She loved the father of her children, but their life together had drifted into the doldrums, she loved her children, and she loved me. She had to make a choice.

The decision she made was for us to break off our affair and for Lucas to return home.

"Christian, I'm so sorry for any pain I've caused you. But the children need Lucas, he's their father and although I really love you, I need to try to make things right…the way they were before."

We were sat on a bench behind the Prince Louis pub, and I could see Mia was broken in pieces. Her eyes were raw and filled with tears and I was also close to breaking down, but she'd made her decision, and I couldn't force her to change her mind. She had to put her children's welfare first.

"You have to do what's right for you and the kids, Mia," I said, trying to sound stronger than I felt.

"I'm going to have to leave. I can't see you together with Lucas without my heart breaking and I might do something crazy if I stay around here. I've decided to go travelling somewhere…anywhere other than here."

* * *

Knowing I had to leave, I decided to travel to France with my guitar. I'd heard from many musical friends that busking was a good option in the south of the country due to its Mediterranean climate. I'd become reasonably good at playing and singing by this time, so why not give it a shot? Better that than hanging around Farnborough with a broken heart.

I spent one final night in Leslie's flat. Despite the fact she could be an evil conniving witch, we still shared a strong affinity. We spent the evening discussing where I might head for once in France, shared spliffs and brandy, and then went to bed.

The following morning, she sent her kids off to school, I packed a bag, grabbed my guitar, and I left Totland Close on a journey into the great unknown—my own Sal Paradise from Kerouac's *On the Road*. I'd read this seminal road trip bible back in borstal and it resonated with my absconding adventures and my dreams of travel.

I didn't have a passport, so I visited the post office, had a photo taken in the photobooth, and got myself a sixty-hour pass to cross the Channel. This was a possibility back in the 1980s. Once in France I'd figure a way to stay as long as I needed to.

19

On the Road Again

(Willie Nelson)

Toulon. Home to the French naval fleet and the city where Napoleon Bonaparte first found recognition with his capture of its strategic fortress forcing the Anglo-Spanish fleet to withdraw.

I'd hitchhiked from Farnborough down to the M20 where I'd met a fellow traveller from Reading. My lift had dropped me off on the hard shoulder and in the fading light I'd spotted a guy with a backpack only fifty yards further on.

"Hey man, where you headed?" I asked once I came close to him.

"I'm off to the South of France. You?"

"Yeah, same. I'm Christian. Why don't we travel together?"

"Sure, why not? I'm Grant." He was a big guy, both taller and more robust than me, and was wrapped in a mountain jacket with his blonde hair tucked into its hood.

"You're a guitarist?"

"Yeah man. I'm heading to the south as I've heard the busking is great…and the weather."

"Well, you've heard right about both. I'm gonna sell cold drinks on the beach in St. Tropez. I did it last summer and earned enough to survive and have some good times."

I said I was headed pretty much anywhere in the south. He had some cash, and I had a guitar. He had experience in travelling around France while I had very little. We also both shared a penchant for enjoying smack, which would soon become clear.

The agreement we came up with was Grant would pay for us until his money ran out and then we'd both live from the proceeds of busking. We took a ferry across the English Channel to Ostend then made our way to the city of Lille where we quickly ended up in a squat and scored some smack. A couple of injections later and we were both fucked out of our minds until the dawn found us both sharing the same sense of disappointment and a desire to get out of Lille.

"Fuck, man," Grant said, "this is one of the reasons I decided to leave Reading."

"Me too, man, I didn't plan this trip so I could continue doing the same shit I've always done at home. It's so I could escape a broken heart and find something new."

We were in accord. We headed for the city centre, found a place to eat and downed a few beers, then tried our hand at a bit of street performance. I had a small repertoire of songs I knew from beginning to end but was very aware I'd need to learn many more quickly.

The songs I had learned were popular Neil Young, Beatles, or Rolling Stones classics most people knew so we didn't do too badly. Something else I realised was this trial by fire method would force me to improve rapidly...or no food, cigarettes, hash, or beer.

Next stop the train station. This was where Grant's experience came especially in handy. He explained to me how to work the system.

"Okay, so you step onto the train and find a seat that doesn't have a 'reserved' label on the headrest. The guard doesn't usually come around for tickets until you've passed a few stations. When he asks for your ticket, you explain, in bad French, you have work at your ultimate destination, in this case Lyon.

"At this point, he'll either say, 'Get off my train,' or he'll ask for your passport, then issue you with a ticket, which needs to be paid later. He's happy because he's done his job by taking your passport number and home address. SNCF (the French equivalent of British Rail) will send letters to your home address, and you throw them in the bin. Simple, right?"

This was amazing. My new companion had saved me hours and hours of waiting on motorways with my thumb out trying to get from Calais to the South of France. This invaluable lesson gave me the means to travel around France for the next several months and I met many other travellers making the most of this same loophole.

We weren't thrown off this first train. Just as Grant had said, it depended on the personality of the guard. We got the busking down as we moved further south and figured pretty quickly how to double our takings. Each carriage had an automatic sliding door at the halfway mark dividing the carriage in two. By playing with my back against the open door I could perform to both halves of the carriage rather than playing to them separately. I'd sing and play a few songs (with the door incessantly trying to close itself throughout) and, during the third song, Grant would travel up and down the carriage with hat in hand asking for donations. I quickly realised the busking game here in France was a far more lucrative enterprise than standing in a street or working the underground in the UK. The secret here was to find a static captive audience. There's an element of peer pressure when donors are sat close together that doesn't exist when performing to a fluid audience on the street. It would be the same when busking the café terraces over the coming months and I proved a fast learner.

I'd just awoken on a bench in the balmy morning sun of Toulon and today Grant and I planned to go our separate ways. He was heading for St. Tropez in a bid to make a living selling cold cans on the beach while I would take my chances busking trains and towns seeking adventure and relief from my broken heart. Our agreement to spend his money first and then rely on my guitar had proven successful and, not only did we both now have some cash in our pockets, we'd also encouraged one another to stay away from dirty squats, smack, and needles.

We rolled up our sleeping bags and crammed them into backpacks, shared a spliff and then set out for the train station to find coffee and breakfast.

Soon we were standing on separate platforms with the railway lines between us. Grant's train came in first and I waved goodbye as his train pulled away east in the direction of St. Tropez. A short while later I was heading west on a train to Marseilles. I waited for the train to gain some distance and speed, stood up and placed my back against the carriage's dividing door then began to play and sing.

* * *

Jumping down from my bunk bed, I stood and stretched at the open window, taking in the spectacular view. The hot bright sun cast its rays down from a pale blue sky onto the town of Sète, a small fishing commune with a thriving tourist industry that boasted terrace after terrace of cafés around the *Centreville* and along the harbour. Colourful houses rolled down the hillside before me until they were met by a river. From this river they climbed a similar hillside opposite up to the blue-skied horizon. I was in my bedroom at a youth hostel where I'd been staying for the past several days. Most residents here paid cash, but I was fortunate enough to have landed the role of house musician. In exchange for bed and board, I simply had to entertain the staff and residents at lunch and dinnertime meals as payment for my stay.

This also meant I didn't need to keep my guitar close to me at all times as I'd had to on the journey from Toulon to Montpellier. I'd lost count of the number of trains, ticket collectors, evictions, platforms, and nights sharing my sleeping bag with my guitar I'd spent before landing here. My guitar was now my lifeline and any carelessness on my part could result in its loss and my descent down to a street urchin—another Gavroche—depending on not just his wits but possibly theft, too.

I climbed down the stairs and enjoyed a breakfast of croissants washed down with hot chocolate in the obligatory round bowl, French style. Looking around I recognised a few faces but the turnaround in this place was incredible with most travellers only staying one or two nights. The only constant was the staff members who were full of warm smiles towards me.

I've often found street musicians in France have a much higher social standing than those in the UK. In both countries, classical musicians are equally revered, yet the street musician in the UK is often treated with a similar contempt as a beggar. In France, especially in the warm and sunny south, it would seem strange to sit at a café and not see and hear musicians entertaining the patrons of the surrounding cafés. I'm speaking of a time long before the wave of migrants Europe has witnessed in recent years—this influx of people has resulted in more beggars and unfortunately changed attitudes around donations. However, as will be seen later in this story (during the COVID-19 pandemic of 2020), the people of this same region could not do without their musical *soirées* despite lockdowns.

After grabbing my guitar from upstairs, I left the hostel and walked down the hill towards the *centreville* (town centre). Upon landing in any French town or city, I'd head directly to the centreville because this is where the drinkers, smokers, street performers, and musicians could be found. It was a hangout for everyone while at the same time being a place you'd need to keep your wits about you. Had I been greener around the ears, I'd probably have lost my shit weeks before.

I bought some beers from a nearby shop and joined a group of musicians playing on the grass near an enormous statue-waterfall feature. There was always a cosmopolitan mélange of music to be found—the North African contingent with their drums, shakers, and their own rhythms, the strong Bossa Nova/Latin American feel to many of the jams, or a healthy dose of reggae—along with French classics like Nino Ferre and Jacques Higelin or the songs of Belgian Jacques Brel.

I watched a guitarist opposite me and figured out the chords and rhythms he was playing and joined in the jam. Once I'd got the hang of the changes and became more confident, he dropped his rhythm playing and began to solo over the changes. He played a couple of choruses then dropped back into rhythm guitar with me to make way for a guy blowing a harmonica. This was the life. Strumming, learning new chord progressions and songs, improving my vocal capabilities.

We continued to drink, smoke, and play together. I'd play guitar for a bit, then finish my song and pass it to someone else to play, then I'd maybe play someone's harmonica. This was early May, the weather was incredibly warm with everyone wearing the barest amount of clothing and, more importantly, not one of us having any sense of responsibility or desire to be doing anything else. This was our moment, and each moment blended into the next and each musician merged into the next and the music was a tapestry holding us all in the right place...the exact place we all needed to be at that point in time.

Fuck Farnborough. Fuck Mia. Fuck The Square. Despite the excruciating pain of my broken heart, I was beginning to feel that providence might have guided me to this place...that Christian could finally escape the destiny imprinted by his father's genes, heavy hand, and sexual deviance; that I could soar above that destiny on my musical wings and become free of that pre-determination, something greater than the story handed down to me.

I began chatting and smoking with one of the guys who'd recently played my guitar. He'd played an impressive rendition of a song from Brittany, *La Blanche Hermine.*

He introduced himself as Pierre Thebault and announced he was a proud Breton. His English was passable, although heavily accented like many French. His face was heavily tanned with equally bronzed arms and a bright gold ring hung from one earlobe. Mousy brown hair fell to his shoulders and a pair of piercing blue eyes fixed on my own with a broad smile. There was an intelligence and humour emanating from this smile that gave me an immediate good feeling, and we'd quickly become friends.

I was surprised and abashed when he complimented me on my own playing and singing but at the same time realised how far I'd come in the few weeks since leaving Farnborough. *I knew this would happen,* I thought to myself, *It's simply a case of playing as many hours as possible and dispensing with fear.*

Pierre had a suggestion. He said we could form a small group made up of me, himself, and a percussionist from Martinique named Marcos. He pointed Marcos out to me across the circle of musicians. He had gleaming white teeth contrasting with the black skin of his face and was throwing some slick moves on a pair of bongo drums.

"We can always make a better show with a few people than we can alone," Pierre sagely advised me, "and then even more *soleil dans la rue* are thrown into the hat."

This was a term I'd heard a few times over recent weeks. It was street slang meaning 'sun in the street' and referred to a ten-franc piece, the equivalent of a one-pound note in the 1980s. The French I was learning from my musician friends was *l'argot* and to this day my reasonably good French instantly gives away which school I learned it from.

This was Pierre's own country, and I realised his suggestion carried a lot of weight. He didn't have his own guitar, which was a concern for me because he might be wanting to steal mine. But he knew the ropes much better than I, so I agreed to give it a shot. Just as I was being taught their language by my streetwise French friends, I needed to also learn their culture from them.

As the sun began to lower and dusk approached, Pierre, Marcos, and I said our *au revoirs* to the gang of musicians and revellers then left the park and headed towards the harbour and seafront.

"We have something interesting for you to see," Pierre said in his strong Breton accent, flashing a mischievous grin at Marcos as he skipped along the pavement. Pierre had a youthful and boisterous energy about him, a *joie de vivre* similar to my own that I found endearing, while Marcos had a much more calm, introverted, and thoughtful demeanour.

I happily followed them, intrigued by what this surprise might be. My mood was good, I had enough cash to last me the next few days and the means to earn more when that was spent, the weather was perfectly warm, I was making new and interesting friends, and I was on the greatest adventure of my young life thus far.

We bought some bottles of cheap wine on the way to the harbour along with some vegetables and dried white rice. Next, we stopped at a bakery and Pierre asked the baker for some empty yeast tins. We passed a place called *Theatre de la Mer* and Marcos disappeared through some gates and into its yard only to reappear a moment later dragging a wooden pallet behind him.

After walking another few hundred yards Marcos left the footpath, hauled the heavy pallet to the cliff edge, and threw it out towards the sea below.

"Follow me," said Pierre, leading the way down a steep winding path that hugged the cliff face. I followed and Marcos climbed down behind me.

A few moments later, all became clear. There was a small cave at the base of the cliff slightly above sea level. In the centre was a firepit and there was a large amount of bedding wrapped in plastic on a ledge, high enough and far enough from the sea to prevent its getting wet.

"You guys live here!" I exclaimed.

"*Bienvenue chez nous!*" they cried in unison and cracked up laughing as Marcos placed his set of bongos on the same ledge as the bedding.

"Wow, this is incredible!"

The pallet Marcos had thrown over the side had broken into big chunks on the rocks in front of the cave. Taking a large rock, he completed its destruction and proceeded to build a fire. There were large bottles of water wedged in position between the rocks so they'd remain cool in the heat yet couldn't float away with the tide. Pierre half-filled one of the yeast tins with water then added white rice and salt.

A wine bottle was opened then passed around. I settled my guitar against the back wall of the cave and rolled a spliff. Marcos balanced a metal grill over the fire, placed the tin of rice on it then collected mussels from the rocks and placed them in another tin while Pierre prepped the vegetables and placed them in a third tin. We sat passing around the spliff and wine while the aroma of the boiling food blended with the salt air playing all around the cave.

We shared an amazing evening together, the first of many in our small and cozy *grotte*. During the day we'd hit the streets and the cafés, drinking coffee early on and then progressing on to wine or beer by mid-morning. This was accompanied by the omnipresent spliff being passed around and this was something I witnessed all the street people doing all day long—earning enough cash to keep the wine, the beer, and the spliffs flowing.

My time at the youth hostel was over. I could either finish my day then climb an enormous hill for thirty minutes to be greeted with a ghostly quiet hostel where people wanted to sleep. Or I could head off in the opposite direction with my new friends playing cafés en route, buying more food, wine and beer then cooking, getting drunk and high, skinny-dipping, diving into the sea, and playing music as raucously and loudly as we liked.

This continued for weeks with the three of us having a fantastic time. I even reached a point of trust with my new companions where I'd sometimes leave my guitar with them. We'd become a close band of musicians bonded by love of music and an equal amount of fun and camaraderie.

Yet beneath this hedonistic surface, there was an overwhelming sadness. One which involved Mia; I couldn't get her out of my head.

I always had pockets full of change so one day, while walking past a phone booth, I stopped, pulled open its door and dialled Leslie's number, something I'd previously been avoiding.

"Hey! Where are you?" she asked.

"I'm in a place called Sète, near Montpellier in the South of France… having a fab time. Lotsa new friends, busking, earning money, living in a fuckin' cave…it's really cool. What about you, how you doing?"

She replied things were fine with her and the kids, shit was still the same in The Square, nothing much to report other than Mia and Lucas were gonna get married.

My heart sank heavily, became a dead weight. I've no idea what I expected to hear but it wasn't this bombshell. This gave everything a sense of permanence.

"They're getting…?" I couldn't voice the question.

"Yeah, but she still loves you. It won't last," the redheaded witch happily informed me.

I said my goodbyes before I fell to pieces, left the booth, and sat on a low wall along the harbour trying to make sense of this unwelcome news. Deep in thought, my eyes following the gulls floating and whirling on the air then dipping down to the sea. I realised I couldn't digest the information there and then, that I needed time, so I very slowly walked back to join the guys. My mind was troubled, and a deep unhappiness stirred within me that my friends could sense. Pierre asked me what was up, but I assured him I'd be okay although it took many days to shake it off before I felt on an even keel again.

We decided to leave town and try our chances further east. Pierre knew the South of France well and assured us every major town and city would be just as lucrative as Sète had been.

We headed for the train station, jumped on the Marseilles train, and travelled steadily eastwards, sometimes staying on the train, sometimes not...depending on the guard. We'd ensure we earnt enough money in the first couple of carriages once the train left the station in case we did get thrown off. There'd be nothing worse than ending up in a small town where it was impossible to earn money for our provisions of wine and tobacco. Hash and weed were scarcely a problem as the south coast of France was flooded with the stuff due to its proximity to the drug routes beginning in Morocco then travelling through Spain and into France.

We were told to leave a train somewhere around a place named Beauvoisin. The guard wasn't having any of our nonsense and evicted us. It was late and there were no trains until morning. The three of us left the station and saw the welcome lights of a bar across the street, customers visible through its windows. We headed over and ordered beers then sat down at the outside chairs and tables, drinking and smoking. We could smoke but had to be discreet.

After another round of beers, a strange sight came towards us—a guy riding a moped with one leg in a cast and a pair of crutches laid across one handlebar. He pulled over beside us and smiled.

"*Bonsoir, mes amies*," he happily said, "you wanna buy some shit?" He smiled even more broadly and then comprehension dawned when Marcos passed a spliff to Pierre.

"Ah, I see you're already well connected. May I join you?"

He successfully dropped the scooter to the floor and managed to stay upright on his crutches.

Pierre pulled a chair out for him, asked what he was drinking then went to the bar and bought him a beer.

"Thanks. I see you're a band of musicians. What kind of style?"

I picked up the guitar and broke into the chords of the Stones' *Sympathy for the Devil* while Marcos rolled out a steady stream of syncopated beats on his bongos. Pierre filled the space between with some melodic "ooh-oohs," and we proceeded to knock this guy almost off his chair with our rip-roaring rendition.

I could see the guy was impressed with our performance and his eyes gleamed as he grinned from ear to ear and said, "Yes! You guys have played together before, no?"

Everybody cracked up laughing then we listened to this guy's story of leaving a bar a little worse for wear, then jumping a wall only to discover there was a two metre drop the other side resulting in a broken femur.

The bar was to close soon so the next thing we concerned ourselves with was how and where we could continue our little soiree. We bought a few overpriced bottles of wine and our new friend, Didier, said he knew of a place we could hang out and party…assuring us we could sleep there too and led the way to some fields outside the town. We partied until late, said goodbye to our friend, and all climbed into our sleeping bags and slept the sleep of the inebriated and stoned.

* * *

We arrived in the Camargue the following afternoon after successfully jumping a train to Arles then hitching a ride south to Les Saintes Maries de la Mer.

Sitting on the Rhône River delta west of Marseilles, this remote commune boasts a population of only a few thousand people that swells to circa half a million during the summer months, giving some idea of its popularity as a tourist destination.

Famed for its tough and hardy wild horses, pink flamingo colony and, most interestingly, a gypsy pilgrimage from all over Europe to carry their patron saint, Sara, to the sea, this wonderful town became the perfect place to spend a few weeks and earn some cash on the terraces.

Making enquiries of fellow travellers and musicians we learned there were strict rules around nomads and itinerants sleeping anywhere within the town, therefore a beach camp a mile east was the best place to spend the evenings.

We took this information in, played a few cafés in the centre then, once enough cash was thrown into the passing hat, languidly made our way along the promenade in the early evening swelter until we found the beach sprawling before us. True enough, after another twenty minutes' walk, we found a bunch of regular musos, backpackers, and hippies variously drinking, smoking, jamming, necking, or collecting driftwood for the evening's campfire.

I left my guitar with the guys, safe now in the knowledge they were happy to share in its proceeds rather than steal it and leave me destitute.

I turned my back on these gathered friends and strangers then walked towards the surf. I removed my shoes, rolled up my trousers, and walked into the cool froth and foam of the freshly breaking waves. As usually happened when I found any time for reverie, my thoughts turned to Mia and my heart sank within my soul. These adventures were a fantastic panacea for my heartbreak as they gave me sparse time for dwelling on Farnborough and all it meant to me.

I could feel tears welling up inside but, being adroit at suppressing such overwhelming feelings, that's as far as it went. I couldn't cry yet there was a silent scream louder than the crashing waves around me that desperately wanted to break free. Mia was going to marry Lucas and there was nothing I could do to prevent it—why, oh why, did she give me such a sweet taste only to snatch it back so cruelly?

I splashed through the surf kicking at the waves and gazing at the flat blue horizon for another twenty minutes, then stoically pulled myself together and went to join the party that was gathering momentum across the sand-whipped beach. I was powerless to change the outcome and could only swallow the bitter medicine.

20

With a Little Help from My Friends
(Joe Cocker)

The couple of weeks spent in this town and on its beach have left me with incredible memories to this day. Just as they did in Sète's youth hostel, the names and faces changed as often as the songs and musical styles each evening.

One night, I became separated from my friends and was so completely drunk from all the revelry I sat down in the town centre, rested my guitar against the wall I was leaning back against, and fell asleep. I wasn't disturbed all evening and woke just as the town was stretching and yawning awake. It took me a few moments to gather my wits and figure out where I was and how I'd ended up there.

Shit, where's my guitar?

"Fuck, man! No!" I wailed out loud.

My guitar was nowhere to be seen yet I knew I would have had it with me when I'd fallen asleep. I couldn't believe my own stupidity. After months of ensuring my guitar never left my side, it was now gone.

I began what felt like a walk to the gallows towards the beach and my friends. How could I have been so stupid?

I arrived at the camp and some guys who knew me immediately asked the same question I had on my own lips, "Where's your guitar, man?"

It was always with me. Either in my hands or slung down my back, body above, neck below, with the strap across my chest. It was a part of me, and these guys' question was testimony to that.

Guitare volée…! I practically cried from the bottom of my soul: "It's been stolen."

We had a multinational community on the beach and the common languages shared by everybody—apart from the music we all loved and played—were both French and English. Some of those on the verge of waking understood what I'd said while others could hear the desolation in my voice and also woke up.

Pierre and Marcos also came awake and both realised what was unfolding. This news also affected them and their ability to continue living here on the beach.

My friends consoled me as best they could, but it really didn't help swing my mood from that of complete misery. Did this mean I'd have to return to the UK?

The fire had been stirred, and people had climbed out from sleeping bags and blankets. Coffee was soon available, so I sat around with all the guys passing spliffs, trying not to think about the loss of my guitar.

There was a car park not far from our encampment and the sound of a door sliding open announced Jean-Paul had risen. He was a regular around the fire each evening, a gentle soul of around fifty years old with long scraggly white hair and a tangled white beard tobacco-stained yellow around his mouth. Unlike us youngsters, he lived in a VW campervan in the car park and had done so for the past couple of weeks. He slammed the van door and came walking towards the camp. It soon became evident he was carrying a guitar in his hand and my heart skipped a beat.

As he came within earshot, he called out in his thick French accent, "Ah, you young ones have a lot to learn, *non*?"

He walked up to me and handed me the guitar.

"I tried to wake you, my friend, but you were too far gone. I knew you'd die of shock when you woke up because your guitar was not there, but this is the better of two evils, *non*?"

A huge rousing cheer rose from all around. I placed the guitar on the sand by my side, stood up and gave Jean-Paul possibly the biggest and strongest hug he'd ever had…with many kisses on both cheeks.

A couple of nights later and the wine and beer were flowing freely. A pretty girl named Eloise was conspiring with me to dispel my pain—somehow, she knew of this pain. She was sitting beside me as I finished my stint on guitar and passed it on. We were huddled together in deep conversation then the conversation turned to sweet kisses. We continued to exchange flashing repartee, warm kisses, and bright white smiles, sharing a bottle of red wine. Then she gently took my hand, lifted the blanket she'd been sitting on and led me down the beach until the sound of our fellow dreamers was indistinct from the howling wind and loud crashing and splashing of the waves. She laid down the blanket on the sand and helped me forget everything other than the moments we shared together that evening in the clear black star-filled night.

And in the morning, she was gone—a glowing, warm, and ephemeral memory on the beach of the Camargue.

We had a throwaway camera on that beach. I remember having a bunch of photos of those weeks and the friends we shared them with for a few years after these events but, as with many people and souvenirs in my chaotic life, they were transient and were eventually consigned to memory…a memory that I'm amazed is so bright and vivid today. Those days in the Camargue were in 1988, thirty-five years ago, but I can still hear the rolling of the waves, the roar of the wind, the laughter of my friends, and all the songs we'd sung together.

* * *

Avignon, a stunning town also sat on the Rhône, famed for several exiled popes, the Palais des Pape they'd resided in, the cathedral where they worshipped, and its bridge immortalized in the song "Sur le Pont d'Avignon." It was also the town where Pierre, Marcos, and I would go our separate ways.

We'd travelled here after leaving the Camargue and had been playing several huge cafes over the past few days. We finished our set one evening, collected our proceeds then headed for the closest park, enjoying the evening's lowering sun while drinking red wine and practicing new songs. A small group of girls came and sat with us to enjoy our music. They brought a couple of bottles of wine with them and said they were grape picking at a local vineyard named *Chateauneuf du Pape*.

"This isn't the really good wine, it's the second-rate stuff we're allowed to drink coz we work there."

I could see how much they were appreciating the music and one girl in particular was giving me all her attention. As the evening progressed, I got chatting with her—she told me her name was Lauren—and when her friends said they were leaving, she said, "Why don't you come with us?"

I agreed, grabbed my guitar, and told the guys I'd see them the next day. They smiled knowingly and wished me luck. I followed the girls to the taxi rank, and we piled into a couple of cabs—we were seven including me.

The cabs dropped us outside the vineyard then pulled away. One of the girls unlocked the entrance gate while a couple of the others were making loud "shushing" sounds in that way only drunk people can. We made it to their dormitory without waking the whole estate, the doors were closed, and the party began.

I sang many songs for them, they kept my glass filled with delightful ruby red wine, and they rolled spliff after spliff.

I'd learned a Cat Stevens song called "Father and Son" a few weeks prior, a hauntingly beautiful song. At this point the song was still new to me. I remembered it from the radio during my childhood when it was a hit and today it seems a strange choice of song when I think about the lyrics and my fucked-up relationship with my own father but, listening to it today, it's still a powerful song.

I dropped this song on them, and Lauren stared into my eyes while I sang. I finished the song and took the spliff she was offering me...

That's the last memory I have of that evening.

"Christian, wake up. You have to go. We need to start work in half an hour." Lauren was shaking me awake.

I grabbed my guitar, tobacco and weed, said *au revoir* to the other girls then followed Lauren as she led me through the gate and out to the road.

She gave me a gentle kiss on the lips, said she hoped to see me again then bade me farewell and went back inside to begin her day's work picking grapes.

I slung my guitar over my shoulder, swung its neck down to my right so the body was against my back, and I began slowly walking in the same direction the taxis had arrived from the night before. I had a stupid grin on my face and shook my head at the wonder of it all. Since that day, whenever I've needed to bring a bottle of wine to anyone's table, it's usually a bottle of Chateauneuf du Pape and is my cue to begin:

"I was busking in the South of France many years ago when I was kidnapped by these girls and taken to the place where this stuff is made..........."

* * *

I'd stayed in touch with Leslie, and she'd kept me updated on Mia's wedding and how things were developing. It was excruciatingly painful for me to think about as my heart was still broken. I tried hard not to dwell on it and was thankful I had plenty of distractions. I was also, however, conscious the summer wouldn't last forever and, after a couple more weeks, I decided to return to Farnborough before the weather turned.

Pierre, Marcos, and I exchanged postal addresses promising to stay in touch and rendezvous the following summer. After sharing big hugs, we said our goodbyes. I grabbed my guitar and backpack then walked the ten minutes to Avignon station and jumped on the first train out of there, heading towards Lyon then Paris, busking carriages along the way.

It had been upsetting to leave my friends as we'd shared many wonderful moments and adventures together, but I consoled myself with the promise I'd given to meet them again. My musical existence in France was reliant on tourism and I realised these tourists would soon be displaced by the approaching colder weather. Also, I was determined to see Mia.

I got lucky and made it all the way to Amiens before a guard threw me off just as it was getting dark. Two more hours on a train and I'd make it to Calais where I could catch a ferry across the channel back to Dover. The next train was scheduled for ninety minutes so I left the station and found a café across the square. Inside many students were celebrating their graduation so I grabbed a stool, ordered some food and beer, then watched music videos on the MTV channel while enjoying my meal.

It wasn't long before a young woman sitting beside commented on my guitar and asked what style of music I played.

"Ah, you know, fairly typical stuff," I responded. "Blues, pop-rock, some French *chanson*, Latin."

"You wanna play something for us?"

"Sure."

"Hey, Estelle, turn the music down, please. We have a live musician in the house."

Estelle lowered the volume, and I played a few songs from my repertoire gleaning rounds of applause, whistles, and offers of fresh drinks between each song.

I finished playing and the evening began to wind down. My new friend introduced me to some of her friends, and they invited me along to a *soiree* and musical jam not far from the bar. Of course, I was up for it as there were no trains now until morning and, besides, these guys seemed cool. We jammed through the night, drinking wine and smoking until daylight came peeping through the cracks in the shutters.

Saying goodbye to my new friends, I left the apartment and made my way to the train station. There was no barrier system as there is today, so I glanced up at the departures board, found the platform number then ambled towards the train that was already waiting. I climbed on board and waited for the train to pull away but was mortified to hear the guard approaching asking passengers for their tickets. This was unheard of and didn't usually occur until fifteen to twenty minutes after the journey had begun.

I decided to feign sleep otherwise I'd find myself out on the streets and I was desperately tired. I leant against the body of my guitar, so it appeared I was sleeping and preventing anyone from stealing it.

"*Reveille-vous...monsieur.*"

I was not going to 'wake up'—no way! I continued feigning sleep, and the guard left me alone. He continued along the carriage checking others' tickets.

What felt like only a moment later, I was being shaken awake... rather forcefully.

Again, there was a *"Monsieur, reveille-vous..."* Another shake of my shoulder. *"Reveille."*

Then, in heavily accented English, "Where are you travelling to?"

I was confused and partly hungover and blearily informed this guy I was heading for Calais.

"Well, monsieur, you've been to Calais...and you've now returned. So you can get off this train and leave the station and try another route. Because if I see you again, I'll call the police."

Aww fuck, what an idiot. I'd feigned sleep so well I'd slept all the way to Calais and returned to Amiens, a four-hour round trip. I now needed to walk to the city's outskirts and hitchhike. This however proved not too difficult, and I was soon waiting for a ferry to Dover after a welcome shower in the ferry terminal building.

21

Back to Black
(Amy Winehouse)

After six months' travelling the South of France, meeting many friends and musicians, and busking the terraces and cafés with them, I felt like a new person. For the first time I felt my dream of becoming a professional musician would become a reality. My adventures had taught me I could leave my homeland, arrive in another country, and make a living with just my guitar and my voice.

I hadn't been exposed to or tempted by hard drugs since leaving the squat in Lille with Grant because I'd been hanging out with a much more functional group of friends. I felt physically strong, and I was determined to keep away from smack and smackheads back in The Square. I was living back at Leslie's flat, and we slipped easily back into our relationship of amity and convenient sex.

Everything was almost as it had been before my departure. Spiritually and emotionally, however, I was anxious around meeting Mia and wasn't sure how I'd react when I did...and even around meeting Lucas, now her husband. Colliding with either of them in The Square below Leslie's flat was a likely prospect.

I first bumped into Mia one afternoon. She'd been to collect her eldest daughter from school. I was exiting the supermarket as she was entering. It was awkward as hell, and I think I mumbled a 'hello' then scarpered back upstairs to Leslie's flat. I stopped on the landing halfway up the stairs to catch my breath with my heart pounding heavily in my chest.

That was the first time I saw her after my return. It soon became obvious to us both we'd need to overcome any feelings we had for one another and would need to accept things as they now were. Mia needed to see her nieces, her daughters needed to see their cousins, and Mia and Leslie had to see each other as sisters. The reason I remained at Leslie's and didn't move on to either a convoy site or some other town to escape the pain was due to Leslie's insistent voice saying, "She still loves you, you know," and who knew her better than her elder sister?

* * *

She was right and within several weeks I was living with Mia back in her house. We'd been unable to keep away from one another, her marriage had exploded, Lucas was living elsewhere, and child duties were divided between them both. Mia wasn't happy with the relationship I had with her elder sister, so she'd asked me to move in with her. It was an insane, complex triangle and the full extent of the damage it would cause could hardly be realised at this point.

Lucas carefully planned his next steps, and these would have far-reaching consequences for all actors, including myself. His parents were affluent and lived in an incredibly wealthy Wiltshire village, so money wasn't an issue whereas Mia's family were working class and had no money—in fact, her mother was no longer alive, and her father was retired with a small pension.

Letters began arriving through Mia's letterbox stating there'd be a court battle deciding which parent would be granted custody of the children.

Love is a powerful force, a force that can clood the mind and blind one's sight. Mia and I were in the giddy weightless phase. We were completely in love, and anything seemed possible. I'd not only just spent six months travelling with my guitar but had also avoided heroin for all that time. I resumed working on the Princesmead site's second phase so was earning a decent wage. We both felt I'd left the drugs/crime nexus behind me and that any judge would also see this as the case.

The day of the hearing arrived. I was looking dapper in a suit and tie, and Mia was also dressed in smart formal. As with most court buildings, hushed voices were bouncing off the hard stone floors and stairs and echoing around the spacious entrance hall. We found the courtroom where the case would be heard and waited outside. Mia's solicitor called her into an interview room and after twenty minutes she returned saying he felt she should dump me and not jeopardise her mother/daughter relationship. As ruthless as this now sounds, he could see the folly of challenging Lucas's well-prepared case.

And, sitting here writing this now, leaden with the knowledge of all that ensued, I realise I should have fled that courtroom as fast as I could. To believe a ruling in Mia's favour was a credible outcome that day was nothing more than self-delusion on both our parts.

The judge heard the case for and against and granted custody of the two girls to Lucas. Christian Austin was a heroin addict with a criminal record spanning fifteen years. It was insane Mia, Leslie, or I thought for a moment the result could be anything otherwise.

The two girls were with Lucas's parents at the time, so Mia and I drove back to her house. She was in total shock and wasn't able to deal with this blow at all. Once back in the house, Leslie came and joined us, and we both tried to console her, but nothing was going to make her feel better. Fuck. This was a catastrophe, an irreversible shift in Mia's life and one from which she would never entirely recover. I remember giving her a sleeping tablet and she thankfully drifted off to a place where the situation was perhaps a little less traumatic.

The next few days and weeks were unbearable. Mia was inconsolable, although I supported her in every way I could—I felt entirely to blame. And as bad as that felt, what was worse was the knowledge that the court's decision was irrevocable and Mia would be in an even worse place if I deserted her now. I took a few days off work and Leslie also came to spend the days with us.

Gradually, the transition to Lucas having the kids full-time and Mia having them on weekends became more tolerable. I spent those weekends at Leslie's flat rather than incense Lucas any further and all of our lives began to adapt to this new rhythm. By the end of December 1988, the worst of the trauma was over. We put up a Christmas tree, decorated it with tinsel and lights, placed presents beneath it and built the open fire to keep the cold evenings beyond the walls of the house. Despite the children not being there most of the time, we enjoyed being in love and Mia never blamed me for the outcome. We'd cook together, listen to music, watch movies, or I'd play guitar and sing but there was a deep undercurrent of sadness that filled each room and could be felt by us both.

New Year 1989 came, the festive season was over, and I returned to work. The winter mornings were bitterly cold, and I was still working on the external groundworks of the shopping centre—laying kerbs and edgings, block paving, and paving slabs. I'd be heavily layered with thermal vest and trousers beneath my work clothes, a woolly hat, and gloves but, despite these defences, each tea—and lunchbreak was most welcome. The most important thing for me was keeping my promise to stay clean and I felt stronger and stronger in this endeavour as every month passed.

I left work early one evening and cycled back to Mia's house. Upon entering the front door, I smelled a familiar stench in the air. I walked into the dining room to find Mia and Leslie sat around the table, both wearing guilty expressions.

"You're home early," Mia said.

"What're you two up to?" I asked, although deep down I knew…I just wasn't ready to confront this monstrous reality. They'd been chasing the dragon, smoking heroin. The air was redolent with the pungent smell of burnt heroin and my brain was reeling.

Mia had always smoked dope and cigarettes, I knew, and had dabbled in psychedelics and cocaine in her younger years as had most of her friends.

This was normalised within the hippie circles she'd floated around for more than a decade. But heroin?

"You've been chasing smack."

They heard my words yet neither of them could look at me.

"What the fuck is going on? Why? Where'd you get it?"

Leslie responded with her typically languid and slow tone I was so familiar with.

"We've been dabbling in it for a couple of weeks. I pressed the buzzer on Dee's door and, when she asked who it was, I said, 'I'm Christian's girlfriend.' She let me in and sold it to me, no problem."

Dee lived on an adjacent side of Totland Close's square to Leslie's flat. She would've seen us together regularly, so I completely understood how easy it had been for Leslie to score as if it were on my behalf.

At this point there was nothing I could do other than join them. I realised it was too late. Leslie, Mia's witch of a sister had once again decided her weaker sister's fate for her and no amount of screaming or shouting on my part was going to turn back the clock. First-time heroin users often have a reaction—whether snorting, chasing, or injecting—that finds them hugging the toilet bowl for an hour or more and results in their putting it down to experience and avoiding its nastiness forevermore. Just as I regretted never having such a reaction, I now regretted Mia not having one too.

She'd evidently tasted the dragon on a few occasions, and she would want more, especially due to its ability to numb emotion and pain. Chasing heroin is nowhere near as addictive as smoking crack cocaine—which would be on our shopping list soon enough—but just as something once seen can't be unseen, this feeling once felt could never be unfelt. And heroin is all about feeling, a feeling of being enveloped in cotton wool with not a care in the universe, the ultimate panacea for one still reeling from the blunt emotional trauma of having her children taken from her. I knew then deep within my soul the salve of heroin would be the perfect poultice to plaster Mia's raw emotional wound.

You can take heroin for months before any signs of dependence, and this was the case for all three of us. Living a functional life while using the drug was simple—after all, the only problem with heroin is no heroin and I had a well-paid job.

We continued dabbling for the next several months. Mia kept it secret from Lucas, Leslie kept it secret from her children and their respective fathers, and my mother and siblings knew the signs far too well for me to try and pull the wool over their eyes.

When the Princesmead job came to an end, I began devoting more time to scoring and smoking than I did to looking for a new job and this resulted in my spending more time at home smoking hash, chasing smack, and generally joining Mia in her quest for oblivion. This was followed by the downwards spiral I was all too familiar with from previous years—whether it was while living with Bob and Ellen or with Heather—where chasing the dragon turned to cooking up in a spoon and injecting. Before long we were both using this route of transmission and then things slowly spiralled out of control.

The absence of a job found me progressing on to shoplifting and credit card fraud to fund the habit that was becoming increasingly addictive and expensive. I would have recognised the signs of an approaching train wreck but Christian 2 was firmly in the driver's seat—destination: more self-sabotage and more prison time. But, before this crisis would overwhelm me, Mia and I took credit card scamming to the next level.

I knew many guys around The Square who were stealing cars or burgling houses, so sourcing credit cards was never a problem. This was when there were more cheque guarantee cards than there were credit or debit cards, and the chip and pin system hadn't yet been developed. When making a transaction, the person on the till would compare any signature with that on the back of the card. Everyone's signature is always different each time they sign so we used this to our advantage. After half an hour's practice in the morning, that day's signature would be as good as it ever could be, and we'd head out. The same card might only be useful for one or two days and sometimes the transaction would be blocked but most times we were successful.

The system I developed was really straightforward and the fact Mia wasn't a criminal attests to its simplicity. We'd leave Farnborough and head for a John Lewes/Waitrose supermarket as this chain was less likely to check a card's veracity than the more budget supermarkets—I'd guess because these stores attract middle-class shoppers, and the checkout guys didn't want to risk offending their patron's sensibilities.

The most expensive popular items were cartons of cigarettes, bottles of spirits, nappies, and baby wipes. There was a limit on the amount that could be spent on a card without needing to provide some form of identification, so we'd arrive at the checkout separately with a couple of bottles of spirits, nappies, baby wipes, a few items from the veg or fruit aisles, then ask for £30 cashback. All going well, we'd sign the chit, be handed £30 in cash then head for the cigarette booth where we'd buy two cartons of cigarettes and collect another £30 cashback. There was always a risk we'd be caught collecting two lots of cashback, which would arouse suspicion, but our luck held out.

We'd hit another couple of Waitrose supermarkets on the way to London and then arrive at my dealer's house with somewhere between £300 and £500 in cash and sellable goods depending on how many stores we'd hit.

Once at my dealers in Wandsworth, we'd exchange the cash and goods for an equivalent value in heroin and then head back home. A few days later we'd need to repeat the process.

Things didn't always go smoothly. I remember one instance where my mind went completely blank at the till when asked to sign the chit. I had no recollection of how to recreate the signature I'd practiced before leaving home. Thinking on my feet, I improvised some pretext around a letter I'd received that morning from the bank, snatched the card from the teller's fingers, and left the shop.

Another time I asked a guy at a petrol station for some cigarettes… no fuel on this occasion, just cigarettes.

"Hey, can I get two-hundred Lambert and Butler please?"

"Sure," the guy responded while reaching for a carton.

"...and two hundred JPS," I continued.

"If you buy four hundred, I'll need to check the card," he helpfully informed me.

"Okay, tell you what, just give me the Lambert and Butler, yeah?"

A nice guy with good intuition. He didn't have to warn me, but he obviously sensed something wasn't right yet didn't want to call the police.

A few days later, my car decided it'd had enough, choked out clouds of oily black smoke, and died. I couldn't function without a car so decided to use a complete ID pack I'd recently purchased to rent one.

I arrived at a rental company's office and handed 'my' driving licence and a bunch of other relevant ID to the girl behind the counter. Within twenty minutes I was driving out of the yard in that year's Peugeot 405, colour white—splendid.

This way of life continued for months. We were living hand to mouth, doing the Waitrose/Wandsworth run every two or three days, and the fact I was driving a brand-new car made me far less conspicuous than I'd been in my Audi—the local police knew that car as mine so there was always the risk of a random stop and search. We were both looking extremely gaunt and our diets weren't ideal because we were moving fast and living on sandwiches and snacks from supermarkets and petrol stations.

It's interesting looking back on this period today because many years have elapsed since then and I've now become a functional, productive member of society. After successfully completing a drug rehabilitation programme ten years after these events occurred, I began working full-time—not sporadically as I did during those junkie years but for extended periods of time—and what struck me most was how much simpler it is to work a forty-hour week. Get up at 6.30 or 7 a.m., go to a place of work, complete your shift at 5 p.m. then go home. Repeat five times, get paid, then repeat each following week for months on end.

I spent years as a dysfunctional drug dependent criminal avoiding the conventional work ethos only to eventually discover what I was trying to avoid is much less hassle, is more satisfying, and doesn't include the risk of being collared and sent to prison for months or years every minute of the day. I know that's a huge oversimplification, and it would have been nigh on impossible for me to hold down a job in the condition I was in at that stage of my life, but it's interesting now to realise what a struggle I created for my own self. Then again, that is the nature of self-sabotage—Christian 2 was driving that rented car and he was headed towards more prison and misery.

22

Isolation
(Iggy Pop)

Sebastian was born in Frimley Park hospital on 14 August 1990. It was a straightforward birth, and I was there in the delivery room. What an amazing experience to witness the long, drawn out, and agonising pain of labour and childbirth resulting in the appearance of a healthy wailing pink baby...my son. Mia was exhausted and dripping with sweat when they laid Sebastian on her chest.

Mia had quit injecting heroin a few months prior to the birth and shifted to chasing the dragon instead. She'd also reduced her intake so, thankfully, Seb wasn't born hooked on smack. The doctors kept mother and child in the hospital overnight and I drove home with a promise to collect them both upon receipt of a confirmation call.

I'd so love to state here the appearance of our son instilled a change within both our hearts and that we left heroin by the wayside that same week. However, smack stories rarely end as happily as fairy tales, so Mia stayed home with Sebastian while I continued working the Waitrose/Wandsworth route to ensure neither of us would suffer withdrawal symptoms.

When Seb was grown enough, we'd strap him into the car baby seat and bring him along. In some ways this insulated Mia from suspicion as she'd arrive at the till with a young baby in a pram, a bunch of nappies and baby wipes, and the checkout girls would drool over the baby. We'd both leave the supermarket with a fully laden car and lots of cash to score heroin with.

There was a problem with my dealer's supply, so he gave me a different address to go and score from. The address was in Earlsfield just around the corner from Wandsworth and, unbeknown to me, this dealer was under surveillance by the Metropolitan Police drug squad—wonderful. I pressed the buzzer on the door that opened to allow me entry and then entered the open door of a ground floor flat. The guy said he was awaiting a delivery and asked if I could return in one hour, so I returned to the car. I'd need to find somewhere to park up and wait.

Just as I pulled out from the housing estate onto the main road, the night lit up with flashing blue neon accompanied by screaming sirens. A police car screeched to a halt in front of me to prevent my escape and another pulled up behind. Coppers jumped out of both cars and pulled my car's front doors open. Fuck, I was busted.

Thank Christ the dealer hadn't had any smack, I thought to myself. This was fortunate for a couple of reasons: firstly, because I wouldn't be charged with possession of a Class A drug and, secondly, I'd have had to swallow the evidence had I been in possession and swallowing the amount I'd intended buying would prove fatal if it burst open inside my stomach.

The police escorted me from my car into the back of one of theirs while a policewoman did the same with Mia and Sebastian. Shit, I hadn't had any heroin for a while; withdrawals would come knocking at my door in the next hour or two.

We arrived at Earlsfield police station, I was processed by the custody sergeant and was assured Mia and Seb were both okay. It was then explained to me a thorough search of my car would be undertaken in the police car park with me in attendance.

It slowly dawned on me these guys had seen me pull up outside the dealer's house in a brand-new car, then pull away again after spending only moments inside, and thought I was the guy delivering a batch of heroin to him. I stood beside the white Peugeot while two policemen began to search the interior of the car. It didn't take long for them to discover a plastic bag containing credit cards and false ID stashed beneath the air filter in the engine bay. Fortunately, they didn't discover the £500 in cash I'd planned on buying the heroin with as it was hidden beneath the gearstick's rubber gaiter. This was recovered from the rental company at a later date after Mia was freed—she pretended she'd lost an earring and was given the keys to look inside the car.

The search continued and a boot full of nappies, baby wipes, cigarettes, food, brandy, and whisky were added to the list of illegally procured items. I was placed in a cell and left to enjoy my withdrawal symptoms.

Next morning, after no sleep but plenty of stomach cramps and aching muscles, I was escorted from my cell to a waiting sweatbox. Next stop, Lavender Hill magistrates court for a remand application containing the usual assessments—escape risk, potentially violent, drug dependent one-man crime wave. Being remanded was a foregone conclusion and I soon found myself in Brixton Prison's F-wing, which in the early '90s, was known amongst convicts as Fraggle Rock.

This name was given because it was the first stop for all drug dependent prisoners as well as any inmates with severe mental health problems; I was amongst some of the craziest, most dangerous, inmates I'd ever met.

One of my new compatriots had tortured then killed the guy who'd informed on his gang members fifteen years previously. He'd purportedly met him in a bar and coaxed the guy back to his flat for after-drinks. The poor sap didn't recognise his nemesis as they'd never met face to face, but the gangster knew who the informant was. He kept him in his flat for days and finally decapitated him.

Another inmate walking freely among us had enticed his gay lover to a property after discovering he'd been cheating on him. With promises of a kinky sexual game, he chained him to a wooden chair in the centre of a room and then, once his victim was secured, stuffed a rag in his mouth then pulled some wiring out of a bag. One end of the wiring was fitted with a 240-volt plug while the other had a pair of crocodile clips. After plugging this appliance into a wall socket and attaching the crocodile clips to the chains securing his victim, he proceeded to flick the switch on and off delivering electric shocks with every flick. Rumour had it the only reason the guy didn't die was the main fuse box blew up due to such erratic usage.

So, these were my new friends and, just as I'd had to in Dartmoor, I needed to be exceedingly wary of who I mixed with and who I managed to piss off.

Up until this point prison had always been a cure for me and I believe this is why I'm alive today and many of my fellow drug users from Farnborough are no longer with us. This, however, changed in the late 1980s and early 1990s, when heroin became widely available inside the prison estate. To me, this was disastrous because it meant prison's curative properties were no more.

I was offered heroin on Fraggle Rock. Fortunately, my money was in the gearstick cavity of a rental car in Earlsfield police station or at the rental company's car park in Farnborough. And, as painful and unpleasant as my withdrawal symptoms were, they were nowhere near as unpleasant as my punishment might be if I scored a bag or two on credit and couldn't pay on time. Such a mistake could easily result in my being stabbed or slashed across the face by one of my crazy new companions.

"No thanks, man, I'm gonna ride this one out..." I'd say whenever dealers approached me on the landings. Besides, the prison £10 bags contained five times less heroin than the street £10 bags and probably wouldn't cure my pain at all much less get me high.

After a week in Brixton prison, I was returned to Lavender Hill magistrates for another bail application. I'd been remanded for seven days but by law could apply for bail again at each weekly hearing. After the usual shenanigans of sweatboxes to different prisons, to the Lambeth hub and then deliveries to various courts, I found myself in a basement cell at

Lavender Hill with a guy I'd never met before. I was planning on breaking the hell out of there and regaining my freedom. I had nothing to lose.

"Hey man, you know the layout of this place? I mean outside the courtrooms, you know, from the other side of the courtroom doors to the street?"

"Sure I do," he said. "I've lived round here all my life and been in here far too many times. Why, you gonna have it away?"

"Fuck yeah, I'm clucking my nuts off. I need some gear."

"Okay, well good luck with that. If you manage to get out of the courtroom doors, you'll find a staircase ahead of you. Down to the bottom then exit left through the glass doors to the street. There's bound to be coppers everywhere though."

"Don't give a fuck…I just need outta here, man."

An hour or so later keys rattled in the door lock, and it swung open.

"Austin, you're on."

I followed the copper up the concrete staircase to a wooden door that opened into the courtroom. I entered the familiar scene of the magistrate sat on the dais in front of me and I entered the dock in the centre of the room. My brief came over and quickly explained the prosecution was opposing my bail application and said he'd do his best to have me freed.

There followed the predictable dull routine of name, date of birth, address, charges against me, and the equally predictable refusal of my bail. My moment was now or never. I'd already spotted where each copper was in the room. I knew the exit door was on my right-hand side behind me as I'd spotted it when people had entered and exited throughout my hearing.

I spun round to fly towards the exit and my head cracked straight into the face of a policeman I hadn't realised was behind me. Fuck. Not only was I now going nowhere other than back to the cell I'd recently been brought up from, but I was also in for a kick-in by these coppers.

They all ran over and violently grabbed me. I was on the carpeted floor clinging to the legs of a fixed bench.

Three or four coppers picked me up by my arms and legs and led me out the door I'd walked through only ten minutes before and then slid me down the concrete stairs with my head bouncing from each step as we descended. They carried me in this way to the same cell I'd come from, unlocked the door, and then dragged me in. Once there, the pair holding my legs pulled them apart so the one I'd accidentally headbutted could stamp as hard as he could onto my genitals.

I got lucky at this point, though only marginally. The angle of the copper's size ten was just a little too acute. My genitals remained untouched and unharmed yet the impact of his heel on my coccyx was very powerful. That moment was intensely painful, yes, but every time I tried to sit down for the next few months I was met with sharp pain from the bruised bone.

The door was slammed closed, and my new friend said dryly, "I thought that was you coming down the stairs."

Unbelievably, after another five or six weeks of repeat appearances and unacceptable delays by the prosecution, my brief persuaded the magistrate to grant me bail if the committal papers weren't in place by the following week's appearance. The following week, they still weren't ready, and I walked from the courtroom a relatively free man. I still had to return to Kingston Crown Court to face the music at some point in the future, but I'd worry about that then. For now, I was a free man.

I returned to Farnborough and jumped straight back onto the smack train, mainly because Mia was waiting for me and hadn't stopped using while I'd been away. I can place the time exactly because REM's song "Losing my Religion" was all over the radio and had been while I was in Brixton prison, so this was just after Christmas 1991.

Mia and I went straight back to the Waitrose scam to pay for the smack and poor young Seb was ferried around in another Audi 100 I'd got my hands on. This predictable existence continued right up to my Kingston Crown Court date. I'd discussed my options with Mia and decided the maximum prison sentence I'd receive would be eighteen months, maybe two years, the alternative would be to piss off back to France and do the same as I'd done the previous year but then I wouldn't see her or Seb, so it was pointless. I decided to face the music—which turned out to be much louder than I'd anticipated.

"Four years imprisonment to run concurrently with all other sentences given out today. Take him away."

I never expected that. Even worse, Mia was sentenced to six months' imprisonment…for her first offence.

Having anticipated a custodial sentence of some form, I'd brought along a parcel of heroin and hash to ease the landing a little. Now I had to figure a way to deliver half of this parcel to Mia when male and female prisoners are separated. Despite this, I managed to divide it and slip it to her beneath a door in the corridor, otherwise she'd have been having withdrawal symptoms that evening. Such symptoms were unavoidable and the small amount we both had would only stave off the inevitable for a few days.

I couldn't believe it, though, six months for a first offence.

I now had plenty of time on my hands, so I worked out roughly how much we'd made and spent over those eighteen months and I'm not surprised the judge threw the book at us. I figured we were pulling an average of £1,500 per week for eighteen months. All spent on heroin, hash, food, and being generous with the friends we were sharing the house with.

* * *

Incredibly, I was sent to Coldingley prison, near Woking. It was a mere nine miles from Farnborough and was the only prison I spent thirty months living in the same single cell, beating my record of twenty months in Dartmoor prison. All cells were single, and they had electronic locks so they could be opened remotely from a central control room. HMP Coldingley is a secure category C prison, which means all airlock doors are both manual and electronic requiring a key and an okay from a screw in a control room with CCTV visuals.

In the evenings we could press our door buzzers and join a virtual queue to use the toilets where, in turn, we could pass drugs to one another beneath the doors or leave bottles of hooch (homemade alcohol) in the toilets for collection…after payment in cash or drugs. Only one cell door was able to be opened at any one time.

After several months, a guy named Barry arrived at the prison. He was also from Farnborough, and I'd met him on the outside a few times before this prison term. He was tall and gangly with long black hair tied back in a ponytail and was also heavily into smack.

I greeted him and suggested he join me on my wing where I had a cell at the end of a short corridor. I successfully managed to install him in the cell opposite mine, which was perfect as it meant we'd both have our backs to the wall in the event of any trouble—either with cons or screws. This would prove an unnecessary precaution because ultimately Barry would become the cause of my woes. I was too trusting and didn't realise then what bad news he'd turn out to be.

Within another few weeks a third guy joined our small gang at the end of the corridor and moved into the cell next-door to mine. His name was Alan J., and he was a well-known heroin dealer from Croydon, a part of London not far from Clapham where I grew up. He was also a much better guitarist than me and we'd play and record some great music together (he was permitted some sound recording equipment in his cell).

Alan was a very slight guy aged around fifty years old with no means of defending himself, so Barry and I agreed to look out for him. In exchange we'd have access to a constant supply of heroin. This protection scheme quickly became common knowledge, and Alan was safe from any sharks…for the moment.

The screws in this prison were a different breed to those in Dartmoor or the many local/dispersal prisons such as Winchester or those in London. Those prisons were for transient prisoners and were therefore geared less towards developed relationships. As a category C prison with prisoners serving sentences the atmosphere was a lot more relaxed at Coldingley.

I achieved an awful lot during my stay in this prison. My evenings were filled with either artwork, learning new songs or practicing old ones on guitar and even learning saxophone so as to pass this knowledge onto a fellow inmate who asked for my help. He'd loan me his saxophone so I could learn it during the evening then I'd teach him what I'd learned. This was the beginning of my finally becoming a saxophonist.

With Coldingley being a liberal prison it was decided a concert would be performed with bands formed of prisoners. This was to coincide with an open day where families could join the prisoners on the prison playing fields, as well as bring in supplies of drugs and alcohol for many of us.

There was an evening guitar class run by a pretty blonde lady that I attended most weeks. I remember there was a slight contretemps between us because she was a folk guitarist whereas I was more into rock songs by The Doors, Janis Joplin, or Led Zeppelin. She'd have a few adherents around her on one side of the classroom learning a "claw-hammer" finger-picking technique she was concerned was slowly becoming extinct, while I'd have a larger group around me begging me to teach them how to play Iggy Pop's *Lust for Life*.

She was an enthusiastic teacher, and she helped us form bands for the upcoming concert. A couple of friends formed a typical five-piece band with me, and we rehearsed a bunch of songs as many evenings as possible. It was similar to my attending Cardiff university years later where our remit was the same: form a band, choose several songs to cover, rehearse and then perform.

The day of the concert arrived, and I had a fantastic feeling inside. My first real performance and something I'd been heading towards for many years now. Our band had rehearsed the set many times and we were confident enough to play before today's audience. A large curtain-sided truck was the stage and was parked in a corner of the prison's playing fields with speaker stacks at either end and mic stands placed ready.

I was filled with much excitement as we climbed the steps to the truck's bed and plugged in our instruments ready for a sound check. I was playing an acoustic guitar with a built-in pickup, had a harmonica rack hanging from my neck, and felt confident as I stepped up to the microphone stand and counted the band in. We performed a song all the way through while the sound man adjusted the levels and were then ready to rock.

I looked out at the sea of faces standing before us in the blazing sun—half prisoners, half wives, children, parents, brothers and sisters of prisoners, and many screws—and spoke into the microphone.

"Welcome to Coldingley…1, 2, 3, 4."

The band followed my count, and I was happily surprised we all came in together. First up was *Bright Side of the Road* by Van Morrison as we'd all agreed it was such a happy song to play in a prison. The bass, drums, keyboard, my guitar, harmonica and singing, all came together in perfect unison. Our teacher was singing backing vocals, and the crowd were immediately swinging and swaying to our music. After the harmonica solo, they erupted into screams and applause and I knew, at that moment, this was for me—the life of a performing musician. My Johnny Cash's San Quentin moment. I remember the feelings I had on that stage to this day, and it was the beginning of a love of performance I've enjoyed ever since, whether playing guitar, singing, harmonica or, later on, saxophone. That pure unadulterated joy of being there in the moment.

The prison open day was a success, both musically and in drug delivery terms, so there was lots to celebrate that evening. Buckets full of home-made prison hooch were brought out from their hiding places and those who indulged were soon out of their minds. I also drank the hooch, smoked spliffs, chased heroin, and continued playing and singing to the lads on my landing until I was too wasted to play anymore. Then, slowly, a quiet hush descended over the prison.

* * *

My next-door neighbour, Alan, suddenly announced he was moving to a different prison named The Mount that same afternoon. He seemed very scared, and it was likely another prisoner was responsible for this fear.

"What's the matter, Alan?" I asked him. "Who's leaning on you, man?"

"No one's leaning on me. I've been offered this transfer, and it feels like a good move."

"Look at yourself, Alan—you're scared out of your wits. Tell me who's leaning on you, and I'll sort it out for you. Me and Barry'll deal with it. You're safe here with us and I don't know how safe you'll be in The Mount. It'll be exactly the same shit so surely you're better off here where you're established. Just tell me who's said something to you…"

It was obvious Alan had been intimidated either by someone here in the prison or through his connections on the street—perhaps via his wife who brought his parcels for him on visits—but he refused to budge and left us that very afternoon.

The following day we heard a newsflash on the radio. There'd been a fatal stabbing at HMP The Mount in Hemel Hempstead. Within another day or two it was confirmed Alan had been stabbed to death by another prisoner.

* * *

A third of the way through my sentence, I was due a home leave. I was allowed a weekend at home with my family, and I'd been counting down the days for months. It was a glorious feeling leaving the prison gates and being driven to the train station. By mid-morning I was walking through the door being welcomed by Mia and Sebastian, my two-year-old son. We enjoyed spending time together and taking Sebastian to the swing park and also chasing heroin and smoking spliffs together—this was still our ultimate idea of recreation and, despite my being imprisoned, I was still addicted to these drugs and Mia was still consuming with all our junkie friends around The Square.

As was standard in prison, Barry and I had borrowed drugs and cash from other prisoners prior to my home leave (with interest, of course), so I needed to ensure I secured a 'parcel' of drugs and cash to return with. The cash was ready, and I was awaiting a delivery of heroin from London that was delayed. Then it was delayed some more and all I could do was wait, despite the knowledge I'd return back to prison and lose the privilege of any future home leaves until my release date. But I knew if I didn't return with the drugs and cash Barry and I owed, Barry would be in big trouble with our creditors.

Finally, the heroin arrived so I said my goodbyes to my Mia and Seb and returned to the prison. As expected, all my future home leaves were forfeited but at least I hadn't left my mate in the shit, surrounded by angry prisoners demanding repayment.

A couple of months later, it was Barry's turn for his home leave. Considering I'd repaid our creditors—albeit a day or two late—we were once again granted credit. Barry left the prison, and I looked forward to his return. I waited…and I waited…and so did our creditors.

After a day or two with no sign of Barry's return, things weren't looking good for me. I couldn't believe Barry was capable of such treachery, but his absence was proof. The following morning, I was in my cell surrounded by three irate, armed, and dangerous prisoners.

"Where's my ting?" said one of them in Caribbean patois.

"And where's my money?" said another.

Two of the guys had home-made knives—made in the prison workshops and smuggled out—while the third was clutching a toothbrush with razor blades welded into it where the bristles had once been. I'd anticipated this outcome and was highly aware diplomacy and my own slick words were the only solution that might avoid blood being shed.

"Look, you're all wondering where Barry is right now, yeah? Well, let me tell you: I'm fuckin' wondering where Barry is more than you are coz I'm the one standing here about to get cut up. You all know I get good visits, and you also know I ain't gonna scream for Rule 43" (asking prison officers for protection).

"So, you can either cut me up right now and you get nothing. Or you wait. And you know I'll pay you back next visit or two…with interest. What's it gonna be? You wait and I'll sort it, or you stab me and lose everything."

I was now either going to be slashed in the face by these guys or they were going to calm themselves and go with the sensible solution. All I could think of at that moment was Alan being stabbed to death in The

Mount several weeks earlier. *Was this it? Was I about to be scarred for life here in my cell or be found by screws in thirty minutes bleeding out on the floor?*

There was a palpable easing of tension as, first one, then all three, agreed to wait for repayment. They left my cell and walked away down the landing, and I could finally breathe. It was only then I became aware I and my clothes were soaked in sweat.

"Fuck you, Barry," I swore under my breath, "I'm gonna fuck you!"

I left my cell and I could see from the faces around me others on my landing were relieved. They all knew I'd been fucked over by my "buddy" —not just my prison buddy but someone I knew from my hometown.

Never trust a junkie.

* * *

I was due for release and the minutes had turned to hours. I was having trouble falling asleep so climbed back out of bed and picked up my guitar, strumming and singing a song quietly.

However, I couldn't concentrate, and my playing kept being interrupted by a host of thoughts flying through my head:

> *I've gotta quit this shit. Somehow, I need to sort myself out and get clean otherwise I'll be serving another sentence before I know it. Smack's everywhere now and therefore prison's becoming a much more dangerous environment for someone like me.*
>
> *Do I really wanna die in prison, either from violence or old age? Never see my child grow up and pass on the baton of dysfunction to him? Never fulfil my dream of playing festivals in a band, hearing the applause, and enjoying the audience go wild after every song? No, I don't want any of this…but, how to stop it?*
>
> *I must return to Mia and Sebastian. I love them, and they love me but how can we escape this cycle of crime/drugs/prison? I've been trapped in this world for so long now I have no idea how to escape its clutches.*

I didn't have any answers. I just knew, unlike many of my friends who couldn't wait to return to the same pursuits after release, I was different. I wanted something more. I'd had a taste of what being a live performer was, both busking around France and at the prison open day concert. I vowed to give it my best shot, to find a job and get off the drugs. I'd had enough.

Mia had been allocated a council flat in Aldershot during the last few months of my sentence, so I had a home to go to, one that was four miles from The Square and all its fucked-up inhabitants. And, as luck would have it, the guy living next door worked for a conservatory company and offered me a job. I had all the necessary skills as I'd been dabbling in the building game on and off now for many years.

His name was Rory, and he had a wife and young daughter. We got on well and he was happy with my work. Soon I got into the rhythm of working five days a week and began to earn a reasonable wage, some of which went on weed and heroin, sure, but I was happy not to be committing crime to pay for the shit.

While my life appeared to be settling into a normal pattern, Mia announced she was pregnant again. This was joyous news—another child would soon be added to our family. In fact, after the first scan, we were surprised to hear it would be an addition of two children. Mia, as a twin, was carrying twins.

Sebastian was five years old at this point and was attending the local school, I had a secure job, and we were spending more time at home and little time in Farnborough. The smack and weed were still a part of our lives—both consuming and dealing a bit—but generally life seemed to be heading in a more functional direction, and I wasn't running such high risks of being sent to prison.

Whenever I went to the local music shop to buy strings for my guitar, my eyes were drawn to a gleaming alto saxophone. I began harbouring thoughts of smashing the window one dark night and running off with it.

What's wrong with you, you fool? I asked myself. *Why not just go in and talk to the guy? Surely, you can pay a deposit then pay it off in instalments until you can take it home?*

Before long, I was practicing blues scales on my shiny new saxophone, a cacophony soon accompanied by a pair of screaming babies. Things were starting to look up (though I doubt our neighbours felt the same way). At this point I hadn't a clue where this inchoate dream of becoming a sax player would take me. In fact, I could never imagine at that point the things and places life had in store for me. But I still had some obstacles to overcome.

* * *

The twins had grown, a boy and a girl. They were perfect. Their births hadn't been easy on Mia and, I'm ashamed to say, they were born addicted to heroin. They've grown even more now, into adults, and we've had discussions around their beginnings and the problems their parents both had at the time of their birth. I try to make it up to them as best I can.

I was no longer working with Rory but had recently gained employment building a new stretch of motorway close to home. It was heavy construction, and I didn't keep the job for long as the heroin use was increasing with the addition of a crack pipe. And the amount of money required for a crack habit is way beyond that needed to maintain a heroin habit.

Once again, I was fucked and heading in a familiar direction—more crime and more prison—although I had no idea at that point this would be the final episode.

My next acquisitive crimes consisted of leaving home in the mornings then driving to a multi-storey car park. Once there, I'd steal a set of number plates and hide them beneath the carpet in my car boot. I'd then drive to a hardware warehouse changing my car number plates for the stolen set before arriving there. Parking the car outside a fire exit, I'd enter the store, grab a trolley, then place two chainsaws into the trolley. Chainsaws always sold well, I knew, and would give me enough cash to support our heroin and crack habits for a day or two. I'd head for the fire exit I knew my car was parked outside, ensure nobody was nearby, then crash the fire exit doors open.

At this point, all hell would break loose with the store's alarm system screaming around the neighbourhood. I'd open my car boot, throw the chainsaws in, jump inside then screech off, finding somewhere not too far away to switch the number plates back again. Next, I'd drive to my local fence, exchange the chainsaws for cash then go and score both smack and crack before returning home.

As well as hardware warehouses, I'd target garden centres. Entering the place, I'd collect a trolley and then choose a Mountfield or Briggs and Stratton lawnmower—retailing at around £400 apiece—then go to the outdoor section and choose some plants, placing them on the trolley. Once I arrived close to where I'd parked my car, I'd throw the boxed lawn mower into the shrubbery and exit the place, leaving everything behind. Back at my car, I'd take a pair of wire-snips, cut a hole in the fence, and manhandle the lawn mower into the car boot. These were acts of desperation, yet I continued this strategy for many months, widening my net to places as far away as Oxford, Newbury, and Reading so as to avoid detection locally.

Despite these subterfuges, I noticed one day I was being followed by a dark BMW. Everywhere I went, this car followed me. So I headed for the motorway. At the first junction I came to, I drove past the off-ramp and then pulled onto the hard shoulder just beyond the on-ramp. The BMW had two choices: to pull over with me and confirm my suspicions, or to continue along the motorway. Once I saw it continue with the flow of traffic, I reversed up the slip road to the roundabout and headed off in a different direction. But I sensed my days of freedom were once again numbered.

I was completely aware the police knew what I was up to and that I was often being tailed, and I wasn't wrong. Early one morning there was a loud crash as our front door was smashed from its hinges and our flat filled with policemen. I was arrested on suspicion of numerous offences and taken away.

* * *

I was remanded once again by Aldershot magistrates and sent to Highdown prison just outside London awaiting investigation and committal to Crown Court. I was back on the merry-go-round. Once back in a prison cell, the lack of heroin soon found me experiencing the worst withdrawal symptoms I'd ever suffered.

During the first week, I felt exhausted but couldn't sleep. I had cramps all over my body and felt as though I'd been stretched on a medieval rack. I'd get undressed and climb into bed because I was shattered but, as soon as my head landed on the pillow, five different trains of thought began scampering around my brain, making sleep impossible. My mind would fly around like a waltzer at a funfair. At this point, I'd get back out of bed, get re-dressed and repeat the cycle over and over until the morning sun shone through the barred window.

The constant climbing into bed, tossing and turning for twenty minutes before getting up and getting dressed again left me with bedsores on my elbows. My mind was in a constant whirl, and it took me seventeen days and nights before I got my first hour's sleep. I know because I counted every single moment.

After that initial hour, I'd then manage a couple…and then a few… and so on, until a regular sleep pattern emerged. It was hell on Earth and was just one of several factors in my life at that point that led me to a huge re-evaluation of everything I had been through, everything I'd become, and everything I was likely to become, and I realised I'd had enough.

I settled into a routine, jogging on the sports field for thirty minutes a day, working on getting fit. I joined a music class and applied to take part in a planned in-house music concert. I began to feel a little better about things.

I was reaching the end of my tether vis-à-vis prison. I'd had just about enough of the guys looking at their second term for armed robbery, the killers, the killings, the weirdos, the stories, the drugs, the victims, the bullies; the screws, the senior and principal officers, the governors; all of it. For these reasons, along with a looming sense of mortality, I decided to write a letter to Alpha House once again.

I'd written to this rehabilitation centre twice over the past ten years and on both occasions they'd voiced concerns I was merely trying to evade a custodial sentence. They weren't wrong.

* * *

"Merry Christmas" were the final words the Crown Court judge said to me. In fact, these were the final words he ever spoke while presiding over Guildford Crown Court.

This was the day before Christmas Eve 1997 and was also this judge's final day before retirement. The atmosphere in the courtroom had been electric all morning for both these reasons and now I was the recipient of this almighty goodwill—I'd been given a two-year probation order with a condition of residence. This condition dictated I reside at Alpha House rehab under staff guidance, and I was not permitted to leave until the staff determined I was ready. Should I leave beforehand, this judge assured me, "You will find yourself before one of my colleagues who will be doling out another four- or five-year prison term." A wonderfully keen Sword of Damocles that I'd feel hovering over me for the next several months.

23

Rehab
(Amy Winehouse)

I lived in the Alpha House community for around eight months. Six of those months were in the main house while the last couple were in the "resettlement programme," a house at the bottom of the main driveway. From this launchpad, residents who'd progressed far enough could slowly integrate back into the local community while retaining the support of the main house with its staff and residents at their back.

Having just re-read my diaries from those eight months, I'm both shocked and surprised I stuck out the programme and didn't abscond and return to Farnborough and the chaos, which had been my life up to that point.

These diaries number four in total and have entries from every day I spent there. Unlike personal diaries, I now realise these are a kind of hybrid diary because our entries would be read and commented upon by either our "keyworkers" (professionally trained counsellors) or by the evening staff who had little professional training. These were more like carers between the staff finishing their shifts and going home and our bedtime.

My contemporary personal life events are within the pages, along with my aspirations that morphed and shifted as I progressed through the programme, and my attitudes towards staff members and other residents… but there's a holding back on intimate thoughts…or even a manipulative slant where I might drop subtle (or not so subtle) inferences that I knew would be passed on to my keyworker. There are also many entries where I stamp my feet/throw my dummy from the pram due to the pressure I found myself under at various stages of the unbelievably intense programme.

But, as a window to the time I spent at Alpha House, these diaries are invaluable.

* * *

On my first morning, I joined what was called an "assessment group" formed of a bunch of new "rezzies" (residents), all of whom had only recently joined the programme. We were evaluated during the first few weeks of our stay and each of us would have a 'care plan' tailored by staff members to suit our specific needs.

Over the next few days, the house rules were explained to us: the systems that were in place to keep one another safe; the consequences of bringing drugs or alcohol into the house; the roles we would be allocated around employment over the coming weeks; visits to a local clinic to test for HIV and Hepatitis C; group meetings; and individual key work sessions—"keyworks" —a whole new vernacular, which I now recall with fondness but that, at the time confused me and, eventually, drove me half insane.

We had all been leading dysfunctional, chaotic lives for many years and our charges knew—either from personal experience or from textbooks and training—it would require the gradual introduction of new frameworks and structures before we could address our multilayered needs. These initial groups were the first steps in remodelling the way we thought about things and, with the help of Alpha's management and counselling team and the senior residents, our resistance to these fresh ideas would slowly evaporate creating space for renewed focus.

Alpha House had a reputation in the drug and prison subcultures as the toughest of them all, just as Portland borstal and Dartmoor prison had *their* reputations as the toughest. My frequenting these toughest institutions seemed to be a recurring theme.

The framework employed at Alpha wasn't the twelve-step programme of AA (Alcoholics Anonymous) or NA (Narcotics Anonymous) with their acceptance of a higher power and the inability to change things. Alpha leant more emphasis on empowerment and enablement, and we were informed early on our employability skills would be nurtured by taking stints in the various departments—office, grounds, gardens, catering, etc.—which I experienced as fantastic opportunities to become a little skilled at each of these vocations.

Every morning residents were required to be up and out of bed at the same time with rare exceptions. This was again about introducing structure into lives that had been accustomed to instability and chaos for years. After waking, residents would head for breakfast in the dining hall and there would follow a community meeting in the main lounge. Any relevant announcements would be made at this meeting and a game of "positive fruit" might be played.

As with many Alpha House experiences, the first encounter would be the strangest. We were all sat on chairs around the perimeter wall of the lounge when someone would gently throw an orange or an apple towards you. Naturally, you catch it.

"I'm sending this positive fruit to you, Christian, because I can recognise in you someone with many years more experience than most of us here and feel we will all benefit from this. Now, you can throw it to anyone in the room you feel something positive about."

Without hesitation, I threw the orange to Angie, one of the residents I'd first met after my arrival.

"I'm throwing this to you, Angie, because I know you've already spent a few months here working on yourself and are therefore serious about the programme...and because you're a fellow musician."

Angie grinned from ear to ear at my last remark. She was a budding guitarist and I'd recently shown her a few chords to work on, so my calling her a fellow musician had evidently filled her with joy.

This "positive fruit" game felt strange to begin with but, like many aspects of the programme, it had been integrated so many years before it was part of the fabric. As the days passed by these new experiences became normalised and I accepted them as part of the Alpha experience.

Us new residents had to learn what were known as "the basics": a set of precepts that had been developed over who knows how many years but that were designed to promote a more harmonious household.

Another aspect of life in this new house was telling another resident you'd "like a word" with them. This mostly elicited a feeling of, "Oh fuck, what have I done this time?" but that's due to the place we all came from as ex-users and is also the way our society is hardwired.

Once another resident told you they'd like a word, the pair of you needed to leave the room and find a place where there was no one else around. This makes sense as peer pressure is thereby eliminated, as is the feeling of "losing face" and overreacting—it became a one-on-one conversation.

At this point, the resident who'd called you out might say, "I wanted a word with you to tell you I liked the way you dealt with John being angry at you. Rather than react to his anger, I noticed you took a deep breath, counted to ten, and refused to get caught up in 'his shit.'"

However, the resident might just as easily have wanted a word to say, "I think you're coasting through this programme, you don't seem to take any of it seriously, and I've never once seen you support another resident who needs help."

Whichever way the conversation might go, neither resident was permitted to speak with the other for a minimum of thirty minutes…at which point they can "check feelings" with the other whether good, or bad.

Having recently spent months in a prison environment surrounded by dangerous and often mentally unstable people—where a wrong look or word might result in a physical fight— Alpha's nuanced and novel environment, although strange, gradually became a different world I realised was geared towards helping me change a lifetime's deeply entrenched behaviours.

I could see the benefits of calling residents aside to provide positive or negative feedback as, ultimately, this would create more harmony within individual relationships and by extension the community. It's not a system we tend to operate with in the real world…although, I have to say, there have been times I've pulled someone aside in the workplace or the UK festival scene and given positive feedback.

My diaries are full of similar concepts I may have completely forgotten over the past twenty-five years had I not kept hold of them. Kitchen standards (KS) were a particularly unpopular but necessary evil. The catering department was responsible for providing the house residents and staff—usually an average of thirty people—with three meals per day but the remainder of the residents were responsible for washing up and cleaning the kitchens after both lunch and dinner…to military standards.

One theme that I see running through my diaries and being often mentioned in the staff's comments is my frustration at their never being enough free time. We were obviously not privy to the contents of other residents' diaries as they were kept in the staff office but, apparently, it was refreshing for staff to hear my frustration instead of the all too common "it's so boring here."

I loved to read, I joined a weekly creative writing class, I was into jogging and weight training and playing guitar or saxophone. But there was never enough time for me to do all I wanted.

After KS, there was an evening event known as "programme cover," the bane of my life at Alpha. This consisted of a rota where each resident would choose an activity for the whole house to take part in, usually in the main lounge. Sometimes it would take the form of everybody playing board games, writing letters home, watching a movie chosen by that evening's resident, or even going for a walk around the grounds during the summer months. Occasionally, if I was in favour with that evening's resident (not always the case), I might be granted permission to go and practice my saxophone for an hour but most often I'd end up being frustrated as I wasn't permitted to pursue my own interests.

Alongside the weird stuff there were also more pragmatic pursuits to deal with such as which department us new assessments were allocated to. In this I feel I got lucky as the first department I worked on was the grounds, which felt perfect as it entailed lots of digging, heavy lifting, and general building and maintenance stuff. Also, a friend I'd known during my festival days was the manager of the grounds department and we got on well.

I was also allocated a keyworker named Bill.

Bill struck me as more a social worker or probation officer type. His sartorial style, his self-effacing demeanour, his manner in a group situation all pointed in these directions—at least to my mind. He was a Scotsman and today I can still hear his gentle accent with its wonderful musical lilt and rolled R's. Another of Bill's idiosyncrasies was a built-up sole on one of his shoes that he explained to me during one of our first keyworks.

Around twenty years previously Bill had been serving in the British army in Burma. Along with his fellow soldiers, he'd jumped from a plane, and everything was going fine until, just as he was landing, one foot landed in a hole and the wind changed resulting in his leg snapping at the knee.

I recall him saying he'd managed to clamber onto a nearby wall awaiting assistance and that the only thing holding his upper and lower leg together was the skin.

"I could've swung it around like a propellor had I not've been in such excruciating pain." He laughed.

Bill had then spent three months in a military hospital doped up to his eyeballs on morphine and had then, once the morphine was halted, endured withdrawal symptoms and cravings similar to my own recent agonies. At this point, my opinion of Bill changed—he wasn't the textbook counsellor I'd pigeonholed him as but had been a junkie himself, although through a freak accident rather than through dysfunctional choice.

* * *

It was a Wednesday afternoon, probably the third or fourth Wednesday since I'd arrived at Alpha. Things had settled down after the excitement of the festive season and a brand-new year had been tolled in. I and the other assessments were no longer the newbies we had been, and another cohort had entered the house to take our place. We'd all learned "the basics" and had begun to use them in our day-to-day interactions with other residents.

Now it was time for our first group meeting. Everyone in the house was present, staff and residents, all sat on chairs placed along the walls of a large rectangular room creating a big oval of chairs.

Silence and occasional fidgeting reigned for the first several minutes and there was a distinct edginess in the air…as though everyone was waiting for a mortar shell to be dropped in the centre of the room. I and the newbies had no idea what was expected of us or anyone else.

"I caught Nathan smoking in the bathroom."

Fuck! So a shell had been dropped…by a nervous-looking slim girl with fiery red hair. She looked to be in her mid-twenties.

I took a sideways glance at the accused. His face was glowing red as he sat with his hands beneath his thighs saying nothing, just gazing into the carpet, hoping it would swallow him up.

"Is this true, Nathan? What do you have to say about Vanessa's accusation?" This from my own keyworker, Bill. Fuck, I was praying they wouldn't send the poor guy down the drive and back into the real world; he'd only had a sneaky fag.

Nathan's gaze burnt more furiously into the carpet, but it was evident to all it wouldn't help. Slowly his eyes crept upwards towards Bill's own.

"It's true. It was only that once and I didn't expect anyone to catch me."

"Well, you'll do this evening's KS on your own and will think twice next time you want a cig in the bath. Thanks for passing this up, Vanessa." ("Passing up" was Alpha's way of normalising the term "grassing up," which in the UK means informing on someone.)

The mortar shell had done its work and now the room returned to silence, fidgeting, and wary expectation. Christ, I'd been told these groups lasted a couple of hours and I was already praying I'd done nothing that would see me being shelled next. As it turned out, there were no further attacks on anyone, and the group became a forum for ironing out many trivial issues such as when was the best time for the local shop to set up in this room on Sundays; when might the senior residents be permitted to go bowling in Fareham; and why couldn't we stay up later on Friday and Saturday evenings?

I'd made it through my first group meeting unscathed. This would not always be the case.

The weeks went by, and I became more used to the ways of Alpha and garnered a deeper understanding of "acting as if" and how to implement the basics. I had more one-to-one counselling sessions/keyworks, more group sessions, wrote diary entries each evening and read the feedback from the evening staff, became frustrated at not getting my own way on many occasions (this mostly revolving around not enough sax practice) and was given a new job as catering manager.

I'd been placed in the catering department after my stint on grounds and the then catering manager, Linda, realised I knew what I was doing. This prompted her to give me more responsibility in the form of tasking me with making the pudding, for instance, which was served with the evening meal; lunches were lighter while the evening meal was the big deal of the day. Word had filtered to the staff members, and I found myself ordering food, creating menus, delegating the chopping of vegetables to my team and being the house chef. I loved it…and so did the residents and staff.

I began with lasagnes, beef casseroles, stews, pie and chips, or thick soups then became a little braver and ordered the ingredients for moussaka or a lamb and date tagine, fish pies, gnocchi with salad. A vegetarian option was always included each mealtime then there was the pudding: rice puddings baked in the oven, spotted dick or jam sponges with custard, treacle tarts. It was fun and I really enjoyed cooking for thirty or so people each day.

In the main entrance hall, immediately visible upon entering the house's large front door, sat a wooden bench. This bench had a dual function, one of which was a place for residents to sit when struggling with the programme or considering walking down the drive (leaving the programme), a means of alerting both staff and residents they were in a bad space.

Its second function was somewhere residents might be ordered to sit by staff, usually when it seemed they weren't serious about the programme or had broken house rules and were at risk of being asked to leave.

So, seeing a resident sat on 'the bench' was instantly shocking and would be the biggest topic of discussion throughout every department. Invariably, at least one resident would be aware of the reason someone-or-other was sat there (often it would be the office manager because his place of work was in the same entrance hall as the bench).

As I've said, Alpha had a reputation far and wide. It was a reputation of not being an easy ride and one of being a "complete headfuck." The task of the team of staff, counsellors, and management was to welcome seriously fucked-up junkies, alcoholics, and self-harmers coming from chaotic lifestyles into a safe environment and then, ever so slowly, impart the rules of the house onto them—the basics, acting as if, passing up, etc. —and then counsel and cajole them over days, weeks, and months until they stand as a blank computer hard drive ready to be written upon.

However, they were dealing with different personalities from different social classes, family backgrounds, with different addictions, histories and varying needs, and therapy isn't a one-size-fits-all science.

I've been avoiding recounting the story of Angie because it's a memory still painful to me. Angie was one of the first friends I made when I landed at Alpha House. She came from London and, like me, heroin was her chosen poison. She'd also been introduced to hard drugs in her teens by those who were supposed to be her carers.

We shared a love of guitar and singing, although I was much farther along the road than she due to my age, repertoire, and greater experience of playing to audiences; I was thirty-five years' old while she was in her mid-twenties. Angie had long blonde hair, bright blue eyes, an infectious enthusiasm, and a presence that lit up the room whenever she showed up.

We'd often meet in the laundry and hang out together while the machines washed, rinsed, and tumbled around noisily beside us. It was one of the few places in the house where we might not be disturbed. She'd bring her guitar along and I'd show her chord shapes, teach her tunes, and give her plenty of encouragement. She was a fast learner, and her enthusiasm reminded me of my own when I'd first picked up guitar. It's upsetting today looking back on the short time we shared together.

Our friendship grew steadily as we came to know one another and the passing of the guitar back and forth along with my imparting musical knowledge soon found us completely relaxed in one another's company.

Throughout the day we'd work in our respective departments and then sit together at mealtimes to swap favourite artists and bands, from David Bowie to Bob Dylan, Cat Stevens to Neil Young, Roy Harper to the Rolling Stones… music our parents had danced to. In many ways she helped me find my feet and reciprocated my musical teaching by encouraging me to stay whenever I felt the pull of my old neighbourhood dysfunctions calling me to abscond.

We planned on supporting one another throughout the duration of our treatment and spoke of meeting after our release and continuing our friendship.

Regular visits from family members were encouraged at Alpha House and were considered part of the rehabilitative process. In many cases these visits were the initial steps towards patching up relationships with mothers, fathers, partners, siblings, and children, relationships that had often been stretched beyond all reasonable limits. The house was filled with residents of varying ages trying to overcome immensely addictive behaviours that invariably left a trail of emotional debris in their wake—family members being stolen from and lied to, the repeated failed attempts at quitting, regular police visits bringing shame, knowing looks from neighbours, and repeated prison sentences. A long and horrible list of disappointments that in some cases were beyond redemption resulting in zero visits, or the terrible sound of "This is your last chance" whispered in a weary voice.

Angie had been excited all week because her mother and her boyfriend were coming to visit her. She'd mentioned it to me several times while we practiced together and as the weekend drew closer, I could see her enthusiasm and excitement gain in intensity. On Saturday morning, we sat together at breakfast, and I could see she was beaming with anticipation. The day had finally arrived. She went upstairs to get dressed up and make up her face and then came running down the stairs, asking me, "How do I look?"

"You look beautiful," I assured her.

She headed for the common room and waited patiently for her visitors to arrive.

A few hours later I was outside in the gardens playing guitar and singing. The sun was shining warmly on my skin, and I was half squinting due to its glare, making the most of this welcome free time. I became aware of another resident, Sarah, approaching.

"Christian, have you seen Angie anywhere?"

"No, I haven't. I think she's with her visitors."

"Nope, they left an hour ago and Angie hasn't been seen since. Everyone's looking for her." Sarah walked off back towards the main house, and I soon found I couldn't concentrate so I followed her footsteps.

Entering the house, I could hear shouts of "Angie!" being called, so I guessed she was still missing. Despite Alpha being a large house, it would be impossible to not hear so many people calling out one's name.

Dinner was called so all residents entered the dining room where there was still no sign of Angie. The general consensus in the room was she'd received some bad news on her visit and had absconded. If that were the case, she was fucked—"Down the road" with no chance of reinstatement. *Damn, after so many months of working towards recovery,* I thought.

Dinner ended and most of us dealt with the dreaded KS. Next everyone headed for the common room where one of the residents would decide on the evening's activities. Reading was chosen, which left me feeling relieved as it could've been board games, image-breaking, charades, or any number of…

There was a sudden commotion outside the common room, raised voices in the hall in front of the staff offices. A resident opened the door to see what was going on.

Angie was there and the staff were telling her to leave the building, that she wasn't allowed back in. A member of staff told us residents to go back into the common room and to stay there. I caught Angie's eye and she saw me, but that was the last we'd see of one another.

We remained in the common room as the door was closed by a staff member but then all ran to the windows to watch the unfolding drama. I couldn't believe it. What the hell had happened to Angie since I'd last seen her? It didn't make any sense. Then I overheard a staff member outside speaking to Angie, and I knew she'd completely fucked everything up.

"Angie, you know neither alcohol nor anyone who's drunk alcohol is allowed in the house. You have to leave."

"But where do I go?" implored Angie.

"That's no longer our concern, Angie. You've completely forced our hand by drinking alcohol and that's it. You have to leave the grounds, or the police will be called to remove you. We must protect the other residents."

Fuck, I thought, *this is serious. Angie's gone.*

But she didn't go, despite different members of staff ordering her to leave. She was now outside the front door of the house that had been slammed closed to prevent her entry and she began to hammer on the door, but it wasn't opened. Then I heard the jarring, crashing sound of glass being broken. All of us residents in the common room could only sadly look at one another, each of us aware this was beyond repair and something we had no power over. Angie had sealed her fate by her actions and was being evicted. But why? What could have happened? Why and how was she drunk outside the front door?

A member of staff came into the common room and explained exactly what we'd already overheard and surmised then added Angie's wrist had been cut when smashing the front door windows and that an ambulance had been called. Jeez, one thing is always guaranteed when recovering addicts fuck up: they seriously fuck up and then the floodgates open.

There was no possibility of continuing with reading at this point, so we all sat and chatted in small groups. An ambulance's arrival was soon proclaimed when a flash of blue light swept the trees lining the drive, turning the common room into a sad and blue disco. It stopped outside the front doors and Angie was helped into the back by one of its attendants, the blue lights never letting up.

We heard over the next couple of days Angie had smuggled in some cash during her visit and had then headed down to the local shop and bought a half-bottle of vodka. I guess, like most of us recovering misfits, she'd been struggling with temptation and, having some cash in hand, couldn't resist trying to alleviate the pressure in the only way she could think of. There was certainly no smack to be found in Droxford.

A few days later during the morning meeting the house manager, Roy, entered and announced he'd received a letter from Angie's mother. He wanted to read it to us while we were all gathered in the same place. Drawing a single sheet of paper from an envelope, he began to read. We could see tears slowly rolling down his face as he read the lines from the page.

"Dear Roy, it is with a heavy heart I must tell you my daughter, Angie, was found dead in a night shelter yesterday morning. She died of a heroin overdose. We're told by the police she'd turned up there the previous evening rather than return home to us.

"She'd managed to find some heroin and had injected herself while others were sleeping and in the morning the shelter staff tried to wake her but to no avail. She was pronounced dead by the first responders when they arrived.

"Yours sincerely, Mrs. Pearson."

"I'm sorry I have to pass this terrible news on to you all. I'm also sorry we had to turn Angie away last week but, as you're all aware, the house rules are here to protect you…until you're ready to leave and not before. Now, let's spend a moment thinking on Angie before we begin our day."

There followed a terrible silence while each of us absorbed this tragic news. I could see Angie in my mind's eye, smiling gleefully as she reached the final chord of a song I'd taught her to play in the laundry.

Roy slowly folded the letter, slid it back into its envelope, and left the room.

24

Feeling Good
(Muse)

Angie's sudden disappearance and tragic ending could easily have sent any one of us tail-spinning out of control and following her example. The amount of pressure we were all under beneath that roof was incalculable: pressure from keyworks, from exploring feelings we'd all been suppressing for years, from "acting as if" around residents we didn't get on with but would secretly like to kill, the pressure to succeed from families out in the real world...the pressure of wanting to leave but knowing such a move would result in another long prison sentence and no end to a fucked-up life of crime and drugs in my case.

I can't speak for any of the others as I couldn't know what was going through their minds but, for me, Angie's implosion reinforced just how dangerous the outside world could be...what sharp, callous, and pitiless teeth it has.

The house slowly returned to its former routine and, sadly, Angie began receding into its history. I'd now been in the programme for roughly four months, and I was being accused of coasting although today's insight allows me to see it differently. As I stated a while ago, therapy isn't a one-size-fits-all science and I think the reason it took so many months for me to break down was due to my being much older than the majority of other residents with a commensurately thicker wall built around my psyche, my emotions.

I'd purposely, albeit subconsciously over many years, carefully erected this wall of defence to prevent any intrusion, to protect myself from any further hurt, and this protective mechanism didn't discriminate. Whether it be companions along my drug-fuelled journey, fellow prisoners, or keyworkers, few were permitted entry.

Bill and I had a keywork around my being so stubborn. We were sat on a fallen trunk in the verdant gardens and Bill was probing me, trying to get inside my head. I didn't recognize back then what I do now so wouldn't allow him entry while assuring him I was giving the programme my best shot.

The following morning at breakfast, I slowly felt a wave of heat wash over me. My shoulders began to shake, and a flow of tears started to fall. I began sobbing uncontrollably and didn't understand what had come over me. Some of the other residents recognised what was going on, though, and headed for the staff office.

I later heard one of them had said, "I think Christian's ready." Within ten or fifteen minutes, Bill entered the deserted dining hall and asked if I'd like a keywork. Finally, Christian was ready to begin dealing with his shit.

And I had a lot of shit to deal with. Aside from the drug use and the acquisitive crime necessary to fund that drug use, the most pressing problem I faced was the issue of Mia and our three children. My diaries are full of angst around whether we could remain together after I'd completed the programme or not. Alpha had a sensible policy of no sexual relations between residents or between residents and staff members (this primarily because we were required to confide in our keyworkers, and the moment we entered an intimate relationship, we would confide in our new partner thereby defeating the object of having keyworks altogether).

So "no couples" was the house policy. My plan was to complete my programme and then return home and take care of the children while Mia came to Alpha to complete the programme herself.

I knew she was still dealing heroin from conversations I had with my family on the phone, I also knew she was still heavily addicted, and that she was using daily. And I knew the council was trying to evict her and the social services were considering taking our kids into care. My mother was there on the sidelines taking the kids for weekends to give Mia a break and I knew she wouldn't allow the kids to be taken away without stepping in and taking them on herself first.

It was a fucking mess, and I'd reached the stage in my programme where it wasn't the desire to abscond and take heroin or cocaine that would find me sitting on the bench feeling vulnerable, it was the situation with my kids.

My family were visiting me with the kids regularly and they enjoyed spending some time with me (especially as I was much more lucid than when I'd been at home with them) so I hadn't completely lost contact but there was a huge question mark over their future.

I personally wanted to stay with Mia once I was free to leave yet I was being told by both residents and staff we can't pull someone out of the mess they're in, they will only drag you down. An analogy that is often employed is that of crab fishing.

Apparently, when catching crabs, they are thrown into a bucket as and when caught. Inside the bucket they clamber over one another attempting to reach the rim of the bucket and haul themselves out and, as one is about to successfully escape, another of those within the bucket will drag the crab back in and the process begins over again.

This quandary was driving me nuts on a daily basis. I was having keyworks around these feelings, was being given advice by different residents, and received advice in the responses to my diary entries by evening staff.

I was also at this time having to consider moving on to the resettlement stage of the programme. This meant leaving the main house and moving into the cottage where only a couple of other guys lived, guys who'd already completed the programme. This was the point where I'd re-integrate with the outside world. I'd have the freedom to leave Alpha House and do my own shopping, to seek employment and decide where

I planned to live, and what I planned to do once I landed back in the real world. I was confident in my decision to remain drug-free, yet I knew how ubiquitous drugs were in every town and city of the UK and knew what a cunning bastard my brain could be. I needed a support circle in whichever town I moved to and would need to keep busy.

The staff at Alpha were planning on helping me find somewhere to live in either Southampton or Portsmouth but I strongly disagreed. A good friend of mine had resettled in Portsmouth a couple of months prior to this and had already relapsed and been allowed to return to the house.

I stated I wished to move to Winchester instead and the staff informed me, "There are drugs in Winchester too you know, Christian."

"Yes, but what does Winchester have that both Southampton and Portsmouth lack?" I asked. My question was met with blank faces.

"I'll tell you what it has: much more affluence and therefore better policing…and better policing means the drugs may be a little more underground and I'll have more chance of succeeding, unlike Gary who's back here after his relapse in Portsmouth."

I'd also chosen Winchester as I'd spent a year or two there in Winton House and Ashborne Lodge whilst in council care. During that period, us youngsters would be allowed to visit the city centre some weekends, so I felt I knew the city a little.

* * *

There was a mountain bike available at the cottage, and I immediately put it to good use. I'd stuff food and drink into a backpack then cycle down to Droxford's church and the River Meon running along behind it or fly along the disused Meon Valley railway line. What a wonderful sensation after six months' being locked in the cage that was Alpha House. Finally, I was free.

It wasn't long before money (or, rather, a distinct lack of it) became a problem so I decided I'd try to find a job. Winchester was twelve miles away, but the route was so hilly it was a killer of a trek. There was nothing

I could do but bite the bullet. I'd decided that was where I wanted to live so needed to find a job there. Public transport was sporadic from Droxford so cycling and getting fit seemed the best option.

As soon as I hit Winchester, I found an ongoing construction job and decided to check it out. I found the groundwork company's foreman and he asked what I could do. I'd seen a lot of steel mesh and concrete slabs being prepared so I pointed at them and said, "I've done plenty of that before, factory floors, power-floating, motorways."

"When can you start?"

"Whenever you need me," I replied.

"I need you tomorrow."

We agreed an hourly rate and I had a job. I knew it entailed a twelve-mile cycle ride in the morning followed by an eight-hour shift of hard graft then another twelve-mile cycle ride home, but I also knew I'd just completed one of the most rigorous rehab programmes in the country and felt I was ready for anything.

I returned to Alpha and managed to catch Bill just as he was about to drive home.

"Hey Bill!" I shouted. "Hold up a minute."

"Hi Christian, how you doing?"

"Great," I told him with a broad smile on my face. "I just scored me a job on a construction site in Winchester."

"Wow, that's fantastic news. How you going to get there each day? Take a bus?"

"No. Mountain bike…I'm gonna get supremely fit and earn lots of money at the same time."

"Good on you. Keep me updated, yeah?"

I agreed to do so and headed towards the cottage to prepare some well-earned dinner. I was famished after all that cycling.

* * *

The saxophone came in a couple of beats before the trumpet player blew the last notes of his solo and new motifs developed around a similar theme. The bass and drums were driving the whole train along and the rhythm guitar was chugging alongside them. Incredible. This wasn't jazz, it was funk, and the guy on sax was the first person I worked alongside at my new job.

I'd cycled from Alpha and arrived on site early, changed into my work clothes in the drying room and then sought out my foreman, Phillip. He handed me a shovel and instructed me to follow him.

We arrived at an open trench and there was a guy there already shovelling soil that had collapsed into the trench overnight.

"Jim, this is Christian, he's just started this morning and he'll be giving you a hand today. Show him what needs doing, yeah?"

"Hey man," said Jim holding out his hand, "nice to meet you."

"Yeah, likewise."

We shook hands then I joined him in the trench and also began to shovel loose soil.

"Where'd you live?" Jim asked me.

"Ah, actually, I live in a rehab place over towards Fareham," I explained. Alpha's basics had taught me well—to make up a cover story would have complicated things. It was far easier to be truthful.

"No way, man." Jim was evidently surprised and stopped shovelling. He fixed me with a pair of intense green eyes then pulled his hard hat off to wipe his brow revealing a shock of tightly coiled dark brown hair.

"That must've been rough," he said.

"Yeah, it sure was. I was on the smack for about twenty years…been clean nine months now. This is my first job since being allowed to leave the place and I cycled all the way from Droxford this morning. Twelve miles of bastard hills."

"Haha." Jim laughed. "I know that route. I'm from Alresford so I know this area. Wow, twenty years on smack, surprised you're still here…"

"Tell me about it," I agreed. "Many of the guys I grew up with are long gone."

We continued chatting while shovelling and then Jim asked thoughtfully, "What made you wanna quit after so long?"

An interesting question I was happy to answer.

"Firstly, looking at my children and knowing I don't want that kind of life for them and, secondly, for myself. I've been banged up or fucked on drugs for so long now, I don't know what a normal life even feels like. I've just spent several months clean, sure, but in a rehab—and that definitely ain't normal life."

I threw another shovel full of soil out on to the ground beside us and continued.

"I wanna see what real life is like. I'm a musician but I've only really ever performed in prisons…or busking here and in France. I wanna join bands n shit like that."

"You're a musician? Whatcha play?"

"I play guitar and sing…and some blues harp and sax."

Jim stopped shovelling.

"You play sax? So do I. Which one?"

"Alto," I responded.

"Me too. I've been playing alto for years and I'm in a funk band. You should come along to our gig this Friday evening."

I could tell Jim and I were going to get on fine. He was only the second person I'd met in Winchester. I had a good feeling about him, and here I was watching him perform with his band at a venue on Parchment Street.

For possibly the first time in my thirty-five years, I felt an optimism that wasn't blighted by a presentiment of doom. There was no Sword of Damocles waiting to descend and find me once again in a police custody suite or a prison reception. I found myself walking along Winchester High Street surrounded by strangers, people who held no expectations of me and I none of them. Strangers who weren't likely to offer me a bag of smack or a crack pipe, or even a spliff.

Surrounded by strangers, yes, but also by an increasingly widening circle of friends. In the evenings after work, I would sometimes attend band rehearsals with Jim where I'd glean some insight into the inner workings of a band and the nuances of musical etiquette. I knew I'd need this understanding for my own future career as a musician, which was still my prime ambition.

Other evenings, I would join some of the Northerners who worked on the same building site in a pub close to site. These guys would leave their homes in the Midlands early on a Monday morning, pile into cars or vans together and drive for three or four hours. This was not long before the large influx of Eastern European labour when the North/South division of plentiful labour was very much in evidence. I met many friends who I'm still in touch with during this period, friends whose accommodation and evening meals were paid for by their respective companies.

These subsidies weren't spent on the hotels or bed and breakfasts they were intended for but would be spent as a one-off payment on a caravan with the following weekly payments being pocketed. As a result, there was a caravan park on our construction site consisting of carpenters, steel-fixers, plumbers, electricians, and various other tradesmen. My time spent in Armley prison, Leeds, enabled me to take the piss, mimicking their accents. I'd join them for their evening meal and sometimes we'd hit a town centre pub for a karaoke session where I'd sing Joe Cocker's *Unchain my Heart*, pull a harmonica out of my pocket, and play a ripping solo through the microphone. My new friends loved it.

I wasn't drinking alcohol during these sessions as I was determined to live a clean and healthy life. This would prove exceedingly difficult over the ensuing months as alcohol is more ubiquitous than illicit drugs and is encouraged at practically every social event, but for now, I was on the straight and narrow.

My favourite pub was the Mash Tun, the most popular watering hole for many of Winchester university's faculty. I spent many evenings and weekends happily reading quietly in the corner surrounded by a wonderful camaraderie, and I was soon noticed by the bar staff who were a close bunch of friends in themselves.

Joe was running the show and he and I soon became friendly along with Will, Karen, Ben, and several others. I wasn't shy about sharing my history and I received an enormous respect from all of these guys.

When I wasn't reading in the corner or buzzing on the youthful vibrancy all around me, I'd play pool and stay on the table until somebody beat me and would then place some coins on the table and vie for supremacy once again. There was also live music at the weekends, and the same faces would be dancing all around me while different bands played and sweated on stage.

In this way, over several months, I was soon embraced by these people who were around ten or fifteen years younger than me. It felt much like the life I should have been living when I was their age. Sure, there was plenty of cannabis in the air out back in the beer garden and there were plenty of other stimulants being passed around and consumed but none of the dark and horrible drugs I'd managed to escape from and put behind me. Alpha House cured me of the desire to consume drugs that revolved around self-sabotage and self-destruction—heroin and crack cocaine. I didn't have a problem with my friends consuming those I'd label "recreational drugs" like hash, ecstasy, acid, or mushrooms.

Mia was also present in my mind during this time. I was aware she was only forty miles away and that she was anticipating a visit from me. Our children were with my mother, and she would bring them to visit me rather than see me return to the perilous zone of Farnborough. But my feelings for Mia were still very strong. One evening, I jumped on a train after work and went to visit her. I should have known what the outcome of this visit would be, but the mind can be cunning and masterfully lead one astray.

I stood at Mia's door and felt nervous at what lay behind it. We hadn't seen one another for a year and, although I was aware of the enormous changes I'd undergone during that year, I couldn't gauge whether those changes would be enough...whether they'd be sufficient for me to withstand whatever emotions assailed me when I was face to face with my lover, the mother of my children...and potentially my nemesis. I pressed the doorbell.

"Christian." I sensed relief in Mia's voice. "I was wondering when you'd come and see me. I thought the rehab—you know, all those counsellors—might've brainwashed you against coming home."

She looked wasted and underweight, but I wasn't surprised. It was the same look she'd had when I'd been arrested a year before—it was only me who now looked and felt twenty times more healthy.

Mia opened the door wider and I entered, pulling her into my arms and holding her tight, her head resting on my chest. We kissed and I held her close, stroking her hair. In that moment, the months I'd been away evaporated and were replaced with her familiar warmth and smell. I realised she was alone, which calmed me a little. I felt I could deal with seeing her alone but had been apprehensive around arriving at a house full of smackheads.

We moved into the kitchen and a new smell filled my nostrils then flooded my mind—the smell of burnt heroin. I tried to ignore it as Mia prepared tea, but it was a smell that had been absent from my life for so long now it seemed to increase in potency.

Within an hour of my arrival, we were back to chasing heroin together. The smell of the smack, the heavy brown rivulet running across the foil, the snug warmth and cotton wool of both the drug and Mia's embrace, all of it so familiar, so comforting, and so fucking dumb. I slept and didn't awake until morning.

Then I ran.

* * *

I was also living in a caravan I'd inherited around this time and, as soon as I arrived back on the Winchester site, I climbed straight into bed. I felt terrible, both physically and mentally, and my friends couldn't understand what was wrong as they'd never seen me so out of sorts before. Many of them kept checking in on me throughout the rest of the day and evening. Next day I forced myself out of bed and managed a day's work.

While working, I thought long and hard about what had transpired with Mia and realised how serious it was. There was no way I could revisit her as the same thing would occur…again and again until I was back to where I'd been a year previously. Back on the smack trail blazing my way to prison for years to come.

The solution to my problem came from a most unlikely source. Before being arrested, I'd been selling smack to a local prostitute named Claudia and a friendship had sprung from this business relationship. She was originally from the Netherlands but had settled in Aldershot and had a six-year-old daughter. I'd never used her services but decided to visit her rather than visit Mia again. Everyone at Alpha House had been correct in saying I could never pull Mia out of the hole she was in—I'd only be dragged back in.

After the surprise of seeing me at her door for the first time in more than a year, she invited me in, fetched some coffee, and we sat chatting and smoking cigarettes. She wasn't surprised when I explained what had happened between Mia and I but understood how easily the situation had occurred.

But, where Mia and I had made a career of smoking smack and crack together, Claudia and I never really had so she offered me a compromise.

"Christian, if ever you need to in future, just come see me as a friend. I promise you—I won't pass you a spliff, silver foil, or a pipe. We can have some fun, you can stay safe, and then you can go home. You've worked too hard to fuck this up. Think about all the hard work you've put into sorting yourself out…the absolute hell you've been through to get clean and think about the reasons you went to rehab in the first place."

This arrangement kept me safe for the next few months and without Claudia's intervention, I've no way of telling how things might have panned out, whether I'd have succumbed to returning to Mia and the certain heroin use that entailed or not. It kept me safe until I met a girl in the Mash Tun one evening who I saw for several months and today I feel a huge debt of gratitude to Claudia who, true to her word, never offered me any drugs and kept me safe until I found an alternative to Mia.

25

At Last
(Etta James)

Jim and the guitarist from his band changed cities around 2001. They'd chosen the city of Brighton as their base. After several weekend trips there—both partying and checking out live bands—it dawned on me I could spend a lifetime in Winchester yet never become half as good as the musicians I was seeing perform at the Komedia, the Concorde, The Albert, or Joogleberries (Brighton's top music venues back then). I made the decision to join them and waved goodbye to Winchester.

Brighton is a bustling city on the south coast of England famous for its music scene, its party scene, and its gay scene, not necessarily in that order. The party scene went hand in hand with a highly active recreational drug scene, and by now I wasn't averse to enjoying some hash, ecstasy, or cocaine with my new friends; it was almost expected in the musical circles I was hanging out in. I wasn't interested in heroin or crack cocaine anymore, but these lesser drugs seemed fine to me.

I quickly found employment on a construction site on North Street building retail units and found a room in a bed and breakfast close to Brighton's pier. My mother often brought the kids to visit me, and we'd all enjoy the beach and pier. The pier has a funfair with a waltzer, dodgem cars, and amusement arcade, and while the roller coaster isn't enormous, it does feel as though you'll fly off the edge of the pier and land in the sea at any moment. I loved being on these rides with my children clinging on to me and screaming with both fear and excitement.

Whenever their mother entered my thoughts, I'd quickly suppress them. I'd so wanted things to work out for us both, for her to complete the course at Alpha after me but it wasn't to be…the loss of all five of her children was too much to deal with and heroin was the only salve that could numb such deep pain. My visit to her after Alpha had revealed to me there was only one road we'd continue travelling together and it wasn't the road best for the children.

I made friends with a fellow saxophonist named Sophie at a local music festival around this time. She was expert on tenor sax, which immediately attracted my attention and was very smiley and confident with long raven black hair and dark eyes. The festival was held close to Royal Tunbridge Wells, and she'd played with a band I really enjoyed. They were playing upbeat gypsy jazz with harmonic minor scales that was fairly typical of Brighton festival bands around that time.

Sophie and I met for food in Brighton one Saturday shortly after the festival and then strolled along the beach close to the pier. I picked up several pebbles and skimmed them across the waves then we stopped and sat on the stony beach.

Sophie reached out and gently laid her hand on my arm stopping me from flinging another pebble. She looked straight at me and said, "I want to ask you something. How come your kids aren't living with you?"

"That's a good question," I answered and thought about it for several minutes, resuming throwing pebbles into the curling tide. I scooped up another handful of pebbles before continuing.

"The thing is, Sophie, I had an unusual childhood and was beaten a lot by my father while still young. This occurred up until I was seven years old. He left shortly afterwards, or my mum managed to persuade him to leave, I'm not sure...

"After that, I was nothing but trouble and didn't spend much time with my mother and siblings. I was sent to care homes at twelve years old. Once there, us bad boys didn't trust adults' judgement nor that of the staff members, so we became our own teachers. I think these experiences left me devoid of a normal paternal instinct."

I threw a flat stone, happy to watch it bounce four times before disappearing beneath the water's surface.

"Don't get me wrong, I love my kids dearly but, unlike their mother's previous partner who took the kids away from her to bring them up himself, I never considered that option. I never considered anything other than their being raised by their natural mother. And, at the point where the social services were going to take them from their mother, I was in prison about to enter rehab for a year, and my mother was making inroads into gaining guardianship rights.

"But it's a good question and one I don't really have an answer for."

She dropped the subject, and we continued our walk alongside the crashing surf. It transported me back to the waves crashing on the shore of Les Saintes Marie de la Mer in '87 and my reverie around Mia back then before the kids had been born. So much water had ebbed against so many shores since then, so many bad decisions on my part and Mia's and her sister's parts. All decisions that were irrevocable yet that affected the lives of so many.

"Are you still considering Chichester?" Sophie's sudden change of subject snatched me back to the present.

She was referring to whether or not I'd decided to enrol on the Chichester College jazz course many of the musical friends I was meeting had completed.

"Yeah, I think I wanna do it. Everything I've heard sounds fantastic… like it's just what I need to bring me up to speed with all the theory."

"Not just that," she said, smiling at me, "you'll be placed in bands and rehearse for weekly gigs. That kinda thing's invaluable for spurring on your practice regime as it's such a competitive environment."

"Okay, I gotta get going. I got a fortieth birthday party to arrange. You'll be there, yeah? Next Saturday at my flat."

"Of course I will, along with half the musicians and party animals of Brighton. I'll see you there."

After we'd parted, I gave Sophie's question more thought. It was still early so I pulled my phone from my pocket and called my mother.

"Hey, Mum, how you doing? How're the kids?"

"Oh, hi," she sounded tired. "They're all good. The twins are in bed and Seb's watching a movie in his room."

"Listen, Mum, I was just having a chat with a friend of mine down here and she asked me, 'Why aren't your kids with you?' What's the plan? It's not something we've really discussed, is it?"

"Well, as far as I'm concerned," she responded, "they can stay with me until they complete their full-time education and then it's up to them."

"Woohooo!" My response was instant and genuine. I'd never been good with responsibility and was pleased with her answer. However, there were also other factors at play: I couldn't return to my hometown of Farnborough because of the drugs; there was also the issue of Mia. I knew from my mother there had been occasions when Mia had stated she'd visit the kids but hadn't shown up. In the world of erratic drug supply, it's always challenging for users to stick to appointments whether in the courts, hospitals, child access visits, or schools. I was sure there would be times when she would show up and I couldn't feel safe around her.

What alternatives were there? The upheaval of the kids and the change of school that would entail? I lived in a two-bedroom shared flat so there was no room for three children to stay. I think my mother went through the few possibilities in her own mind and realised the children remaining with her was the best option. Also—and this is pure conjecture—I have a feeling today she wanted to see me experience a bit of real life after the years of incarceration and drug use.

At last, it felt like life was mine to live.

26

Bad Guys
(Paul Williams)

On my first day at the Chichester College's jazz course, I pulled my truck into the campus car park and found a small stream to park beside. I'd bought the truck to use as my home while at college, to save on paying the extortionate rents in Brighton, and also for the summer festivals.

That first day I met my fellow students, a mixed bag of different ages and nationalities who all shared a passion for their instruments and different styles of jazz. We all got on really well and spent that first year being thrown into different bands that were a mix of novices and semi-professionals.

These bands varied from four- to five- to six-piece and would include soprano, alto, tenor, or baritone saxes, clarinets, trumpets, trombones, electric or double basses, electric or acoustic guitars, violins, drums, and various other percussive instruments. Many of the students travelled from Brighton daily and I soon discovered many of us shared mutual friends.

Weekly lessons on our chosen instruments were included in the package and we all shared classes in theory, improvisation, history of jazz, aural training, composition, and band practice. Each Friday afternoon we'd be handed two tunes to perform as a band the following Friday, tunes drawn mostly from the Swing and Bebop eras of jazz. We'd then spend the weekend juggling our social lives while needing to learn the tunes ready for our Monday morning rehearsal. I wasn't the only student who'd occasionally turn up on a Monday morning with no idea what the tune we were playing sounded like.

The jazz course really was everything I'd been assured it would be and I could see why so many friends had recommended it. Alumni were being accepted by Middlesex and Leeds universities in their droves.

Bands would perform their rehearsed tunes on Friday afternoons, each band taking turns. Those not performing were sat at the back of the hall on tiered seating giving encouragement and applause to their friends, both after solos and at the end of each song. It was a really supportive environment and someone hitting a bum note or two wasn't denied their applause.

* * *

In midsummer 2005, I pulled my Dodge truck up outside The Big Green Gathering and came to a stop with a loud hiss from its air brakes. This was a huge festival held not far from Cheddar Gorge in Somerset, England, with its focus on the environment and social justice, including workshops and talks on permaculture, politics, ecology, and crafts, as well as art, live music and spoken word performances. The site held capacity for around 20,000 visitors.

Having been a UK festival habitué for twenty years by this point, I can attest to this festival's uniqueness and magical charm. It was one of those rare festivals that had something for everyone: those looking to get off their face on ecstasy and writhe in the dance tent all night long; a more mature reveller seeking a long weekend of live bands; a family seeking a place to bring their young to have their faces painted and enjoy quality time away from the city; an eco-warrior researching a variety of information around sustainability; a dyed-in-the-wool hippie searching for like-minded willow-basket weavers; or a black anarchist wanting to connect with other proponents of the Reclaim the Streets/Stop the War campaigns.

I was there mostly for the live music and to join my friends for a good time. My truck had plenty of crates of beer hidden beneath the bed and I was handed a "live-in vehicle pass" by a Brighton friend so I could get my truck on site.

The weekend was as wondrous as I'd expected and I shared it with many friends old and new, from both Winchester and Brighton. On the final day I watched a gig by a band named the Don Bradmans. The band consisted of a lead singer who played banjo, a fiddle player, a guitarist, and a keyboard/melodica player. An electric bassist and drummer completed the lineup.

Once the sound check and its bursts of feedback were out of the way, they began to play. There was something noticeably different about them. The lyrics were humorous—as were the musicians themselves—and they had a great musical rapport, bouncing off one another with ease. I later learned three of these musicians had all completed the same Chichester jazz course I was attending. They finished their set with a cover of *Bad Guys* from the movie *Bugsy Malone*, which was inspired as the majority of the audience had watched and loved that movie in their early teens.

I returned to the Chichester college routine where my progress was becoming increasingly evident to, not only me, but also to my fellow students and even my course leader.

The reasons for my quick progress were manyfold: I was keen to become a good musician as this had been my dream since learning to read music back in borstal in 1978; I had no family at home distracting me when I wasn't at college nor any neighbours limiting the number of hours I could practice; and as was the case for all us students, the information being thrown our way in classes and band rehearsals was coalescing into a system we could manage.

During this period of intense learning, I'd often wake in the night and catch my brain processing the information being thrown at me. There'd be a light bulb moment where I'd think, *Ah, so that's why that scale works so well over that particular chord progression,* or a similar realisation. At forty-two years old, my brain was still as sharp as it had always been, despite all the drugs I'd consumed over those years—or perhaps because of them?—and I could feel my dreams of becoming a live performer slowly and unstoppably becoming a reality.

And this reality came from a totally unexpected corner. Towards the end of my second year at Chichester, I was asked if I'd like to join The Don Bradmans. I was blown away and agreed without hesitation. Their fiddle player had a love interest in Sheffield and was changing cities to be with her new partner, hence an opening for a new soloist. This was the work of the universe paving the way for me once again, I was certain.

I met with the guitarist in Brighton, and we had an impromptu audition at his house with the lead singer and bass player joining us. We went through a few numbers I'd only heard once before at their gig, but they were happy with my sax improvisation and agreed I would replace the fiddle player. I was handed a CD containing all their tunes and was given my instructions.

"Learn all the fiddle lines and practice soloing on everything."

This was the moment I'd been dreaming of and working so hard towards for years.

* * *

The second year of the jazz course was coming to an end for all us students, some of whom I'd spent the past two years learning, playing, and partying alongside. We had a couple of assignments and a final live performance assessment to complete and would then go our separate ways only to meet occasionally at festivals and gigs. I'd had an amazing time performing and socialising with them all, but it was time to move on.

I received a call from the Don Bradmans guitarist, and he explained the fiddle player didn't want to leave the band but would instead travel to and from Sheffield for gigs. I was completely disheartened as I loved their music and had learnt to play on half the tunes from the CD already.

Oh well, I stoically told myself, *I'm certain the learning process has helped improve my playing.* I was disappointed though as I'd been looking forward to being in my first band. I put my head down and concentrated on completing the jazz course. Something else would come up. I was certain my musical career was about to take off.

2007 was in many ways an incredibly good year for me though not without a few hiccoughs. The most significant of these was being stopped by the police in my Dodge at the bottom of Elm Grove in Brighton after leaving a pub and being breathalysed. I completely kept my cool until I failed the test and was being read my rights. At this point I decided to shoot myself in my foot.

"Drink driving? Let me tell you about drink driving—I've been drink driving since you were at school and can probably drive better drunk than you can sober."

I was soon lying on the tarmac road with my wrists cable-tied behind my back. Next, I was bundled off to the police station, kept in a cell overnight, charged for driving over the legal limit and then released. The court date I was given was a few months away and I could still legally drive until that date.

Once again, my guardian angel came to the rescue. I was offered a job as a gateman on a building project just outside Brighton. The main contractor was building a new wing and swimming pool at a female mental hospital, and my job was to sit in a large metal container signing people in and out mornings and evenings, taking down car and lorry registration numbers and in between I could read all the books I wanted.

The site was in an affluent area and staying in my truck each evening outside the site's main gates was becoming conspicuous and out of place. After a few days, I approached the project manager and suggested I might park my truck in the car park and double up as a security guard—a deterrent to any would-be thieves. When he agreed, I heaved an enormous sigh of relief. The job was projected to last another eighteen months to two years, which was potentially longer than the eighteen-month driving ban I was eventually awarded by the magistrate.

So I was now living on the site and acting security guard. The irony wasn't lost on me: poacher turned gamekeeper.

At the same time I was living and working on this site, my dreams of performing onstage in a band also came true…and it was the year I met my next long-term partner. In fact, these two were inextricably linked and revolved around the Big Green Gathering festival.

The fiddle player performed only one gig with the Don Bradmans after her move to Sheffield. The band had agreed to pay her travel expenses and did so only to discover there was little money left over for the remaining band members. I was asked a second time if I'd like to join the band and I immediately replied, "Only if you promise not to sack me in the first week again."

And that was that. I was a Don Bradman.

* * *

Tommo, the Don Bradmans' guitarist, and his girlfriend, Bela, had travelled with me to the festival a day before the rest of the band. Bela, an accomplished cellist, joined us to form an impromptu trio that evening, and I named us "Bela Artois." We were playing some regular jazz standards and some Eastern European tunes to an audience in Weirdigan's Café, a marquee with a bar, small low tables, and scatter cushions for seating.

We reached the end of a song, and I felt a light tap on my shoulder.

"What did you say your name was?"

"Don Bradman," I replied to the young woman who'd asked.

Another woman came over and asked, "Did you just say your name's Don Bradman?" She had an accent I couldn't place, and a friend who also seemed interested in our conversation.

"Yes, it is," I laughed, "and so is his." I pointed at Tommo. In fact, all six of us DBs were called Don Bradman.

"Oh, you *are* playing this weekend then?" she said. "My friend's gonna be so pleased. He checked the programme and was really disappointed you're not in it."

"Let's say we're here in an unofficial capacity." I laughed. These girls hung around while we played a couple more songs and then Tommo and Bela left to erect their tent before it got dark. The advantage of having a live-in vehicle is never having to deal with tents.

I offered the girls a beer, which they accepted, then I dismantled and cleaned my sax before placing it in its case.

"Let's find somewhere to sit, yeah? You two have names?"

"Sure. I'm Emma and this is Sam." We grabbed a few scatter cushions and found a spot on the floor by the walls of the marquee. The place was busy, and all tables were occupied.

"Do you smoke?"

Emma said she did.

"Wanna skin up?"

"Yeah, go on then."

I passed her my tobacco, cigarette papers, a tin filled with hash pollen, and a lighter and she proceeded to skin up with a dexterity of someone who's been smoking for years. I watched her as she licked and stuck the papers. She had the finest straight blonde hair I'd ever seen and a pair of green eyes with tiny brown flecks in them. I guessed she was around five feet tall, and she had a cute accent.

"Where you from?" I asked her.

"Newport, South Wales…where all classy girls come from," she quipped with an ironic smile. She had a great smile.

"And what do you do when you're in Newport?"

"I'm a personal banker but I'm fed up with that so I'm doing an access course to get into university. I'm also a single mum."

"What?" I burst out laughing. "You can't be old enough."

"Her son's eleven years old. He's back at our camp with the friends who love your band," Sam offered.

"Eleven? How old are you?" It was hard to imagine she had a *two-year-old* son.

"I'm thirty-two."

"Wow, I'd've put you down as twenty-two, no more."

"Thanks." She smiled that smile again with a flash of her eyes. This girl had something about her...real character.

We chatted for hours, me drinking all the beer I'd brought with me and all three of us smoking. When the place had thinned out and was closing up, I arranged to meet Emma and her other friends the next day so I could explain where they could see us play. Even *I* didn't know where that would be yet.

* * *

The thing with the Don Bradmans is they're an eclectic bunch with a great sense of humour, rich and diverse musical tastes, and a penchant for the ridiculous. Fancy dress was the norm and, although I wouldn't say bum notes were encouraged, they weren't criminal offences either.

Influences ranged from The Bonzo Dog Doo Dah Band to Frank Zappa, the world of swing jazz, funk, Eastern European, the punk/New Wave era of the late seventies/early eighties, and we'd often change genre three times in one song. It was insane and our festival audience loved it.

As I'd said to Emma, "All six of us are called Don Bradman," and over the fifteen years we played together, we'd call one another Don whenever we were together. While there's an incredible camaraderie within bands that isn't easy to convey to laymen, I feel what we had in that band was even more special than most.

* * *

"And on saxophone, Don Bradman," Tony, the lead singer, purred into the microphone as I wound my way through my solo. The audience was loving it.

My solo over, I flew straight into the next lines of the song that required me to imitate a police car's siren. The song then segued into the chorus of The Ruts' iconic *Babylon's Burning* before returning back to the original song, *Bill Oddie's Body*.

I could see many in the audience completely blown away by this random behaviour from such a strangely garbed band of musicians. I could also see Emma and her friends dancing in the middle of the crowd obviously having a great time. Tommo flew into his solo next.

"On guitar, Don Bradman. Look at him goooooooo!" Tony was in his element, a shaman to his adherents, holding them in his spell for the duration of our time on stage.

The audience formed an undulating wave of faces bathed in the reds, blues, greens, and whites of the spotlights, writhing frenetically and harmoniously to the rhythms of our music. Those closest I could see clearly but the farther back I tried to see the more the glare of the spots blinded me. I needed to concentrate on the next line I had to play, the next cue from Tommo so I didn't miss the beginning of a phrase. I was the newbie here and I was still learning some of the songs. The sweat was pouring from me, a combination of my black top hat and tails, the heat generated by the multitude of dancing people within the huge marquee, and the blaze of the spotlights above our heads.

The naming of the band has a rather humorous/ridiculous story to it, a story I'm still not jaded with telling despite having told it a thousand times.

Don Bradman is possibly the most famous cricketer in the history of the sport. The drummer, Doug, had a friend at school who owned a pet spider named Don Bradman and he thought it would make a fantastic name for a band and so it had. However, people would often ask, "What's the cricket connection?"

To begin with, Doug having no idea about cricket, would confusedly ask, "Cricket?"

"Yes, Don Bradman the cricketer."

"But Don Bradman's a spider…" Doug would respond ingenuously.

Which sets the tone for one of the most entertaining bands I've ever come across…and I was now their sax player.

We finished our gig then left the stage, smoking and drinking beers, and chatting with many people who'd enjoyed the gig. We weren't on the festival's programme because we were still trying to make a name for ourselves, to become better known to the festival audience in general. And this festival was the best vehicle to offer such an opportunity as there were so many indie stages to choose from. We managed to play twelve or thirteen gigs over the festival's four-day duration and my soloing on each of our songs had noticeably improved by the Sunday evening.

Our final gig on the Sunday evening was a triumph. I think the knowledge it was our last of the festival added impetus and we all played with fire and passion. Emma and her friends had been in the audience for every gig we'd played over the weekend, and I was aware we'd all part our separate ways that evening.

As the final notes of our last song faded away, I pulled a page of sheet music from my sax case, scribbling my mobile number on it, and then motioned Emma to come closer. I knew she and her son and friends were leaving early in the morning and that they'd need an early night.

"Hey, here's my mobile number" I said, handing her the page. "I want you to have learned the song on it by the time you call me, okay?"

She laughed, said she'd call me, threw a sparkly smile at me then headed off through the crowd. The way I felt as I watched her back disappear attested to how fond I'd become of her over the four days since our meeting at Weirdigan's Café.

27

Tent
(Bonzo Dog Doo Dah Band)

My life at this point was the most functional it had ever been. My dream of becoming a musician in a performing band had come to fruition due to my diligence in practicing my craft and pursuing all opportunities related to it. I was also playing a lot of guitar and singing but wasn't as confident around microphone technique yet—but I was slowly getting the hang of it.

Okay, I was drinking a fair amount, smoking lots of cannabis, and popping the occasional ecstasy tab but didn't feel out of control. The thing about rehab's conventional wisdom is there's this idea that goes like this: "Once you've been an addict, you will crave your chosen poison every day until you die ergo you'll need to attend Narcotics Anonymous (NA) or Alcoholics Anonymous (AA) meetings forevermore." I just can't subscribe to this mindset.

Some will disagree, and that's fine, but here's my take. I feel this is no better than a heroin addict being given a maintenance prescription of methadone that is then that addict's crutch for eternity...or a smoker quitting cigarettes today only to become addicted to nicotine patches, E-cigarettes, or vapes. This is substitution...one habit for another. I know a guy who attends five or six AA meetings per week, regardless of which country he's in.

I've attended two of these meetings in my life and was speechless witnessing attendees take turns in bemoaning the fact they are "helpless" to change their situation, imploring a "higher power" for sustenance and assistance. Each to their own, right? Sure, but not for me, thanks. At that stage of my life, I preferred to stay away from the hard stuff yet still be able to have a drink or get high at a party, pub, or festival.

While on the subject of drug choice, it was at this point many of my friends in Brighton were turning to the latest fashionable substance, ketamine. An animal tranquiliser. Jeez, when I saw them on it, it reminded me of heroin. It was the same when I heard them on the phone, desperate when none was available.

I was still living on site in my truck at the hospital, and in the evenings, I'd often remain in my gateman's metal container practicing sax. It had been a few months since the festival, and I'd not heard from Emma… until my phone alerted me to a text message and I saw it was from her apologising for taking so long to get back to me and asking how I was.

I called her immediately—"Hey, did you learn that song yet?" —and we chatted for a couple of hours, catching up on one another's news with much laughing and joking. It was the most natural and easy conversation but we both had to be up early for work so agreed to speak again soon. This we did and these conversations continued for weeks until I said I'd come and visit her.

"That's gonna be really difficult for you as you can't drive. Listen, why don't I drive to you on New Year's Eve? I'm sure there's plenty to do in Brighton, right?"

"Wow, really? Well, if you're up for it, that'd be fantastic."

True to her word, Emma drove over. We had an amazing New Year together beginning with a gig at Brighton's Joogleberry's and then a party in central Brighton before returning to my truck.

Next morning we found somewhere to have breakfast, and the easy conversation continued. We returned to my truck then ambled through the nearby woods, exchanging details of one another's lives, and enjoying being together. We agreed to see each other again.

Work continued, as did our long phone calls. After several months of my visiting Emma in Wales using public transport, my driving ban was over. This was fantastic news but there was no way I was driving my truck all the way to Wales as it has a four litre six-cylinder engine and the cost in fuel would be astronomical.

Over these past months our relationship had become well established, and we both felt closer each time we met; love was in the air.

While things were going well for us, however, they weren't going so well for the UK's economy. Something was about to go badly wrong, and my bosses could see the writing on the wall.

"Christian, it's looking likely there's gonna be a financial crash, and we'd like to offer you a position in the company."

"Whaddya mean?" I asked, genuinely bemused.

"Well, there are certain trends within the sector that give clues as to something being wrong. For starters, lots of sites are being mothballed and lots of plant is being off-hired and staying in the yards. This probably means there's gonna be a recession. Now, you've been good to us here for eighteen months …

"How would you like a job as a general foreman? You know lots about the building game, you've proved this over and over, you can drive most of the plant and you're a great people person."

"You missed out my sterling personality, charm, and wit." I laughed. "Okay, so what's the deal?"

"A contract, reasonable salary, company car, fuel card, family healthcare, and pension."

"Where do I sign?"

Once again, this seemed to be the universe providing for me, as though there were some kind of equilibrium metric going on. Karma, even—now I was involved in lots of positive pursuits, I was receiving these rewards in return.

My friends were stuck on a crazy ketamine merry-go-round, and I'd met and got together with Emma at exactly the right moment. My weekends now consisted of either a long drive to Newport, South Wales, or a long wait for Newport, South Wales, to come to me. My only business in Brighton at this point was with my band, so I'd drive my company van into town and we'd sometimes rehearse our set list and other times write new stuff.

We'd just been invited to play the Shangri-La stage at Glastonbury so were focusing on polishing our set as much as possible. Glastonbury is the biggest festival in the UK and would be the pinnacle of our musical success up to this point.

Another offer to play the Glastonbury Red Bull stage over the same weekend came our way and we prepared our set in earnest.

* * *

Since being employed by Leadbitter, I'd risen from general foreman to assistant manager and my company van had been replaced with a car to reflect this new status. The hospital team remained together to build Eastgate Square, Chichester, a mixed residential and retail project.

By 2012, my company had valiantly managed to stay afloat since the 2008 financial crash. They survived the crash, yes, but then signed up with a savvy couple of developers who ran the Waterhouse development company. These guys were next-level clever, rang rings around Leadbitter and in many ways became the architects of their doom.

Waterhouse contracted Leadbitter to rebuild Dorchester's Brewery Square. Phase I of the project would cost an estimated £300 million and would take eighteen months to complete.

I'd been moved to the Dorchester site and had been given the responsibility of supervising the conversion of a hundred-year-old building into a Carlito's restaurant, a Nando's, Costa, and other retail units. I was back living in my truck on this new development.

This was an interesting project where I'd learn a great deal more about construction site infrastructure and politics. I was involved in meetings with the architects and design team, had to deal with the materials procurement team, attend management meetings, and liaise with a crazy Italian structural engineer named Gino. It was interesting and satisfying watching the transformation of this historical building that was a part of the former Eldridge Pope Brewery.

This all came crashing around my ears, however, when Leadbitter was bought out by a huge French infrastructure company and I was made redundant.

28

Break on Through (To the Other Side) (The Doors)

"Can you improvise to this?"

The guy auditioning me was named Rob and he was sat at a piano in one of University of South Wales's rehearsal rooms on the Atrium Campus in Cardiff. He was a fellow saxophonist. His fingers sprang and danced across the keys and the familiar sound of Herbie Hancock's "Watermelon Man" filled the room.

Of course I can, I thought, and proceeded to blow my horn.

I felt our interview had gone well but now my acceptance rested on my ability to play. In the UK's university system, UCAS points are the metric by which proficiency is determined. In my case, however, I didn't have enough points due to my unorthodox education in care homes and my leaving Chichester's jazz course early to join the Don Bradmans.

We wrapped up the song and Rob pronounced, "You're in."

I was elated. None of my family had been to university and here I was about to begin a three-year undergraduate degree in music only ten miles from home. I couldn't wait to tell Emma and her son, Liam, the good news.

The first weeks of uni were incredible. What a joy to be shuttling to and from the library, classrooms, the lecture hall, rehearsal rooms. At fifty years old, I was a mature student surrounded by nineteen- and twenty-year-olds with a similar energy to my own. We were placed in bands and assigned to choose a bunch of songs to cover for a live concert we were to perform in six weeks' time.

I was attending lectures on the history of music by a tutor I immediately clicked with as he was familiar with the festival scene, the battle of the beanfield, Hawkwind, Nik Turner, and the joys of mushroom picking in the Welsh hills as a youth. There were seminars on computer-generated music from a lecturer who related to me as he'd also been a mature student when he'd attended his university. Improvisational explorations with a tall, thin, chain-smoking rock guitarist dude, and musical cultures classes from a guy who dressed as though he was in an episode of Miami Vice. A fantastic range of subjects from an array of interesting teachers.

Rob, the course leader was so steeped in music it bled from his pores. His improvisations oozed passion, and he was a prolific songwriter…still is today. He'd formed a New Orleans style street marching band named Wonderbrass twenty years previously, so I joined the band and attended rehearsals every Tuesday evening.

I'd had some musical sightreading practice on the Chichester jazz course in the big band sessions but was still at novice level. This began to improve in Wonderbrass. I was playing my alto and, just as in Chichester, I was surrounded by many other saxes, trumpets, trombones, clarinets, electric bass, and drums. Rob would be there in the centre calling the tunes, stopping us all when things weren't going well, giving advice on which scales to use when improvising on certain songs.

I played Wonderbrass gigs for the three years I was studying at The Atrium and what a fantastic vibe we created. We played St. David's Day parades, Cardiff Castle gigs, restaurant openings, Stop the Cuts demonstrations, all manner of street events. We also recorded lots of material at The Atrium, taking advantage of its superb recording studios.

I also joined a ska band one of the Wonderbrass saxophonists was a member of, not on sax myself but on guitar. I bought a Hot Rod Fender amplifier and a slick walnut Gretsch guitar then joined them for rehearsals and gigs around Cardiff, the valleys, and at festivals.

This was my musical dream coming to fruition and I'd worked extremely hard to attain it. The hours and hours of practicing scales alone, memorising tunes, learning which scales work best with which chords, diving deep into music theory. A journey that had begun in borstal with a fifteen-year-old boy discovering a book on the rudiments of music theory. I was now regularly performing to large audiences in three different bands, working towards a degree in music, and couldn't be further from my former dysfunctional lifestyle.

I'll never forget the wonderful moment a neighbour validated the relentless hours' practice I'd put in. Whenever moving into a new house or flat, I'd knock on the neighbour's doors and introduce myself.

"Hi, I've just moved in next door and I play saxophone. Just wanna say if it's ever driving you insane or the kids are trying to sleep, just bang on the wall and I'll shut up, okay?" I felt it was the least I could do considering I was still a beginner.

A year or so later, I came out of my flat and saw a guy come running down the stairs.

"Is that you playing the saxophone?" he stopped and asked me.

"Yeah, man. I'm sorry…"

Before I could finish, he interrupted me, "Don't be sorry. It's really cool, like living on the Lower East Side or something. I gotta go. Just keep blowing that thing, yeah?"

And he left me standing there with a growing smile on my face.

I'd always felt an affinity with music. My brother and I would play my mother's Tamla Motown and Trojan ska records over and over until we knew every scratch or jump, even exactly where a song would get stuck. At the closing bars of any song, I'd know which song was up next. As with any subject I dig deeply into, I'd become obsessed, and I don't feel I'm exaggerating when I say music saved my life. Sure, throughout this narrative, I've proclaimed many times "the universe seemed to be on my side" or "this was the universe taking care of me/looking out for me," which may account for my not dying young as so many of my peers did. But my passion for music and my investment in every aspect of it was the vision that drove me.

I was invited to give a talk at Birmingham University's Department of Social Policy, Sociology, and Criminology a few months ago. The audience was comprised of mostly students from these disciplines, those who need to hear my story as they might be the future policymakers of this country.

The title of my talk was "Maintaining a Vision of a Future," and this encapsulates the ethos of that passion that saw me never giving up, never becoming too despondent in solitary confinement, singing in police cells and being beaten by the police for refusing to stop, wanting to smash a shop window to steal a saxophone, enduring the pain of blisters on my fingers from practicing guitar yet continuing to practice, often not joining my friends partying but rather staying home to practice scales on my sax.

Perhaps those I left behind in Farnborough and on the wings of different prisons never had an alternative to their lives of crime…no other drivers. In functional society, stakes in conformity are the guardrails that prevent backsliding into dysfunction. The family unit is the imperative that sustains functionality.

In socially disorganised neighbourhoods, however, it's often hopelessness that is the main driver. Hopelessness and no vision of a future. It's the difference between my fellow prisoners and junkies saying, "I can't wait to get back on the streets and bang up some smack" and me saying, "Fuck that, I can't wait to get out and have *no* smack." The former is a consequence of hopelessness while the latter that of hope and vision, a hope that was instilled in me by my mother. As I explained earlier in this story: my father inserted a chip in my brain that programmed me towards dysfunction, self-sabotage, and self-destruction, while my mother provided me with an insatiable thirst for knowledge…and knowledge is power.

29

When You're Smiling
(Louis Armstrong)

I spent three years studying at the Atrium campus of the University of South Wales situated next door to Cardiff prison. This irony was impossible to ignore because each day of those three years I would climb and descend an open plan staircase with a glass wall before me; a window into my former world.

I'd witness the familiar sights of the kitchen inmates pushing food hotplate trolleys across open yards, laundry inmates with the same style trolleys I'd manufactured in Portland borstal as a seventeen-year-old, screws escorting these same inmates and unlocking numerous gates for them. My former world played out before my eyes while I hurried from rehearsal rooms to classrooms, from lecture halls to libraries.

The time for me to consider work experience came in my third year of study and an inchoate idea had been forming in my mind, an idea linked to my former life.

I'd not mentioned my history up to this point as it had not seemed relevant; also, it might have compromised my being accepted by the university. Now, however, after having completed two years' study with no problems, my idea for work experience lent it relevance. I gave my course leader, Rob, a concise version of my delinquent, criminal, prison, drugs story and asked if there'd been any collaboration between the university and the prison next door. He replied there hadn't.

"Okay, for my work experience I'd like to gain access to the prison's learning department and teach inmates how to play guitar or piano, or how to use Pro Logic, if they have access to computers. What do you think?"

"I think it's a fantastic idea," he replied.

I contacted the head of Cardiff prison's learning department and was invited for an interview within a couple of weeks.

I arrived at the prison's front gate and, after security clearance, was provided with a visitor's pass. This hung around my neck on a lanyard, and it felt strange to be escorted by a screw within a prison, having gates unlocked then locked behind me in the capacity of visitor as opposed to prisoner, feeling on equal terms with the screw instead of being his charge.

I felt light-headed, and a real sense of destiny pervaded me. This was the beginning of something huge; I could sense it. The turning of the tables. Christian Austin on a path to helping those in the same situation he'd found himself during his formative years. I felt as though this could be the doors opening to an exciting career change, one where I could offer my own example to a new generation of prisoners, the example of possibility, of change...of escape from the dark cycle of crime/drugs/prison.

I continued following the screw. The hollow echo of the huge prison wing reverberated around us as we walked—so familiar yet so far behind me since escaping its clutches. A metal gate slammed somewhere, and the sound rattled and bounced all around the cavernous Victorian building. Muffled voices of prisoners shouting to one another from windows or through walls drifted down from the landings above. I could smell the terribly familiar smell of the prison kitchen's offerings and of bleached laundry in the air, the unmistakeable stench of prison.

We reached the learning centre, and I was handed over to the head of the unit by my escort who then receded beyond several locked gates on to his next duties.

Mrs. Dynes was a woman in her mid-fifties sagging beneath the weight of hundreds of rejected proposals. The years had etched lines of defeat into her face, the disappointment of meaning good in the face of a voracious monster more concerned with retribution than rehabilitation. I'm certain she'd arrived at the prison years previously with a bubbling enthusiasm at the number of lost souls she could save with her boundless energy and optimism. The same optimism I'd felt on the walk from reception to her office suddenly left me just as I guessed it had left her during her tenure.

I explained my proposal to enter the prison once or twice a week to teach music, and she seemed keen to have someone with my experience and history interested in trying to help. She explained the music programme was run by a third-party initiative working out of Bristol called Changing Tunes. She also explained how difficult prison access was to gain from the Home Office, especially for one with my atrocious police and prison records.

Once our discussion was complete, she led the way to the classroom. The walls between this classroom and the next were so thin that soundful music was forbidden so in the centre of the room was an electronic hub with an array of headphones spidering out from its many ports. Three young men sat around this contraption, one playing an electric guitar, another drumming sticks onto an electronic drum machine's pads, and another with a small digital piano. Mrs. Dynes explained the department had acquired this kit because of complaints from the next-door classroom. Each guy had a volume control, and a mixer ensured the "band" could all hear one another.

Across the room another student held an acoustic guitar and was strumming some chords quietly. Along the left-hand wall one other student was wearing a pair of headphones creating beats using a software programme on a computer. There was scant evidence of the interaction conducive to collective creativity I would associate with making music or being in a band.

Mrs. Dynes said she had to attend to some matters in another class, introduced me to the Changing Tunes tutor, and left the room. This guy explained the budget for musical equipment was small and that there was much initial resistance due to noise concerns. He said trying to get more funding from anywhere was highly challenging because the whole world seemed to be trying to get straight after the financial bubble burst. He invited me to chat with any of the guys in class and then went to check on the progress of the beats creator.

I pulled up a chair beside the acoustic guitar player and saw he was learning, *Wish You Were Here* by Pink Floyd (oh, the irony…I remembered learning the same in Dartmoor prison a lifetime ago). He was reasonably good and was stumbling on one part that stalled him each time, so he'd start at the beginning again. I didn't want to take the guitar from him and show him I could play it but rather encourage him and enable his progress.

"Hey man, I might be coming to join the class as a part-time teacher in the next few weeks. How you doing?" He nodded his head to indicate he was fine.

"Can I make a suggestion?" I tentatively asked him.

"Yeah, what?" he responded defensively.

"Why not concentrate on the part you're stumbling on? Practice that one bar over and over until it's perfect, then start again from the beginning. Seems to me you've got it perfect up to that point."

I sensed he felt self-conscious with me standing beside him so stood up and left him to his practice. I walked around the room looking at different posters on the walls—suicide prevention, bullying awareness, vocational training, support for quitting cigarettes or drugs—until Mrs. Dynes returned and led me to the prison reception. Before I entered the airlock, she explained how I could download a Home Office application form for gaining prison access then shook my hand and left me. I walked out into the sunshine with blue skies above me and felt a crushing weight lift from my shoulders. Jeez, I'd forgotten just how fucking dark those places were.

I returned to the learning department one more time after that first visit but couldn't get involved with the Changing Tunes initiative until my prison access was confirmed. A phone call from Mrs. Dynes explaining the Home Office had denied my application soon put a damper on my plans and I was back to square one.

Shit, I thought, *what the hell do I do now?* I had a 10,000-word dissertation to write, access to my research project had just imploded, and time wasn't on my side.

I eventually managed to circumvent this absence of prison access. After all, a dissertation can contain as much on the failure of research and its causes as it can on its successes.

Contacting the Changing Tunes guys at their Bristol office, I discovered they continued encouraging those they taught in prison post-release and was informed they held gigs in Bristol. I managed to complete my dissertation by attending one of their concerts in a Bristol church. I interviewed some of the participants and Changing Tunes staff and made a point of decrying the exclusion of one as experienced as me trying to help those trapped in the prison system.

The single most thrilling aspect of my dissertation-writing experience was a response I got from an email I sent out to one of the authors of an academic paper I discovered. The paper in question is titled *F*ck It! Matza and the Mood of Fatalism in the Desistance Process.*

This paper discusses prisoners' attempts to go straight after being released from prison. Most prisoners don't want to return to prison but are met with insurmountable odds from the moment they walk out of the gates. I'm not siding with ex-offenders in any way here, nor acting as their apologist; these are well researched facts.

Most prisoners lose their "stakes in conformity" —families, wives, jobs, accommodation—within the first few months of their prison terms. They are then, after eventual release, ejected onto the streets with little money and yet are expected to find somewhere to live, find a job, and never commit a crime again. After weeks and months trying their hardest, they say, "Fuck it" and return to their former means of making money whether burglary, robbery, drug dealing or shoplifting. Some might say they deserve this because they committed crimes in the first place, but this is one of the largest contributions to the 60% re-offending rate that leads to the revolving doors of more crime and more prison…at enormous expense to the taxpayer and further harm to society.

This paper really struck a chord in me…such a chord I sent an email to one of the authors. Of all the papers I read, this was the only one I responded to and, looking back today, this was another moment of synchronicity. I explained to the author what my research consisted of, a little of my history, and asked whether he or she could point me in the direction of any similar papers because I'd found it so relevant to my research.

I was very surprised when I received a response.

> Hi Christian, I was so happy to hear how much you enjoyed the paper I co-authored with some of my colleagues here at the Institute of Criminology. I was also surprised to hear about your research because one of my students—I've copied her into this email—is also writing her dissertation on music in prisons. She sings with King's College choir here at University of Cambridge and is taking small choirs into HMP Whitemoor and HMP Grendon with the "Sing Inside" programme.
>
> We are having a seminar here at the institute next month called The Subversive Good. Perhaps you would like to attend, and you could meet Kay in person and compare research notes?
>
> Signed, Karen

This certainly piqued my interest. I'd inadvertently contacted a professor at Cambridge University and was now being invited to attend a seminar there. Me, ex-criminal, ex-junkie, ex-prisoner, Christian Austin BA (Hons), being invited to one of the most prestigious universities on our planet.

A month later, I arrived in the city of Cambridge, parked my car, found the seminar room, and entered with moments to spare before the door was closed. I found a space to sit in the back row just as a choir began singing *a capella* behind me. I have no idea what they were singing. Perhaps it was Handel's *Messiah*? Whatever it was, these guys were top shelf. They finished singing and Kay leant down and asked, "Are you Christian?"

"Yes, lovely to meet you. Wow, that was…spectacular."

"Okay, we'll start the seminar. I'll catch you at the end and we can talk, okay?"

The speakers were interesting, Kay outlined her idea for the Sing Inside music programme and described its progress, there was a Q&A session, and then it was over.

I searched for Karen outside in the corridor and found her in the midst of a small crowd.

"Hey, Karen, thank you so much for inviting me here today…so interesting! Listen, could I grab ten minutes of your time before I head back to Wales?"

"You see all these people? They all want ten minutes of my time…"

She pulled out a piece of paper and began scribbling on it, "Here, this is my address. I need to pick my daughter up from school. Kay will give you the Cambridge guided tour—King's, Trinity, Queens' Colleges—and then come to my house in an hour. We can talk there."

"Okay, that's great. I'll see you soon."

I found Kay and we escaped from the throng then headed out into the warm sun.

We chatted as we walked, she answered my questions regarding Sing Inside and then switched to tour guide once we arrived at Queens' College, the first of several colleges she led me through. I was stunned by the architecture of the buildings, little changed over hundreds of years, dripping with archaic tradition. Punts filled with students and tourists lazily slid along the flat surface of the river Cam as we crossed stone bridges while many bicycles meandered in every direction through the crowded streets.

After an hour exploring the colleges, we parted company, promising to exchange ideas around our respective prison music research. I found my car and drove to Karen's house.

Once inside, she introduced me to her four-year-old daughter, asked me if I had any dietary requirements, then started to prep food while we chatted about my tour with Kay and the Sing Inside initiative.

"So, what about you?" she asked. "I'm interested to hear how you managed to turn your life around to the point where you're studying at Cardiff Uni. At what point did you decide to change...what drove you to that change?"

"That's easy. My children. Well, my children, yes, but also a desire to not end up spending my entire life banged up or dying in prison, and a feeling my life could be so much more..."

I gave her a short version of my life story and, at some point, was enlisted by the four-year-old into a game of tiddlywinks.

I finished my story and began another game of tiddlywinks then heard the front door open and Karen's husband entered with their son. After introductions, we all sat down and ate.

"Christian, you've an amazing story and you've done an incredible job in managing to claw your way back to life. I know because I research prisons and crime every day.

"I tell you what—do well in your degree and then apply to do a master's here at Cambridge and I'll be your supervisor. Then you can continue on to a PhD."

I was stunned and almost choked on the food I was chewing. Cambridge University? Me? Working-class criminal junkies from Clapham don't apply to study at such an elitist institution much less get invited.

But, then again, why not? Isn't this where all the study in every prison cell over all those years had been leading to? Wasn't this possibly the "something else" I'd always felt awaited me, the "destined for more than a life of drugs and crime" idea always lurking in the back of my mind?

We finished eating, I said my goodbyes and told Karen I'd do my best at my degree and would stay in touch with her. I then had a four-hour drive back to Brecon, enough time to digest both my food and the events of the day.

30

Just a Gigolo
(Louis Prima)

This had been a fantastic year for achievement and musicality, but my relationship had paid the price. Emma had moved to Bognor Regis in pursuit of her social work career months previously. Despite our breakup, she'd left me living in her house so I could complete my undergrad degree in Cardiff and be there for Liam. Confirmation had come through I'd achieved an upper second class with two prizes: Best Business Project and Best Dissertation of 2015–2016, and Cambridge University's Institute of Criminology was interested in me studying for a master's degree.

I'd also just spent a week erecting and dismantling the three-pole marquee at Into the Wild festival in Sussex as well as helping my friend, Michael, sell pizza all weekend. I'd returned with a full wallet and the knowledge I had nothing in my diary until the Glastonbury Festival in several weeks, when I'd be erecting more marquees. I needed to get away and figure out what was going on in my life. To get away from Emma's house with all its memories on every wall and surface…from Newport in general, because, without Emma, it had reverted to the shithole it always had been. And to celebrate the completion of three years' fucking hard work.

I packed some clothes into a backpack and threw them in the back of my Audi 2.5 TDI. Next, I added a sleeping bag, some pillows and blankets, my guitar and saxophone, and I was ready to set off. I said goodbye to Liam and told him I'd be back in a few weeks. He'd be fine; he had his own university work to get on with, and he'd love having the house to himself. His mates and his girlfriend would probably move in, and he'd have no stepdad on his case telling him to "stop playing that bloody computer game," tidy his room, and wash up his dishes. Things were never all that bad between us, and we'd been getting on much better since his mum had left—we'd get stoned together and watch movies.

I jumped in the Audi, fired up the engine, and pulled off, heading towards the M4 junction. I lit a spliff, wound up the stereo, and felt the bite of the tobacco and hash in my lungs. Mick Jagger was screaming "Let it Bleed" from the speakers, and I jumped straight in the eastbound fast lane as soon as I hit the M4.

I bought the car from a friend I'd been working with for a mere £400—an incredible price. The car was fantastic and, although twenty years old, it had a monster beneath the bonnet (a similar engine to the five-cylinder found in the old Audi Quattro). Before I'd split up with Emma, I'd sometimes leave her place in Bognor at three in the morning and take the car up to 125 mph along the M4. I'd be home in Newport within a couple of hours. I drove all the way down to Dover without incident and bought a ticket for a single crossing.

I've always loved the ferry across the channel and refuse to take the Eurostar for this reason. Under normal circumstances, I'd have hit the bar and sunk a few beers during the crossing, but I had no one to share the driving so I had to abstain. I pulled into the harbour at Calais, and I went below deck as soon as I heard the announcement on the tannoy. The ramp was lowered, and I was off, driving between the razor-wired fences of the Jungle that held thousands of migrants all trying to reach the golden-paved streets of the UK. I headed for the E15 that would take me south. My destination was Sète on the south coast close to Montpellier, and it was a thousand-kilometre drive.

The reason I'd chosen this as my destination was because of my previous love affair with this beautiful fishing port. The reader will remember my 1988 adventures when I'd left Andy in Toulon and then travelled to Sète and teamed up with Pierre Thiebault and then, later, with Markos and Mikhail. I had fond memories of the place and felt certain I could make a similar living busking the cafés with either my guitar or saxophone.

The drive took me the whole day with power naps in a couple of *aires de service* en route to ensure I didn't fall asleep at the wheel. I had enough money for fuel and the multiple *péage* (tollbooths) I encountered and then arrived in Sète late in the evening. I considered eating in a cheap restaurant but I was pretty shattered, so I made myself a bed in the back of the car. Being an estate, there was plenty of room for me to sleep, and I shared my bed with my guitar on one side and my saxophone on the other—a musical *ménage à trois.*

I woke up early due to the hot sun blazing through the car's windows. I threw the blanket off me and opened the doors to let some air in, but this didn't really help as the ambient temperature was also warm. I got dressed, grabbed my coffee pot and left the car for the shade of some trees. I'd parked close to the *théâtre de la mer*, close to where my friends and I had previously slept in the cave located in the cliffs below.

I drank my coffee and smoked a spliff, then went back to the car and grabbed my saxophone. I covered the guitar with a blanket and locked the car. Leaving the guitar in the car was fine, but the sax was coming with me. It's a 1954 Keilwerth New King, and I was terrified of losing it. I walked the twenty minutes into town and found a café where I had some breakfast and grabbed a wash. Feeling much more alive, I headed towards the town centre and looked out for familiar sights, but it had been almost thirty years since I'd last been there, so I didn't recognise much at all.

Sète really is a beautiful fishing harbour with many cafés along its terraces and promenades all advertising a delicious array of foods, especially oysters—*les huitres*—and *moule marinières.* Such a *cliché* but with good reason. I remembered collecting *les moules* from the rocks with Pierre and my other friends so many years previously. It felt good to be back here breathing in the salty sea air surrounded by the constant bustle of fishermen hanging and fixing their nets, winding rope around marine bollards along the quayside, and laughing among themselves. The sky was that beautiful azure so common to the South of France. Yes, it felt good to be away from Newport and the UK and on an adventure once again.

A few hours later, I approached a café in one of the town centre parks. There was a dry warmth in the air and people were sipping drinks and holding relaxed conversations, some smoking cigarettes.

"Bonjour, Mesdames et Messieurs," I said to the customers sat at the tables. Several people looked up from their conversation, and I began to play "La Vie en Rose" on my saxophone. I gently blew through the melody a couple of times and then followed it with an Eastern European tune "Talijanska" while meandering around and between the tables. I finished off with "Work Song," a jazz standard written by the cornet player Nat Adderley, soloed for a few choruses, and then went around with my hat. The people smiled and said thank you, and most of them gave me a donation.

Smiling, I packed away my saxophone and thanked the audience then walked off towards the shopping area to find a *boulangerie* and buy some lunch. Before I'd walked far, a guy with very curly hair and a huge smile fell into step beside me.

"*Bonjour, je suis Christian et je joue du saxophone aussi*," he told me, which translates to "Hello, I'm Christian and I play saxophone too."

"*Non c'est par possible—c'est moi*," I replied.

"*Non, c'est moi!*" this impostor retorted. "*Allez, on y va! Suivez-moi.*" The guy certainly didn't seem threatening at all, so I did as he suggested and followed him.

"*Tu parle Anglais*?" I asked him, as speaking in French would very quickly give me a headache. I hadn't spoken it for many years.

"*Oui, oui, un peu*," he said with the *oui* pronounced as "way" as they do in the South.

"Cool, so where are we going?" I asked this Christian.

"Come, I will show you. Have you cigarette?"

I passed him one and lit his and then my own and we continued walking.

"You are from London?" he asked.

"Yes, London," I agreed. It's often easier not to get into specifics when there's a language barrier. I may even have told him I was also from *Pays de Galles*, which is French for Wales.

Christian turned into a doorway and walked up a few stairs. I followed him and we entered a small bar and the bartender said "Salut" to him and they kissed one another on the cheek. The bartender nodded and smiled at me, and Christian ordered.

"Deux Pastis sans glace."

Ok, fine. Pastis is one of those aniseed-flavoured drinks the French love so much and I don't mind it at all. We grabbed the drinks and went outside to sit at a table in the sun. Another cigarette was asked for, and I handed my new friend the tobacco and cigarette papers.

This was the way I always love to travel—purely by chance. We had a couple of drinks at the bar and then Christian asked if I wanted to come back to his place and eat. I said, "Sure," so we walked back to the seafront and along the top of the cliffs past my car. Christian even offered to carry my saxophone case for me. I thanked him but I wasn't going to hand my vintage sax to someone I'd only known for a few hours. It turned out his place was only a mile or so beyond where my car was parked. He lived in a small apartment on the ground floor and the place had the ambience of a Bristol squat. There were beer cans everywhere and he certainly didn't have a cleaner.

There was a saxophone on one wall that looked like it had been driven over and flattened. It really was an eye-catching *object d'art*—fantastic. I asked what had happened to it and he said he'd smashed up an old saxophone specifically to hang it up as art. Very cool. I asked him where his saxophone was, and he replied he didn't have one at the moment. That kind of set off alarm bells in my head, and I made a quick mental note to keep my own very close to me.

It's interesting what a fantastic judge of character I had become after all the care homes, borstals, prisons, and the drug scene. To this day, I can tell within a few seconds whether I'm faced with a friend or a foe. It was about survival in my formative years, and it's all about survival when travelling alone in foreign lands, going to places with new people I'd meet, and generally having half an eye on all my stuff and the nearest exit at all times.

I didn't feel Christian was going to steal my saxophone—after all, he evidently did live in this place and had freely shown me where it was. But my guard was still always up, and I'd need to ensure I didn't get too stoned or drunk as that could leave me vulnerable. My saxophone was expensive and was also my only means of survival there in Sète.

Christian cooked some dinner for the pair of us, and we shared a bottle of wine then he suggested we go to a late-night bar along the beach. *Local people, local knowledge*, I thought. This was the way to do it.

The bar was fantastic. It was very busy and the music was loud, lots of vibrant youngsters loving life. The surf wasn't far off and could be heard whenever there were lulls in the music and raucous conversation. Beautiful! I could feel myself relaxing. I'd just worked so hard for the past three years. Christ knows how many essays and assignments. I'd not got over the break with Emma yet—that was still really raw even though it had been four months ago. Then there was the drive nonstop from Wales all the way down to the South of France; it felt good to relax.

I walked away from the bar and into the darkness closer to the sea to pee in the sand. I could see Christian laughing with some friends at the bar behind me. Spliffs were being freely passed around, and the beer was flowing. I could hear the crashing of the waves and dimly see their white crests. The wind was blowing my dreadlocks across my face, and I simply smiled. I smiled and felt the alcohol and the weed coursing through my veins, and it felt a good time to express my gratitude for all of this—all the things I had going for me. *Life! Life! Life*, I thought. *Thank you, Universe. Thank you for saving my sorry ass from the same fate as all my friends years ago. Thank you for giving me the strength and power to endure all the travails of my life. Thank you! For the good and for the bad, all of which have moulded me into the man I am this evening pissing on this beach.*

I zipped myself back up after my prayers and headed back towards the revelry at the bar. Christian saw me coming and came over.

"Play some saxophone, man. The barman wants you to..."

"No problem. I'll play along to this...it's cool."

I took my case and opened it, put my neck strap on and hooked the sax to it. I blew a few notes to find the key of the song and then began to blow, softly and slowly at first, complementing the music blasting from the big sound system. People began to notice a change and then some saw me playing. Yes, this was where the magic happens. I blew some more and a whoop went up. Here we go! I found a groove and played for the crowd, enjoying the looks on the faces of the crowd and the smile of the bartender. This was good for business, and I knew I wouldn't need to pay for beers or spliffs for the rest of the evening here. The wandering minstrel. The entertainer. The magician of sound. This is what I loved living for so much.

We stayed until the bar was almost closed and then Christian and I ("C'est moi!"—"Non, c'est moi!") walked back along the beach the way we'd come. The moon was lowering. We'd stayed out late and the downside to that would be the sun blazing through the car windows in the morning, turning my Audi into an oven. Christian and I said our goodnights. I thanked him for a great evening and said I'd catch him the next day at the same bar.

I was right about the sun. I woke early and had to get out of the car and find some shade. I didn't feel great, that's for certain. I'd probably only managed four hours' sleep. I made some coffee with my trusty little camping stove and stovetop coffee maker, cleaned my teeth, and then grabbed my sax and headed for Sète town centre to find a café to sort myself out. Once I'd had a wash and a light breakfast, I returned to the same café as the previous day and earned some money playing music. A second café gave me enough money to keep me going until the evening, so I hung out in the shade of a park and met a guitarist. We knew some of the same tunes and jammed for a while before he had to leave. He went his way and I went mine, and we were never to meet again, which is the wonderful nature of such spontaneous and transient musical moments.

I met Christian again in the same bar that afternoon and he took me to a BBQ in a friend's back garden. There were lots of different people eating, drinking, and mingling, and I played saxophone for them on a stage that was a permanent feature in the garden. A couple of guitars came out and we played some music together. I think I played some guitar and Christian played my sax. There was mention of a gig in a bar that evening and it was decided we'd move on to there after the BBQ. Some people with children left early, and then a very merry group of us left the house and walked along the streets singing, smoking, and drinking.

I remember the venue was very hip with a cool band. Another thing I remember is a portrait artist sat outside the place. He drew a very good sketch of me, which I still have today.

Someone mentioned there was a saxophone in the house, so the band asked me if I'd like to play.

"*Bien sur*," I said. "Of course." And I played a few tunes with them. Christian was blown away and couldn't believe how well I played. Obviously, that left me feeling great, and I explained to him that was really my *forte*—playing with live bands. He'd only heard me play tunes from my repertoire and on the beach a couple of nights previously, playing along to dance music. The band slowly wound down then so did the evening, and everyone said their goodbyes. I walked back through the town towards the harbour with Christian and he suggested we go back to his for a smoke. A perfect way to end the evening.

I stayed the night on Christian's sofa as I was pretty stoned, and it was preferable to walking back to the car. The next morning, we awoke, and Christian went to the shop and came back with some super strong beer. He offered me a can, but I declined as I'm not keen on waking up first thing and drinking. I'm not a Quaker, as I'm sure my tale so far attests to, but I also needed to keep an eye on my compulsive behaviours so they didn't run away with me again; waking up and drinking alcohol is not a great idea.

We left Christian's apartment and headed back towards the town centre. Christian had some stuff to attend to, so I stopped at my car and he continued on towards Sète town. I went through my usual morning ritual of coffee and teeth-cleaning and then sat in the shade drinking coffee and smoking a cigarette.

I saw a car pull over to the roadside a hundred yards ahead and two girls got out. They headed to the back of the car, got a suitcase out, and then one girl got back in the car and drove away. The girl with the suitcase walked back along the road towards me and, when she got closer, asked if I was driving to Cap D'Agde. She was wearing shorts and big sunglasses, had curly black hair to way below her shoulders and was pulling this enormous black suitcase. I didn't think she looked French. I told her "sorry" in reasonable French and said I wasn't going anywhere so she thanked me, crossed the road, and stuck her thumb out, waiting for an "autostop."

I continued sipping my coffee and smoking my roll-up. Then I boiled some water and had a shave, using the car's wing-mirror to see my reflection. I finished shaving, cleaned up the equipment and was then ready to lock the car and head back into town. I noticed the dark-haired girl was still standing with her thumb out and, on the spur of the moment, I shouted over, "*Hey, Allez! On y va,*" which, roughly translated, means, "Hey, let's go!"

I remember thinking to myself, "Do you wanna get stuck in this town with a musician who doesn't have an instrument and drinks the French equivalent of Special Brew for breakfast, or do you want adventure?" I chose "*l'aventure.*"

"*Salut. Parle vous Anglais?*" I asked my new companion.

"*Si, si,*" she responded. "*Nessun problema.*"

Ah, Italian. But she spoke English. A good start.

I helped her get the huge suitcase into the back of the Audi, struggling with its weight.

"What's in the case?" I asked. "Your ex-boyfriend?"

"*Si!*" she replied with a laugh. "*Andiamo.*" ("Let's go.") And she climbed in the passenger side.

I got behind the wheel and asked where she was going. Now, this girl could talk a lot and her English wasn't bad at all—much better than my Italian. Her name was Isabella. She told me she was from someplace near Venice in Italy and that she'd hitchhiked all the way from there. Impressive. She'd hitched around a thousand kilometres. And now she said she wanted to go to Cap D'Agde, which is a bit of an expensive destination. I turned the key and pulled away.

"Do you smoke?" I asked her while lighting a joint and winding down the electric window. She said she did, so I passed her the joint after a few tokes. I asked her what she did for a living.

"I'm taking shoe samples to different shops, trying to gain sales so I get some commission. I decided to hitchhike to save money, but now rain is forecast for the next three days."

I looked out of my window and gestured to the sky with an inquisitive look on my face. It must have been thirty degrees with no sign of a single cloud. She passed me back the spliff and said she hoped it stayed like this too.

I followed her directions to a swanky-looking hotel and parked the car, then helped her get her suitcase out. She offered to buy me a beer, so I agreed and followed her and her suitcase. The bar was the first place we came to with palm trees and tables beneath rush leaf parasols. I said I'd grab a beer and wait for her while she checked in.

A waiter came and took my order. I made a cigarette and checked my surroundings—it was a very nice place with a sense of class to it. Not somewhere I'd be able to afford at that post-student stage of my life. Perhaps back in the crooked days, yeah. I sipped on my beer and blew smoke into the air when I saw Isabella coming my way.

"It's so expensive," she said and told me the price of a room.

"Why's it so expensive?" I asked her.

"It's a nature beach where you can sunbathe without clothes on, but it's too much money."

"Yeah, my beer was eight euros," I told her.

"Okay, I'm going to check back out," she said and sauntered off again.

She returned with the big black suitcase ten minutes later and suggested we find a different beach, one where we didn't have to pay for the privilege of being naked. I was easy—I was on holiday and had no plans at all. After a few miles, we pulled over and found our very own private beach. It was empty, and we were skinny-dipping and laughing our heads off within minutes. This girl was crazy and didn't give a damn about getting naked. I didn't mind either so long as she was the right kind of crazy.

There are many different types of crazy.

We sat back down on the beach, and she held up a towel to shield me from the wind so I could roll a spliff. I'd made sure I'd brought plenty of hash with me before leaving England. There's nothing worse than arriving in a foreign country only to discover the only stuff you can get isn't up to standard. While we smoked the spliff together, Isabella asked me a question.

"You know you said you're up for adventure?"

"Ye-ees," I replied uncertainly.

"Well, how about you become my chauffeur? It's going to rain for three days, and I have stuff that I need to do in Toulouse then Perpignan and then Marseille. You drive me and I'll pay for the fuel, hotel room, food, and drinks."

"Why didn't you say so sooner? And I'll supply the hash and you can roll the spliffs while I drive. Done, it's a deal."

We agreed this was a plan and I was blown away that, as per usual, the gods were smiling on me. We drove back to Sète, where Isabella said she'd treat me to *les huitres* (oysters) as I'd mentioned I'd never tried them before. I parked the car back in the free parking space where I'd first seen her, then we walked to the harbour and had lots of oysters. Seriously, lots. Fantastic, and it was only lunchtime. I felt as though I'd known this crazy girl for weeks.

After we'd eaten, Isabella said she had to be in Toulouse the next day and asked if I could drive there right away, saying we could stop somewhere and find a hotel *en route*. No problem. We put Sète behind us, I said goodbye to Christian in my mind and wished him all the best, but I'm guessing he's probably still drinking super strong beer for breakfast each day. *Adieu, mon amie!*

We followed the sun and drove west in the direction of Toulouse, my old favourite from back in '88 where I had fond memories of Place Wilson and Place St. Georges, and where I'd cut my teeth busking at the tender age of twenty-four years. *Wow, twenty-eight years ago*, I thought. *Where'd the time go?*

Isabella was rolling spliffs while I drove and not telling me all that much about herself. I didn't discover until later that she had a big secret, and I'm amazed she didn't reveal it to me in the car during all the hours we drove together; she was actually famous.

We pulled off the autoroute slip road for Carcassonne, and Isabella found a reasonably priced hotel for us to stay the night using her mobile phone. I pulled the car into the hotel car park, then we both went inside, leaving the suitcase in the car. I brought my saxophone case in with me but left the guitar hidden beneath a blanket.

After showering, we headed for the main part of town and checked out the watchtowers and the double-walled fortifications. The sky was dark but the whole town was floodlit, which looked amazing. I now have a good friend who grew up there, and I get her point that it wasn't a great place to be raised—it's simply great for tourists.

We found a café serving Middle Eastern dishes, and I had an exquisite couscous dish with lamb and harissa. We had some beers with our dinner and then smoked some hash at the table, which was outside the front of the restaurant. The proprietor didn't mind, and I remember his chef or waiter joined us for a smoke. It was a nice balmy evening, and Isabella and I were pretty tired. It had been an incredibly full day. We said goodbye to the proprietor and his workers and headed back to the hotel.

I was in the double bed first because Isabella took forever in the bathroom. Then she climbed into bed and said, "There's a line down the middle of this bed, okay?"

Great. The same thing had been going through my own mind—Isabella seemed lovely and was as full-on as myself, but she wasn't my type at all.

"*Si, si. Tutto bene. Dorme bene,*" I responded, and I quickly fell asleep with a big smile on my face. I liked my new friend.

The morning brought another beautiful day with the sun already warming the room when we awoke. We had a quick breakfast of coffee and croissants then headed towards Isabella's first destination, a hunting store in Toulouse. I waited outside in the car park while she went in to exhibit her shoe samples.

I was feeling fantastic sat in my Audi surrounded by bright sunlight, blue sky, and the warmth of the Mediterranean air. I wound the stereo volume up and smiled while marvelling at how fantastic my life had become. I really felt blessed more and more each day and thought back to my fucked-up heroin and crack years. The freedom and happiness I'd discovered since then had exponentially become more magical. Sure, there were ups and downs, as there are in everyone's lives, but there now seemed to be mostly ups. Was this simply because my life had got so much better? Or was it because I'd changed my perspective and was therefore more able to deal with stress with greater maturity? My frame of reference most certainly helped; the constant knowledge that I was no longer dependent on heroin or crack, no longer in prison, and didn't have half a county's police force searching for me always lifted my spirits and dispelled any sense of doom around anything. Now here I was in the South of France once again with no idea of what today or tomorrow might bring. Pure spontaneity and freedom. I flicked the end of my spliff away and patiently waited for Isabella's return.

She exited the building with her huge black suitcase in tow, checked both directions for traffic, and crossed over to my side of the road. I climbed from the car and opened the boot and slung her case into the back for her.

"How'd it go?" I asked.

"Yeah, it was okay. They are going to place some orders soon. Okay, we go to Perpignan now, yes?" she asked. We got back in the car, and I gave her all the gubbins to make a spliff.

"*Perfetto. Andiamo.*" I impressed her with my perfectly accented Italian.

"What's this music?" she asked while sticking some cigarette papers together.

"Leningrad," I informed her. "My favourite band. From St. Petersburg in Russia."

She didn't seem all that impressed with my musical choice, and in fairness, Leningrad do sound like a gang of Orcs teamed up with John Barry's horns.

I pulled away and headed back out to the ring road. The sign for Perpignan said it was roughly two hundred kilometres, so I relaxed into the drive. Isabella explained that the owner of the shop there was more a friend than a client and that she hadn't seen him for almost a year. Her English was pretty good, which was fortunate because, had we been reliant on my Italian, we wouldn't have communicated much at all. We discussed our respective families and friends, and I told her some of my history. She started to joke that she'd been picked up by an English psychopath, and I had to remind her I hadn't been all that keen to pick her up in the first instance and that psychopaths probably weren't that fussy. She said she came from a city named Vicenza, an hour west of Venice.

I pulled up outside the shop in Perpignan, and Isabella indicated I should follow her into the shop. She introduced me to her friend, Nicola, once inside, and I mooched around, checking out the hunting paraphernalia while they discussed business.

There were guns everywhere. Guns and knives. All kinds of rifles and automatic pistols, shells, different-sized knives, knuckledusters, hunters' jackets and trousers, and boots and hats. A bazaar for every hunter's needs. I'd never been to such a shop previously so was intrigued and hardly noticed Isabella and Nicola calling me over. They'd finished their business, and it was time to go. Nicola set the alarm, locked the doors, and then pulled the shutters across.

"*Bene*," said Nicola, "let's get some beers." We hit a store, and he bought a pack of beer and handed Isabella and me a bottle each. We found somewhere to sit and make a spliff, then continued chatting. It was still a nice evening, and Nicola said he could chill for a while before having to head home to his wife and child.

We finished smoking and drinking, said goodbye to Nicola, and then returned to the car. Isabella said Marseille was next but it was three hundred kilometres away, so she searched for a hotel on her mobile and we drove there. This time, we had a twin room, so no need for imaginary lines in the middle of a double bed. We agreed on not getting up too early as the traffic would be bad, so we enjoyed a lie-in. This hotel had a pool so, when we did eventually get up, we had a swim, then some coffee and breakfast, and were heading east on the autoroute by around ten.

I remember the traffic was still terrible. Most of the way there, we were driving very slowly. I don't recall why it was so bad. What I do remember, however, is entering Marseille at the beginning of afternoon rush hour around three o'clock, and this meant that by the time we found the shop Isabella needed to visit, it was closed.

Okay, no problem. She wasn't too fazed by this. We found a wonderful restaurant to eat at, and Isabella ordered a huge platter of *fruit de mer* to share with a nice red wine, Chateauneuf du Pape, one of my favourites.

We finished eating and then went outside so we could smoke. There were a couple of girls giggling and having far too much fun at a table close to us, so we joined them and were soon smoking and drinking together. They were local and spoke some broken English, so between my Franglais, Isabella's Fritalian, and English, we had a whale of a time together. We finished our drinks, exchanged contact details with the girls, left the restaurant, and walked to the car.

Having missed the store in Marseille, Isabella's working trip was at an end. Now she was concerned with getting home to Vicenza in time for a party. She explained she'd missed her sister's last two parties and that there was another in two days that she felt obliged to attend. She asked me if I'd mind driving to Nice next, where she could get a train direct to Vicenza. It was another two-hundred-kilometre drive, but I had no plans other than following chance and seeing where I ended up—so I agreed.

I headed north out of the city until picking up the A8 autoroute, direction Nice. Isabella slept while I drove. The miles rolled by, and I kept my eyes open for speed cameras and cops although, being quite late, there weren't many police around at all. The Audi ate up the miles and I pulled up outside Nice's central station just after midnight. Isabella woke when the car came to a halt.

"We're here," I told her as she rubbed sleepy eyes.

She flung both arms out and stretched, then said, "Okay, wait here, please. I'll go and check out train times." She climbed out and headed across the road.

Ten to fifteen minutes later she was back.

"No good," she told me. "The next train is at eleven, nine hours from now. That's too late. I need to be at the party by then."

I didn't say anything and simply let her mull over whatever options she had.

"You want to drive me there?" she asked. "I mustn't miss her party—it's her first wedding anniversary, her husband's birthday, and a national holiday this weekend, *La Festa della Repubblica* [a celebration of the birth of the Italian Republic in 1946]. I'll pay for you to drive me to Vicenza and the fuel money back to here if you can do that?"

Incredible! I couldn't believe my luck. I said I'd happily drive her there and help her and her friends celebrate the formation of their republic and anything else they invited me to celebrate. It was more than five hundred kilometres to Vicenza and the satnav said it was a six-hour journey; we'd need to take turns driving to get there in time for the party. I pulled away from the train station and drove east, following signs for Sanremo and Imperia. Isabella and I chatted and smoked while I kept my foot down on the accelerator. The Audi was doing really well for a twenty-year-old car, churning up the miles with no effort at all. I'd always owned Audis, my favourites. We pulled up at the final péage before the Italian border, and Isabella once again handed her card to the teller. Then we crossed over and were in Isabella's country. As we progressed, we encountered tunnel after tunnel and often the tunnels were longer than the gaps between them.

We exited one of these tunnels and saw the sparkling lights of Genoa like so many jewels in the night far below and to the right. Miles and miles of tunnels were followed by tall mountains and ravines, which slowly changed to rolling hills and greenery. The light of the sun began to glow on the horizon before us, and it was time to swap roles. I slept while Isabella drove for some hours.

I awoke and it was daylight. Isabella was nowhere in sight, and the car was pulled into a lay-by alongside a forest. I sat up and noticed trees all around. Then Isabella returned from the trees and climbed back into the driver's seat, fired up the engine, and pulled back onto the tarmac.

I yawned and stretched and reached for some water to drink. I was hungry.

"What's the time? Where are we?" I asked her.

"*Buongiorno*, Christian," she said without even a hint of tiredness. "We have just passed the city of Milano. We have about two hours of driving left. Are you hungry?"

She'd read my mind—I certainly was, and I told her so.

"Okay, we'll stop at the next place."

I slowly awoke some more and reached for a cigarette. The CD in the stereo ended so I put something else on: Goran Bregovic's *Champagne for Gypsies* album with its raucous version of the Italian partisan song, "Bella Ciao." Isabella recognised it instantly, and we both sang along with the Italian lyrics. I knew them from memory as it was a song I had learned on guitar previously.

Three songs into the album and a roadside café with lots of articulated trucks outside it appeared ahead on the left side of the road.

"This'll do, pull in there," I said, pointing at a few spaces between the trucks.

I crawled out of the car. Stretching my legs, I walked about on the gravel car park a bit, then stretched my arms and tried to ease the aching from being cramped asleep in the car seat without respite for so long. Once I felt my true height again, we walked into the diner and found the place full of men, almost twenty of them. The only women in sight were the two ladies behind the counter. I scanned the menu for something I might recognise but no, not a chance. I let Isabella translate and describe what each dish was and went for some kind of sausage and chips with the biggest, strongest coffee they served. We grabbed the coffee—I loaded mine with sugar—and we found a free table to sit at.

The coffee was as good as I'd expected; we were in Italy, after all. Very hot and very strong. Exactly what I needed to clear the fog from the hash I'd smoked the night before. The truck drivers were pretty rowdy, laughing and joking with that camaraderie one finds in any familiar group.

The waitress shortly brought our food, and I attacked it with enthusiasm. I really was hungry. Within minutes, I'd polished most of it off while Isabella also waded into hers. One of the truck drivers smiled over at us with a "*buon appetito*" and I smiled back. We finished the food, and I made a roll-up. The truck driver who had spoken asked me something, but I had no idea what he'd said.

Isabella responded in Italian and the single word I recognised was *musicista*—musician. Then *sassofono*. I could see where this was heading, a special concert for a bunch of truckers. Great. Their ears pricked up at the word saxophone, so I went to the car and brought my sax in and played a few tunes, melodies followed by improvisation. The room went wild after each song. These guys spent the best part of their days driving all across Italy and Europe and their evenings parked up in places like this either sleeping or waiting for their tachographs to tell them their break was over.

For a stranger to enter their domain and start playing live saxophone was unheard of. They absolutely loved it. Isabella grabbed an ashtray from one of the tables and placed it in front of me. They all began dropping coins or notes into the ashtray and thanking me for *la musica*. I was having a fantastic time doing what I love most, entertaining people. I finished a song and Isabella said, "Go and get your guitar."

I did. I returned with it and began serenading them all with blues numbers and Tom Waits covers and, again, they went wild, and the ashtray filled with more coins and notes. When I stopped playing and put the instruments away (which wasn't easy among the nonstop calls for encores), Isabella went to pay for our food, but they wouldn't have any of it.

We made our apologies, explaining our urgency in getting to Isabella's sister's anniversary party in Vicenza on time, then jumped in the car and back onto the autostrada heading east.

"Thirty-seven euros," she told me after counting the notes and coins from the café. Not too bad for an impromptu gig that had left a café full of truckers buzzing with excitement.

"Whoop whoop," I exclaimed. "Skin up." I pushed my foot to the floor. "Next stop, Vicenza."

31

Ederlezi
(Patrizia Laquidara)

It was lovely to wake up in a bed with clean sheets. I wasn't able to relish the feeling for very long, though, as those setting up the party had already arrived with crates of Bacardi, plastic bags full of ice, and bushels of fresh mint leaves. The noise of their arrival had woken me.

I got up, washed in the en suite bathroom, got dressed, and headed downstairs, where I was introduced to Isabella's sister, Rosanna. She and a couple of friends had brought the initial provisions for the party—those things I've mentioned and around a thousand bread rolls and frankfurter sausages. This was a mojito and hot dog party. I felt amazingly good considering it was eleven o'clock; Isabella and I had pulled up at the house and gone straight to bed only four hours previously.

I helped with preparations where I could, and slowly, people began to arrive. There were probably twenty guests in total. Rosanna's husband was really nice, and the guests had obviously known each other for years. They were super friendly and wanted to know how I knew Rosanna or Isabella, and Isabella told them of our incredible meeting and the "thousand-kilometre friendship" from Toulouse to Vicenza, which they found incredible.

Isabella called me away from the crowd and asked if I could play something on the saxophone. "Of course I can," I told her. She primed me when the cake was being brought into the garden, and I came out of the house playing "Happy Birthday" on sax. There were two enormous homemade tiramisu cakes (probably a square metre in total), and it was the best I've ever tasted. Absolutely divine. Champagne and toasts were next and then more hot dogs and mojitos—spliffs and a jam for the musicians in one of the bedrooms upstairs. The party continued for hours, and once the last of the guests left, I helped Isabella tidy some of the clutter. We left most of it until the next day as Rosanna was due to return to help, so we shared one last drink and a spliff, then I went upstairs and collapsed on my bed.

* * *

After helping Rosanna with the debris from the party next morning, we visited a musician friend of Isabella's who lived practically across the square from her house. He had a piano in his lounge that I briefly played a tune on, but he was busy and kicked us both out. He said he'd see us the following day at a nearby party—apparently, he'd be playing there with another friend and asked me to bring my saxophone. I agreed, and Isabella and I stepped back out into the blazing Italian heat.

"Okay," said Isabella, "let us visit Patrizia."

During the drive from Sète, Isabella told me about her friend, Patrizia Laquidara, a Sicilian who'd lived in Vicenza since she was a child. She told me what a gorgeous voice she had, how she sang in Portuguese as well as Italian, and how famous she was in many parts of Italy, as well as in Portugal and Brazil.

Patrizia lived in Vicenza proper, whereas Isabella's house was in a small town on its outskirts called Malo. We jumped in the Audi and headed for Vicenza's town centre, and I pulled the car up where Isabella directed me. After entering Patrizia's garden through a large set of double doors set in a stone archway, Isabella pressed a bell.

The door opened after a short pause and Patrizia stood there, smiling and moving her head from side to side to look at each of us in turn. My immediate impression was she was charming, and I guessed she was probably in her mid-forties. She had an impish air, was very pretty and, I would soon discover, extremely talented. She was dressed casually, as if she had neither plans to entertain guests nor to venture outside.

"*Ciao, Isabella.*" Patrizia spread her arms wide, and Isabella moved towards her. They kissed one another on each cheek and then Isabella turned and introduced me in Italian; Patrizia spoke almost no English.

"Patrizia, this is Christian, who has driven me all the way from Toulouse so I could be at my sister's first wedding anniversary party. He is a musician."

"*Ciao, Christian,*" said Patrizia, kissing me on both cheeks.

"*Piacere*" ("Nice to meet you").

I noticed how small she was as I returned her kisses. She must have been a little over five feet tall, with a slender figure and eyes of the darkest chocolate.

Patrizia asked if we'd like coffee and we both said "Si, grazie" at exactly the same moment. We all laughed together, and Isabella said something I didn't understand.

I took a look around while the girls headed for the kitchen. This was a pretty big place and was quite quirky—I liked it. The walls were all pristine white and there was a skinny silvered tree branch covered in fairy lights hanging on the ceiling. Paintings were everywhere. I don't mean just on the walls; they were literally placed everywhere. They were on chairs, on tables, and sitting on the floor. It felt like an impromptu art gallery with many African scenes and images of African men's and women's faces.

"Wow, whose paintings?" I asked Patrizia. She asked Isabella what I said, and Isabella translated. They belonged to her housemate, who was an artist. I continued exploring all the different images while the girls chatted in the kitchen. There was a big glass door that opened onto the garden, so I went outside to smoke a cigarette.

I was called back inside, given a cup of coffee, and then followed them to a smaller room, which was Patrizia's space for making music. On one of the chairs, I saw an "At home with…" magazine with Patrizia's photo on the front cover.

There was a guitar leaning against the wall, and Patrizia indicated I could play if I wanted. It was a classical nylon string guitar. Perfect. I played a ballad and then something a little more upbeat and Patrizia sang along with the melody. Just as Isabella had said, she had a lovely voice with crystal clear tone, light and bright.

It was decided we'd head for the city centre and eat at a restaurant. Fab, my favourite sport. Patrizia said she'd drive, so once we finished our coffees, we walked through the garden and climbed into her white Fiat Brava. Isabella sat in the back, and I was in the front passenger seat. Patrizia opened the electric gate, and we were on our way into town.

The pair of them chatted in Italian and I had no idea what was being said. After a few exchanges, the conversation became heated and I thought, *What the hell are they arguing about? Shit.*

It seemed Patrizia was telling Isabella to do something, but I couldn't quite catch her meaning. Then Isabella spoke to me.

"Patrizia says I have to tell you something."

"Okay…" I said.

"She says I must tell you about myself."

Curiouser and curiouser, I thought.

"I was in the Winter Olympics as a snowboarder in 2002 and 2006 and also competed in a few World Cups. I didn't want to tell you this, but Patrizia insists. Now I have told you, and maybe she is happy."

"Wow, why didn't you tell me this before?" I asked her, confused as to why somebody would want to keep such a thing a secret.

"I don't know, it's embarrassing," she replied to me. Looking at her on Wikipedia now, I guess maybe it's because she didn't win any championships but, hey, professional snowboarding—to me, that was pretty amazing.

Patrizia parked the car and the three of us walked arm in arm through some narrow streets and then entered the *Piazza dei* Signori—this was another of those moments when I had to pause in my mind and compare it with my younger days when life had seemed such a permanent struggle. Now, here I was with these two lovely Italians simply enjoying life with ease. No heroin, no crack, no police, no threats of violence. Just total freedom, the balmy Italian breeze, and a beautiful girl on each arm. I grinned to myself and expressed gratitude to the universe without missing a beat.

We entered the square, and I was instantly and completely blown away. I'd say it was almost a hundred metres long and fifty wide with a huge pair of floodlit pillars at the far end of the *piazza* with a griffin-type creature atop one and a man atop the other. The sides of the square comprised many residential buildings of different pastel colours with Juliet balconies and many different types of lush green plants. There was a red brick arcade on my left-hand side and the stunning white stone of the Basilica Palladiana on my right, with an enormous tower at its end. This tower was twice the height of all other buildings and reigned supreme in the square, with a clockface halfway up and a bell tower at the top. Known as the City of Palladio (after its architect, Andrea Palladio), Vicenza is one of Italy's wealthiest cities.

Walking across the softly lit square on that warm June evening, it certainly felt like a wealthy city along with my life feeling an extremely wealthy one. Our voices were bouncing off all the hard stone surfaces, and Isabella asked Patrizia to sing something for me. She mentioned she was recovering from a sore throat or a cold but agreed to sing something brief.

I wasn't sure what to expect, but what came from Patrizia's tiny frame amazed me, filled the square, and stopped people in their tracks.

"Sa o Roma babo, babo,
Sa o Roma, o daje,
Eeeee...Ederlezi...Ederlezi...
Sa o Roma daje"

Patrizia finished on "*daje,*" and the vestiges of her voice bounced around the square then diminished into silence. I'd mentioned how much

I loved the Romani Balkan song, "Ederlezi," to Patrizia back at her house but didn't realise she not only knew it but had recorded a version of it quite recently.

A few cheers and a round of applause went up around the square, and I had the impression some of these people recognised this beautiful songbird.

We continued to the restaurant, and I had a wonderful dish of gnocchi while the girls had different types of pasta. Red wine flowed and we discussed different topics with Isabella acting as interpreter. After food, we went to a bar and sat on some steps behind the Basilica, drinking beer while Isabella massaged Patrizia's shoulders. I have a beautiful photo of this that I found recently when flicking through my albums—a beautiful moment frozen in time.

Patrizia didn't smoke cigarettes or hash, but Isabella and I wanted a smoke, so we went and sat by the river and Isabella made a spliff while translating for Patrizia and me.

Patrizia had been told a little about my Cambridge University offer and some of my early life story by Isabella. She was interested in how I'd successfully turned my life around to the point where I'd been accepted by one of the world's top universities and was also interested in how my children now were and what they were doing with their lives. I filled her in on all she wanted to know and then we slowly walked back to the car and drove back to hers to pick up my Audi. We said our goodbyes with lots of kisses on cheeks, and I drove home with the realisation I was probably a little in love.

* * *

The following morning, I returned to the town centre alone and it didn't take long to find other musicians—there are always many itinerant musicians travelling Europe in the summer months, so it's easy to find musical companions and jam together. This often meant differing levels of talent would join in, which was sometimes fine and sometimes not, depending on whether the object was to earn money or simply create a party vibe and have some fun.

The weather became too warm around midday, so we found some shade and began playing and dancing along a street busy with shoppers and outdoor cafés. Some people would join in with our dances and throw coins into the hat, while others would throw open their shutters and hurl abuse from above. This was normal. Playing during siesta could get you in trouble with the police as it was supposed to be a quiet time, but by two in the afternoon, there were maybe eight musicians singing and playing guitars, saxophones, a violin, and congas, many of us jamming jazz or popular tunes. We played some fantastic music together, in the streets and in restaurants.

I had to stop playing and go to meet Isabella, so I said goodbye to my new friends. They gave me some money from the takings before I parted, and we agreed to meet in the same street the next day—especially my two new friends, Michael and Nicolò, who were incredibly talented at playing gypsy jazz in the style of Django Reinhardt.

I found Isabella in the café she'd mentioned. I asked the waiter for a beer, then lit a cigarette.

"*Ciao, carissima! Come stai?*" I asked her.

She said she was fine and told me we'd been invited to dinner that evening by a good friend of hers named Peppe. Apparently, he was a fantastic chef, and I could park my car inside his place, which was a relief as parking charges in Vicenza were sky-high.

"Here is his address and mobile number. Just call him when you are parked outside his gate, okay, *carissimo*? Now, I need to go as I have a meeting with my father. I'll see you at Peppe's at eight this evening."

"Sure," I said, "that's great news. Thanks." And I sat back and enjoyed my cold beer in the shade.

I found the address without too much difficulty and pulled up across the street from the gates, then called Peppe's mobile number. Behind the gates was a tall, beige apartment block with green or red awnings pulled down over large balconies to keep the heat at bay. A dark-haired man walked onto the third-floor balcony and put a phone to his ear. At that exact moment, a voice on my mobile said, *"Pronto? Ciao."*

"Peppe?" I asked. He responded by pointing a remote on the end of his arm down towards me, which caused the huge black gates of his parking area to part. I drove over and found a place to park as the automatic gates closed behind me.

"Third floor," he shouted down to me, and I made my way up the stairs; the whole place seemed built from marble. Very plush.

I found a door already open, so I knocked gently, walked in, and placed my saxophone case on the floor.

I found Peppe still on his balcony, and we said *Ciao* to one another and shook hands. His English was as fluent as my Italian—i.e., not very—and, interestingly enough, we became fantastic friends very quickly as we shared a love of good food, wine, coffee, gelato, grappa, and music. And Peppe, it turned out, was all about food.

I sat at the large table on the balcony and accepted my new friend's offer of wine, then lit a cigarette and enjoyed the wonderful view from my seat. It turned out we were sat in the most expensive real estate in Vicenza. Hence my free parking and the gated compound.

* * *

I'd gone for a walk around the city and left Peppe to prepare for that evening's dinner. When I returned just before eight, some guests had already arrived and were mingling on the balcony. It was another very warm evening, and there was no need to wear anything other than a shirt. I checked in with Peppe in the kitchen but he was busy, so I stepped out onto the balcony and introduced myself to the guys who'd already arrived. It was four years ago, so I've little recollection of the names of the guests, just photographs that reveal faces but not names. They were professionals and not my usual crowd at all. Fortunately, I'm very good at mixing in all strata of society and one great thing about the language barrier in Italy, France, Portugal, Georgia (anywhere I travel, in fact) is my accent doesn't give me immediately away as it does in the UK—pure South of England working class.

Isabella showed up with some other guys, and Peppe brought the starter in. As expected, it was wonderful, some kind of roasted red and green peppers with balsamic vinegar and then a main course followed by different-flavoured gelati and sorbet. To finish, my favourite part of the meal: very strong Italian coffee and grappa.

We all got chatting over drinks once the food was out of the way, and the guys were asking me what I smoked. They were quite strait-laced, and just as they weren't my usual company, a musician with dreadlocks wasn't theirs. I admitted to smoking a bit of weed and made a spliff to share with Isabella. It wasn't long before most of the guests smoked too. This added to the tipsy ambience, and I got my sax out and played some tunes on the balcony. Great responses from all the guests and even some neighbours out on their own balconies. I remember us all having a fantastic evening, and when asked by Peppe if I wished to stay the night instead of returning to Malo with Isabella, I agreed. It meant I'd already be in the city to meet my musical friends in the morning. Fantastic.

After the guests left, Peppe showed me to a bedroom with a beautiful double bed and white sheets. I gratefully fell immediately asleep.

I woke the following morning, climbed out of bed, and headed for the kitchen, rubbing my eyes. Curled up on the living room floor in a sleeping bag I found Peppe. I couldn't believe he'd given me his own bed while he slept on the floor of his own apartment. Christ, these Italians!

I was playing saxophone with Michael and Nicolò's jazz band at a festa the following evening, so I decided to stay at Peppe's one last night. I was playing the festa in a small town named Marano Vicentino. First, though, one final party at Isabella's, one she'd invited a bunch of musicians to attend and play. It was a great night. Probably a total of eight people in Isabella's basement—it really could've been in any one of her house's eight rooms, but the basement had an open fire, and most importantly, a large piece of slate next to the hearth for cooking on.

Isabella played hostess, and us musicians took turns jamming together between drinking and smoking. We partied and played until around one or two in the morning, then everyone slowly began to leave. I hung around helping Isabella, but she was concerned I didn't get back to Peppe's too late as he'd be sleeping.

"Fuck it, I'll stay here tonight," I told her. "I don't need to be in Marano until the evening."

She agreed that it was fine, and I said I'd help tidy up in the morning. I was asleep in seconds.

I woke around nine in the morning, and my immediate thought was *Today I am leaving Vicenza*. I'd be leaving Isabella, and Patrizia, and Peppe and the hospitality of these wonderful Italians to drive back to the UK. I had commitments elsewhere, otherwise I would've loved to stay longer. I needed to make preparations for Glastonbury 2016 and my move to Cambridge to start my master's degree.

What wonderful people I'd met. Such a beautiful culture and such a warm and embracing people with a climate to match.

I had breakfast with Isabella and helped clear up the previous night's debris, then we exchanged big hugs and I told her I'd return the following year around the same time. She closed the door behind me, and I caught the bus back to Vicenza to see Peppe.

He was at home and my car was still in his parking space. Peppe rustled up some ragù and pasta and we drank some coffee and grappa together, then I chilled on his balcony all afternoon. He was busy inside the house doing some stuff on his laptop while I surfed the net and social media and posted some of my latest photos. It was incredibly warm, even with the blinds pushed out to their full extent, so I went to a store and returned with some chilled beers. Cold beer and spliffs while waiting to drive over to Marano suited me.

The time came to leave, and Peppe insisted we have one final toast of grappa to celebrate friendship. I simply couldn't argue against such a toast, so he poured a good measure for each of us, we clinked our glasses together, "*Alla nostra*," and I grabbed my sax and headed down to the car.

Peppe opened the gate for me, and I was back on the road. Next stop, Marano Vicentino and my friends' concert.

It took me ages to figure out the place I was looking for wasn't a concert hall, it was the town square.

"Of course," I said to myself, "this ain't the UK. It's totally bloody warm, it's not gonna rain, and the main stage is in the open air in the town centre."

I parked the car and headed over to where the stage was set up. There were many small stalls offering different Italian foodstuffs, a couple of bars selling beer, and the obligatory enormous Catholic church with its doors yawning wide open.

The sound techs were testing amps and mics and DI boxes and all that other stuff they do pre-gig, so I grabbed a beer and sat on one of the hay bales that formed the seating for the evening's auditorium. My phone alerted me to a message, and it was from the guys. They'd arrived. I found them ready to lug amps and other bits of kit to the stage and gave them a hand.

As the sun lowered, the uplights illuminating the buildings on either side of the stage began to do their work and, I must say, it was a very impressive effort. Purples and pinks mingled with different shades of blue and the stage was bathed in white spots ready for performers to do their thing.

Me and the band were chatting, smoking, and laughing together when a short burst of feedback announced something was imminent. I turned to see a guy on the stage with a mic in his hand. He mentioned some names I didn't quite catch and a duo walked onto the stage, one carrying a hang drum and the other an electric guitar. This was the first act, and my friends were on next, so I got my sax out and made sure she was in tune, ready for our performance.

The duo finished their set, which was quite mellow and mystic, and they left the stage to much applause and appreciation. My friends then climbed onto the stage and set themselves up—one double bass and two Selmer Maccaferri guitars. They began with "Limehouse Blues," a Django Reinhardt favourite. Very upbeat.

That's it, wake the audience up, I thought. The previous guys had been good musicians, sure, but now people were twitching in their seats and it wouldn't take long for them to get up dancing. Next, they played "After You've Gone," another Reinhardt classic. A few people stood up and began to dance where they were seated. These guys were amazing musicians and had all trained at the Vicenza Conservatory. It was there they'd all discovered a passion for the Belgian gypsy guitarist.

My Italian wasn't so bad I couldn't understand what was being said after that last song. Nicolò was announcing the meeting in Vicenza with an English saxophone player, and I made my way over to the stage and climbed up to join the band. The crowd's response sounded very enthusiastic at the word *sassofono* with cheers and whistles before I'd even landed on the stage.

As a band, we'd not had a rehearsal in any real sense of the word; we'd simply jammed on the streets together, but we knew a few of the same songs.

Once I ensured my microphone was working and got the okay from the soundman, the band jumped straight into the traditional Russian favourite, "Dark Eyes," one I used to play with the Don Bradmans regularly, so no problem. I jumped straight in with the head and stood back while Michael went into a solo. As he approached the end of his second chorus, he subtly indicated I was to solo next, so I stepped up to the mic and blew a couple of choruses. It went down really well. People were dancing within the confines of the hay bale auditorium. We played two more songs together, I thanked the audience and the band (just oozing professionalism right there; did you notice?), jumped off stage to clean my saxophone, and accepted a few compliments from some lovely strangers who enjoyed my work. Awesome, a great way to finish my tour of Northern Italy.

The guys played a few more numbers, then also got off stage and packed their instruments back into their van. The festa slowly began to wind down as people took children home and vendors and bars gradually closed. We grabbed a couple of drinks before they did. Adrenalin was high and driving home straight away was not really an option. It was still really warm, so we spent half an hour drinking and smoking together and slowly watching ourselves become the final stragglers. Then the last spliff was finished and we had big hugs. Again, I told these wonderful Italians I'd return next year, and we'd play together again. They jumped into the van and pulled away with a spray of gravel. Now I *was* the final straggler. Just me.

I walked to my car, realising this was going to be the first night I'd sleep in it since meeting Isabella when panic suddenly hit me. Fuck, I didn't have any cigarette papers. I had tobacco, I had hash and a lighter, but no papers. The whole place was deserted, and I couldn't....

But wait. A light. There was a light on fifty yards beyond the dark silhouette of the church, a light from someone's open front door. It looked like a dog had been allowed out for a moment. I walked briskly to the source of the light and saw a girl standing in a small garden before the house.

"*Buona sera,*" I said to her, trying not to frighten her. "*Carte per sigarette, per favore?*" I asked in my best Italian.

A guy came from the house to see who this stranger in the night was. "*Buona sera, sei un musicista?*" he asked me.

"*Lei parla Inglese?*" I asked.

"Yes, I speak some," he replied. "Are you a musician?"

"*Si, si, un musicista.* I played an hour ago at the festa."

"I thought it was you. Yes, I watched the performance. You want to come in for a drink? We're having our own little festa, it's Saturday night, no?"

The joy of being a musician. *Here I go again,* I thought. This was actually standard procedure for a musician in a foreign country. I could see tomorrow's headline all over Vicenza's tabloid press: "British musician kidnapped and forced to consume wine, beer, grappa and spliffs for eighth night in a row."

* * *

Yet again, I hadn't slept in my car but woke up in a comfortable bed in a spare room. I was up quite early and had a wash as quietly as I could because no one else was stirring. I made coffee and ate some bread, then left a thank you note on the kitchen table. It had been a small festa, and I had made up the fifth person. Nice guys. Even the town mayor had been there (a very young mayor, too, or perhaps it's me showing my own age).

I left the house and walked out into another beautiful warm and sunny morning. I got some *Qigong* stretches in before jumping in the car. I would be driving all day and wouldn't get much exercise done.

"Calais" I typed into the satnav. The machine told me it was a little more than 1300 kilometres and thirteen hours.

"Cool, let's go," I said to myself, and then gave Marano Vicentino a kiss goodbye through the open window. The mountains looked a gorgeous, lush green ahead of me as I pulled away and drove past the church. The main square where we'd performed the night before sailed past on my right, and I gathered speed, heading west in the direction of Milano where the route would then take me north towards Switzerland. The roads were clear as it was a Sunday. Most of the vehicles I did encounter were haulage trucks.

The wind gusting through my open window was delicious, a welcome antidote to the sun's heat magnified through the car's window glass. I made good time, and after a few hours, I saw a sign for Lake Maggiore. This was a wonderful surprise, taking me straight back to my reading of Hemingway's *A Farewell to Arms*—the part where Lieutenant Frederic Henry and Catherine Barkley flee across the lake to Switzerland. I couldn't believe the coincidence wasn't some form of providence working in my favour, so I decided I'd make the detour to visit this place. I had no idea whether I'd drive this route ever again.

I took a turn at a sign for Cannobio then drove towards this mythical place with mountains surrounding me on all sides. I wanted a glimpse of the lake to take some photos as well as find something to eat. Parking the car opposite a large and colourful market, I crossed the road and bought sliced pizza, then headed towards the lake.

Cannobio is a gorgeous town with cobbled streets and typical pastel-coloured Italian architecture surrounding the lakeside and sprinkled over the sides of the mountains circling the lake. Yachts and small boats were dotted about on the choppy water with many tourists and locals walking among the open cafés and restaurants along the promenade. The weather had changed, and the air was now full of brooding clouds and wind—so typical of mountainous areas.

I headed back to the Audi, climbed behind the wheel, and found my way back to the autostrada, where I picked up the satnav's route once again. Straight on—towards the Swiss border, which was only a few kilometres ahead.

32

Candidate
(David Bowie)

I was living in my truck and working in Brecon in mid-Wales after completing my degree and in my free time I did exactly as Karen had suggested. I applied to study for a master's in criminological research and began seeking funding. The application process had begun, and I have never experienced anything as complex and frustrating.

I had to write a personal statement, partly giving reasons why I should be included in the master's programme and partly a research piece, fully referenced. Karen and I pinged the draft back and forth until she felt it was strong enough to submit.

Next came Cambridge University's Self-Service account, which consists of several tick boxes. I would log in online and watch over six or seven months as each box was slowly ticked, one for application, another for degree certificate confirmation, funding, acceptance by one of the colleges. The administrator at the Institute of Criminology was an absolute angel who I shared many phone calls with. I'm not sure I'd have made it without her tireless energy and assistance. Finally, every tick box was filled, and I received confirmation I'd been accepted for interview.

I returned to Sidgwick Avenue, Cambridge, and parked my car outside Newnham College, across the road from the Institute of Criminology. I was dressed completely differently than I was when I'd attended The Subversive Good seminar—this time I looked much smarter wearing a suit, shiny black shoes…and my dreadlocks?

Fuck, what about my dreadlocks? I thought. *Well, they're a part of me and I ain't cutting them off, that's for sure. Just go in there and be yourself, man. It'll be fine…or it won't…ain't no amount of worrying gonna change a thing.*

This monologue was echoing through my mind as I walked towards the Institute building. I realised I was right: only authenticity would shape the outcome.

I walked in through the glass doors and the receptionist directed me where to go. I walked up a flight of stairs, found the correct door, sat, and waited. Before long, the door opened and a woman with blonde hair and an American accent ushered me in. She was one of my interviewers and was also one of the lecturers at the institute. She sat behind the desk next to a black guy who directed a disarming smile at me. They were both super friendly throughout the interview and did everything possible to make me feel at ease.

The American girl did most of the talking and began with a few simple questions. I sensed she was trying to gauge my mental acuity by the questions she was asking. The black guy said nothing. He was sitting there, quietly observing.

"So, what makes you think you're suitable for this programme?" the blonde woman asked me.

"Well," I began, "I'm reluctant to use the word destiny but everything that's happened in my life up to this point has seemed to lead me to this place. I spent years locked up in prison and all I did was study, both in the prison learning centres and in my cell. I taught myself how to write to a level that found me accepted by Cardiff University, and then I got a respectable mark in my degree. I sent one email to a random author of an academic paper, and she invited me to a seminar and then suggested I do well at my degree and apply to study here.

“Most people studying here at Cambridge University have probably always had an inkling they may study here. I’ve never considered it… until around a month ago. But, now I’m here, it’s like all roads have led me to this chair.”

“What are you doing sat in that chair?” This from the black guy, the first words he spoke to me.

I’d seen this in the list of possible questions when I’d googled “Cambridge University interview questions” and felt I’d already half-answered that earlier, so I shifted gears and asked a question I’d prepared.

“Hang on, I have the answer right here in my notes. ‘How do I go about becoming a lecturer in criminology?’”

They could both tell my brain was fully functional and sharp despite a lifetime of drug consumption and they also, most importantly, seemed to be on my side. The atmosphere eased a little and they asked me some lighter questions, about my funding and accommodation prospects.

With the interview over, the woman opened the door for me and said, “We know you’re having trouble getting funding together, but we’ll try and get an answer to you as soon as possible…hopefully by tomorrow.”

I’m not sure why but, to this day, I felt she was telling me it was going to be fine. I got a good vibe from that woman, and she soon became one of my lecturers.

33

The Only Way Is Up
(Stornoway)

"My name is Christian Austin, and I spent ten years in prison and seventeen years on heroin between ages eighteen and thirty-five..."

You'd be forgiven for thinking I was attending an AA meeting but, no, I was stood up in my first class at Cambridge University's Institute of Criminology.

I wasn't the first to stand up. Many of my classmates had already introduced themselves and what an incredible assortment of characters I'd be sharing my learning experience with: a police chief from Singapore, a petite and pretty public prosecutor from Bogotá...a South Korean girl, who'd grown up in Australia and excelled at a double undergrad degree in criminology and psychology in the US, a stunningly gorgeous half-Indian/half-Italian girl named after a character from a Puccini opera whose research was around prisons. I was among some of the top brains in the world gathered in this place to increase and share their knowledge.

* * *

I'd arrived in Cambridge early to organise accommodation in my college. I was living in my truck and would stay in it until things were sorted, after which I'd found a place to store it on a friend's driveway.

Interestingly, I remember the first time I saw Darwin College. It was a dark evening, and I was surprised at its modern architecture. I then headed for King's Parade and saw some of the more traditional colleges with much older architecture and eventually found myself in the Pickerel Inn, an old pub (with a history beginning in 1608) where C.S. Lewis and J.R.R. Tolkien used to meet and discuss their respective fantasy novels' progress.

I had a couple of beers then headed north along Magdalene Street and turned left towards The Backs. I pulled tobacco and rizlas from my pocket and sat on the flagstones across the river Cam from King's College. I could see the lights of Darwin College sparkling only a hundred yards away and knew my department, the Institute of Criminology (IoC), was situated the other side of the trees before me. What I didn't know at this point was this was one of the last spliffs I'd ever smoke; in a matter of days, I'd discover I needed my brain back.

* * *

I walked into the Porter's Lodge of Darwin College, University of Cambridge, for the first time in September 2017. The porter asked my name then directed me to the Old Library where registration was taking place. The first Darwinian I met was a girl from Lebanon who soon became a good friend. I was registered, my Cambridge email was set up, and I was given passwords to access the university Wi-Fi. I was then an affiliated member of one of the world's most exclusive clubs and was free to take a walk around my college.

I found the reading room where the daily broadsheets were laid out on tables and several students were reading from their laptops, headphones rendering them oblivious to my presence.

The Parlour is a remarkable sight and seems to have been transplanted from an episode of Downton Abbey. Well upholstered wing-backed chairs are scattered around the room along with small tables for tea and coffee cups. A large gilt-framed painting of Charles Darwin gazes down from above a fireplace. The house had been the residence of the Darwin family many decades previously until it became Darwin College in 1964.

The Common Room held wonderful surprises for me in the form of a piano, pool table, ping pong, and bar football tables. Adjoining the common room was Darwin College's bar—fondly known throughout the whole of Cambridge University as DarBar—where I would spend most evenings over the next twenty months either regaling fellow students with anecdotes from my life or letting off steam after a day of lectures, seminars, presentations, or writing essays.

Up a dark varnished wooden staircase to the Richard King Room with its laid-out tables and cabinets filled with trophies and Nobel Peace Prizes awarded to erstwhile Darwinians. Next, I walked through the servery and into the dining room. Large paintings of previous Darwin College Masters gazed down benignly from three walls while the fourth was mostly a glass wall with French doors opening on to a spiral staircase that brought me down to the college gardens.

These gardens are extremely well-tended and numerous events and outdoor activities are regularly held there. In May, the lush and abundant wisteria curtaining the parlour walls steals the eye of any passers-by. In the balmy evenings drinks can be bought and drunk beneath several canopies erected for both eating and drinking. Graduation meals are held in large marquees on the lawns.

During one of my first visits to DarBar, I met a student named Leah. She had auburn hair, long and often worn in tight plaits. Her cocoa brown eyes held mine with a frank yet daring gaze and she stood at almost the same height as me—that is, six feet. And she could hold her drink. We hit it off instantly and made a beeline for one another in DarBar most evenings after our first meeting.

Initially, I was uncertain about revealing my story to other students as it was galaxies away from the average Cambridge story. Leah was one of the first I confided in, and she congratulated me on my evident strength and sense of purpose.

"How on Earth do you not only survive a life like that but manage to land here at Cambridge University? And to study criminology? It's unheard of," she said, and I knew she was right. It *was* unbelievable and her response made me realise I wouldn't be pilloried for my chequered life story but would rather gain respect.

A couple of days later, I returned from my department to discover a book in my pigeonhole in the porter's lodge.

As I pulled it out, the words on the spine leapt out at me and my heart sank.

Borstal Boy by Brendan Behan.

The game was up. I'd been exposed, and in that moment, I realised my stay here at Darwin College might not be the cakewalk I'd anticipated. I slid the book beneath my arm so no one else would see it and headed for the reading room to sit down and gather my thoughts. I found the room empty, which served my purpose, and I took a seat.

I opened the book and saw a name written on the inside cover—*Leah Barber*.

* * *

"Jesus, Leah, I was completely fuckin' freaked. I thought some Cambridge toff had placed it there and it was the beginning of my downfall. Then I saw your name on the inside cover."

Leah was mortified and couldn't believe she'd inadvertently unsettled me via such a generous act. I informed her she was obliged to pay for my beer all evening and she happily agreed. More students were pouring into the bar and soon we were all laughing together and trying to forget whatever the day had brought. DarBar is the place to forget failed experiments; bad data; upcoming assignments, exams, or essays; the imminent PhD viva, whatever. There's a reason drinking's so ubiquitous in universities.

We continued to drink until the bell announcing no more beer was rung then Leah said she had to leave. Some friends and I had lined up a few beers at last orders so we could continue drinking for another hour. We said our goodbyes, she apologised once again for the book thing, and I jumped straight back into a conversation regarding the pros and cons of drug consumption in academia—i.e., marijuana, microdosing LSD, psilocybe mushrooms, etc.

"Nope, doesn't work for me," I piped up. "I was in the lecture theatre in the mornings thinking, *Shit, am I the only one in here without a brain?* You know, that foggy head thing?"

"It totally helps me," this from a machine learning student I'd met in DarBar several times before. "Helps me retain information, write my essays, even deal with my supervisor."

This was met with much laughter.

"Also, you know the guy who invented the PCR? He was a California surf bum dropping acid and smoking weed like there was no tomorrow."

My phone pinged at this moment. It was a message from Leah.

"Hey Christian, I've left my cardigan in the dining room cloakroom. If you get a chance, would you mind grabbing it for me?"

The evening wound up and I left the bar to find Leah's cardigan. It was dark at the top of the stairs, so I slid my hand along the wall until I found a light switch.

I switched it on and my ears were shattered by the sound of an incredibly loud siren reverberating throughout the whole college.

Fuck, I thought, *that ain't the light switch!*

I bolted down the stairs and exited the building as fast as I could, then made my way south along Silver Street heading for King's Parade but, ultimately, a late-night bar called Novi. I couldn't deal with the situation and took the only recourse I could in that moment—more beer now, worry about the fire alarm later.

I looked back along Silver Street and saw maybe fifty students, mostly in their nightwear, filing out of Darwin College to stand on the street awaiting the fire brigade.

Fuck!

I headed for Novi.

* * *

I awoke to the sound of an alarm in my head. I sat bolt upright.

The previous night came rushing back to me and I knew I'd need to confess my crime rather than await the inevitable accusation. I quickly dressed and headed downstairs.

"Morning, Nick."

"Good morning, sir." This was Nick's catchphrase. I'm not certain it was a throwback from his former career as a copper or an affectation adopted since becoming a Cambridge porter, but he never greeted me in any other way.

"I've a confession to make," I said sheepishly.

"A confession?"

"Yeah. Last night I was in the bar and Leah asked me to retrieve her cardigan from upstairs…"

I noticed a hint of a smile at the corners of Nick's mouth and wasn't sure how to proceed.

"I went upstairs, went to switch the light on and all hell broke loose."

"It's okay, sir. I know what happened as you're all over the CCTV footage. There should've been a pane of glass over the fire alarm, and it's been rectified by maintenance this morning. Perhaps next time you could report it to us here in the lodge? Have a good day, sir."

Whoa, I hadn't expected that. I'm not sure what I'd expected but this was fantastic.

DarBar was the most popular bar throughout Cambridge University with students flocking there from many of the other colleges. Monday evenings were extremely popular due to 'Recession Session' with many drinks only £1 rather than the usual £2.50. Tuesdays and Wednesdays were noticeably quieter with a quiz night and a drawing group then there was a gradual build-up from Thursday to Saturday. Friday evenings meant formal hall dinners and a sudden influx of tuxedoed, frocked, and gowned diners descending on the bar from the dining hall above.

However, socialising, and drinking beer were for evenings only. I was also required to study and have my head crammed full of knowledge. This was Cambridge, after all. I was studying for a master's in criminological research that meant my course was twelve months long. I could have opted for the straight criminology master's at only nine months but as I was to be involved in prisons research the course was longer. This was to account for the prisons access application, a very long and arduous process.

Darwin is an international college, and I learned there were 660 students from 76 different countries in my year (2017-2018 academic year). These students' lack of awareness around the British social class system granted me an anonymity that would have been absent in any of the more traditional colleges. Their friendships, however, now offer me the opportunity to visit them in countries as diverse as Brazil, Canada, Mexico, Australia, Japan, Singapore, South Korea, China, Vietnam, Russia, as well as most European countries. One post on the Facebook group—"Hi, I'm in Rio. Who's around?"—might find me being hosted at a friend's place there for a week.

Arriving at the IoC for lectures each day was the most exciting aspect of this whole trip, whether being taught criminological theory, organised crime, nodes of criminal gangs stretching from the mid-African continent and up through the Mediterranean, or even statistics. My penchant for learning had found its ultimate classroom.

My fellow students were all as enthusiastic as me, and there was never any stigma directed towards me due to my history. We were all in the same boat, rowing as hard as we could to the same destination of securing a master's degree in criminology, helping one another to achieve that goal, and then visiting one another's college bars to relax in the evenings.

I discovered there was a programme within my criminological MPhil called Learning Together that I could take part in if I wished. This initiative had been devised and created by Karen and one of her colleagues a year or two previously. It involved IoC students attending classes in HM prisons Grendon and Whitemoor where subjects as disparate as philosophy, theology, criminology, and history might be studied and researched by prisoners and IoC students together. The prisoners were able to achieve a degree certificate on successfully completing the course. The moment I heard about this, I wanted to take part in it. The learning department of every prison I'd done time in had been my haven, the place I always applied for during the first few days of every period of remand and every sentence and my subscribing to it felt like a full circle moment.

"Hey, Karen, can you put me down for the Learning Together programme please?"

We were in her office on one of the upper floors of the IoC and I felt completely relaxed as I always did around Karen. There wasn't a teacher and pupil vibe between us, more a burgeoning friendship based on mutual respect. The bookshelf behind her was stacked full of criminological literature with a healthy dose of theological tomes thrown in. This made sense to me as I'd learned Karen held a strong Christian faith.

There were some framed photographs of her and her family on the desk, one with winter clothing and a half-built snowman while another boasted warm blue skies and sunglasses. She caught me trying to get a closer look at the second photo.

"Turkey, last summer. I feel like I need another break, get away from researching and writing papers…

"Okay, Learning Together, yes. It's not a part of your master's programme so is what you might call extra work. Just a 3,000-word essay and the time spent within the prison classes, not too much. I'll need a copy of your criminal record for both prison governors to see before you're permitted access. I'm really happy you're going to join us because of your history; you'll be an example of what can be achieved post-release to all these guys still serving their sentences."

That evening, I searched for my criminal record in the Dodge truck. I knew it lay inside an A4 envelope because I'd received a copy from the police when Emma and I were planning on visiting her uncle in Sydney. I'd been granted permission by the Australian government, but we'd changed plans and taken the three kids to the Sahara and Marrakesh instead. I knew the envelope was in my truck…somewhere. I also knew I'd had a big clear out at my mechanic's yard near Brighton before leaving for Cambridge. A lot of rubbish, including paperwork, had been thrown onto a big fire in his back field.

"I think I might've accidentally burnt it."

"I need it by Friday otherwise you won't be able to participate." Karen wasn't at all happy I couldn't produce the documents and neither was I, but their absence kind of dictated subsequent events. I never did join the Learning Together programme and soon accepted a little less work in the midst of an excruciatingly intense twelve-month degree might not be such a bad thing. Sitting here today, carrying the knowledge of what transpired around Karen's Learning Together initiative a few years later, it's yet another example of the universe doing its utmost to insulate me from danger.

* * *

I joined Darwin College's music society and soon came to the attention of the Darwin College band, *The Galapagogos*, who seemed in need of a saxophone player. I was auditioned and I got the gig. This new opportunity was particularly funny because I went from playing jazz, funk, rock, and punk with the Don Bradmans, then jazz with Wonderbrass to playing with a band formed of guys in their mid-twenties. The choice of music reflected this consisting of a range of songs from James Brown's "I Feel Good" to Britney Spears's "Toxic," from Bruno Mars's "Uptown Funk" to Nelly's "Hot in Here."

Regardless of this diverse assortment of tunes we practiced long and hard, I learned the repertoire, and we had plenty of fun playing all the different college May Balls throughout the summer season. Free entry to the balls was included as well as financial gain.

I also joined the Darwin debate society but only took part in one debate, a debate that seemed tailor-made for me: "Us Cambridge Elites Will Never Understand the Working Class."

Only months prior to arriving at Cambridge, I'd spent the summer working with a friend, erecting marquees at different music festivals and weddings. I did this sort of work for ten years or so. Often these weddings are for married couples hailing from a similar social status as the friends I was now rubbing shoulders with at Cambridge. My friend and I were working and joking together when I suggested we ought to have T-shirts printed bearing the logo "Posh as Fuck Marquees." This never came to pass, but I did discover how easy it was to create my own T-shirt online and have it delivered so I designed and paid for my own "Posh as Fuck" T-shirt.

I then found myself leading a team of two in the debate held in Darwin College's Old Library wearing said T-shirt and defending the working-class corner. To my surprise, my attire was greeted with much good humour and laughter and, needless to say, my team won after I argued not one of them could ever understand the absence of a financial safety net after finding oneself and one's family living in a bus shelter two weeks after being made redundant.

The first six months of my master's degree were spent attending lectures, seminars, and classes within the institute. We'd been divided into two manageable groups, so I didn't spend as much time with half our cohort as I did with my own group. Also, at the end of these six months, we no longer had any lectures, seminars, or classes and had to read for our dissertations so no longer saw each other as often. I now wish I'd been made aware of this sooner because, overnight, I no longer saw much of my criminology student friends who were scattered across many of the other Cambridge colleges.

I decided to continue my focus on music in prisons for my dissertation research. At the time I felt a huge excitement in combining my love of music with its potential for rehabilitating those who had fallen foul of the law, were addicted to drugs, or just found themselves ensnared in a cycle of drugs, crime, and prison as I had been. However, I would soon discover a huge difference between those incarcerated in the West Country and those locked up in London prisons...and it had to do with gang and drug culture.

Gaining access to prisons in order to conduct my research was almost as difficult as escaping the drugs/crime nexus itself. Of course, that's a huge and flippant overexaggeration but, seriously, it was reminiscent of a game of ping pong with my supervisor who repeatedly returned the application form to me for revision and improvement. If it hadn't been such an important part of the process, I'm certain I might have given up the idea and changed my dissertation subject. But I'd already found a music in prisons initiative keen for me to research their programme. They were so keen they already had plans to publish some of my research on their website.

Eventually, I was permitted access to HMP Belmarsh where the music programme was being held and I once again found myself in a prison airlock after successfully passing security clearance.

A screw led me through a maze of corridors and my nostrils were soon assailed by the familiar smells of prison food and laundry. We arrived at the prison chapel and I met Sister Agnes, the chaplain, and Howard, the music programme leader.

"Hi, nice to meet you again. Hope the journey down was okay? I'm setting up ready 'cause the inmates will arrive shortly and then we can get to work."

Howard had the typically laid-back personality of many of the musicians I know. I left him to his plugging leads into amps and keyboards and turned to Sister Agnes.

"Hello, Sister, do you get involved in these sessions in any way or do you simply spectate?"

"Oh, my singing days are way behind me." She laughed. "I do enjoy watching the inmates spending their time working on this creative stuff though. They spend almost all day locked up in their rooms and the programme encourages them to write lyrics."

These lyrics I'd soon hear were all centred around drugs, BMW cars, street gangs, and "hoes and bitches." And, just as I had discovered in the Lambeth holding cells forty years previously, the London prison population consisted mostly of blacks. (Again, refer to Loïc Wacquant's *Punishing the Poor* and Michelle Alexander's *The New Jim Crow* for an understanding of these disproportionate number of blacks in London prisons; although written around US prisons and data, the principles also apply over here—prejudice targeting blacks over whites in 'stop and search' and assumptions of drug-dealing.)

The chapel door creaked open and the participants slowly entered, led by a screw. Twelve guys walked in and ten of them were black. I soon realised one of the two white participants was speaking with the blacks in Caribbean patois that meant in reality there was only one white guy among the participants. This guy would very quickly be excluded from the group due to his musical tastes not aligning with the rest of the group's—i.e., hip-hop and rap. The white guy with the dreadlocks seemed to be tight with the blacks and evidently had a rapport with them.

"Hey guys, come in, come in. We're gonna get some great stuff down today. You brought your lyrics with you, yeah? Linton, Ben, you wrote some more lyrics?"

Howard's enthusiasm was evident while the participants' energy seemed more lacklustre. They were taking their places sitting on chairs with small shelves containing bibles on them while nudging and pushing at one another.

"Okay, let's start with a listen to what we got down during last week's session.

"Oh, but first, hey, this is Christian. I mentioned he'd be coming to research what we're up to, yeah? He's here to take some notes and after a few weeks he'll interview you guys on your experiences within this programme."

I received a few cagey looks from a couple of the guys and I'm guessing my dreadlocks went a long way towards being accepted over the ensuing weeks. I tried to remain invisible, sitting as far away from the action while making observations in my notebook.

After listening to the previous week's tracks, Linton placed a set of headphones on his head, picked up a microphone then began rapping along to the music only he could hear. These were the lyrics he'd spent all week writing in his cell awaiting today's session to get them down.

Not all the lyrics to the songs that were created were about drug and gang culture although most were. I still have the recordings from my research and a few allude to tenderness, love and loss, or about a missed son or daughter at home. I quickly understood the guys' approach to the sessions was their common bond around black culture…their young minds gravitating towards the gangs and drugs that had caused their imprisonment. What had changed significantly since my own carcerative experience was gang culture had become ubiquitous within the London prison estate…and would likely migrate to other urban prisons.

While interviewing these inmates in isolation they were more prone to being honest with me, removed from the bravado and braggadocio exhibited among their peers and so a few confided in me. They said it was safer to join the gang once placed in prison than it was to refuse joining because of the protection it afforded. Without such protection, you might become a victim. There was also often an element of discovering many members of your street gang being on the same wings within Belmarsh prison so there was already a place waiting for you.

My whole research experience did nothing other than reinforce my belief that the UK prison estate is all about compartmentalisation, extracting the judiciary's pound of flesh for the offender's crime then spitting them back onto the streets with less hope and chance of escaping the cycle than money in their pockets when released. It is now far worse than it was when I was imprisoned during the '80s and early '90s. It wasn't in much better shape during my research in 2018. And today politicians speak only of more prison spaces needing to be built rather than placing emphasis on how to prevent the causes of crime—the whole purpose of criminology.

The participants in my research were all in their mid-twenties. This brings to mind the "age crime curve," which describes most offenders becoming involved in crime during their teens and then that involvement slowly fizzling out in their early twenties due to various factors including meeting a girl, settling down with her and finding a job, having a baby. There's a saying in the world of criminology: Today's prisoner is more likely to become tomorrow's father than tomorrow's life sentence prisoner. I'm hazarding a guess eight or nine of those participants have their alarm set for work tomorrow morning.

Just as I was finishing my research in Belmarsh prison, my eldest sister, Serena, died from lung cancer. Having been removed from the family home at age twelve, my relationship with both my sisters obviously changed and we became less close. As I became more and more embroiled in crime and drugs, I became an embarrassment to this sister and I'd sometimes meet her in Farnborough town centre when she was walking with work colleagues during their lunch break. I could see the look on her face as we neared each other, she with her swanky Diner's Club friends and I with my gaunt "skin care by Heroin" look.

However, we are family and had the same blood flowing in our veins. Over the years we didn't exactly become close but close enough for me to describe what happened between our father and me, so she had a greater understanding of the root causes of my dysfunction.

It had been around my birthday in January we had our last telephone conversation. I was wrapping up my research and getting ready to write up around July or August, I guess, so that call had been several months prior. I remember it was me who called her.

"How you feeling?" I stupidly asked.

"Well, you know, not planning any clubbing this weekend," she quipped. She'd always been into her jazz-funk weekenders, driving stupid distances to dance all weekend with her fellow "Saxmaniacs," as her gang was called.

I remember she asked how my master's/Cambridge experience was going, and I told her I was loving every minute of it, to which she replied, "Well done, you!"

I think we both knew it was goodbye as we never spoke again, and I'll always remember the way she said that "Well done, you!" It was a serious affirmation from her to me, a recognition of how much I'd turned everything around. Bless her.

The funeral was a form of closure. It was followed by a wake in her favourite pub where I met many of my old schoolmates who couldn't believe the news I was studying for a master's at "WHERE?!?!"

But, after the funeral once I returned to Darwin College, Serena's passing was affecting my ability to operate and function. I began sleeping in until 2 p.m. every day. I'd still hit the bar each night at 9 p.m. and drink until 1 a.m. but this because it helped numb the pain. I was supposed to be writing my 20,000-word dissertation yet all I wanted to do was sleep, eat dinner, hit DarBar, repeat *ad infinitum*.

It was Leah who came to the rescue. My old friend of the cardigan/fire alarm incident. She encouraged me to meet her at a different Cambridge pub each day around lunchtime and impressed upon me I wasn't allowed a beer until I'd got down 1,000 words. I have no idea whether I'd have completed my master's degree without this sterling assistance.

Thank you so much, Leah!

Next came submission then the waiting game. Same as my undergrad degree but way more intense—*You don't get accepted to study at Cambridge and fail!*

Right?

34

Out on the Weekend

(Neil Young)

Darwin College had loaned me a sizeable sum of money to ensure I could complete my master's. The combination of this debt and my love of the college, its bar, and the friends I'd made prompted me to ask the head of the catering department for a job serving food to all the college fellows, master's and PhD students. My friend who already had a position in the catering department encouraged me a fair bit, so when I walked upstairs from the bar and asked the question of the catering manager, he announced, "Ask me again tomorrow when you're sober."

Once it was established I wasn't joking and would seriously take up such a position others might find untenable, I was given a contract to sign, a waiter's penguin outfit, and was then taught how to stack a ridiculous number of empty plates on one arm while collecting more plates, knives, and forks with the other.

Many of the friends I'd made over the past year couldn't believe it when they saw me behind the servery, but I took it in my stride and then saw them in DarBar that same evening where we'd laugh it off over a beer or two.

The singular thing about my new position though was I'd not only serve food and wine and collect empty plates at formal dinners in my penguin outfit, but I'd also attend them wearing a tuxedo and bow tie!

While serving my friends wine at the table, they'd encourage me to misbehave by allowing me to drink the wine from their glass while "keeping dog" for the catering manager. I'd often feel quite tipsy collecting the dishes and serving the cheeseboards before joining my friends in DarBar downstairs after the formal clear-up.

This remaining at Darwin College had an added benefit when the 2019 cohort of new students arrived as it meant I doubled the number of Darwinian friends I had. It also meant I was offered the position of Food Officer for the 2019 Darwin May Ball. I'd thoroughly enjoyed the 2018 Ball, had played a fantastic set with The Galapagogos, and had enjoyed the food and beer immensely but had nothing to do with its organisation. 2019 was different.

I guess it came about simply because I was working in the servery. I was sat in the parlour one afternoon when a new friend came in, saw me, and said, "You'll do it, won't you?"

"I'll do what?" I asked.

"You'll be food officer for the May Ball, won't you?"

This new friend was one of the new students and she'd been given the role of May Ball Committee President because she had experience from a Girton College May Ball the previous year.

"Er, what do I need to do?"

"Okay, I'll give you an £18,000 budget and you organise the food providers for the party. It's easy," she replied with confidence.

"For how many people?"

"Six hundred people. Cater to all diets. Ball runs from 9 p.m. until 3 a.m. due to it being a residential part of town. You'll do it?"

"Yeah, sure I will."

And that was that. I'd been given the task of spending more money than I'd ever legally spent in my life to organise the food for a party that lasted only six hours for 600 people. Apparently, there were more minor details to follow.

The May Ball was a huge success. Nobody went hungry and, as well as food, I'd organised plenty of sweets, gelato, ice cream, and a chocolate fountain. I played sax with The Galapagogos and the crowd went wild, which was a perfect ending to my stay at Darwin College.

* * *

The 2019 Darwin May Ball was over…done and dusted. And what an incredible party it had been. I'd never have guessed back then it would be the final Darwin May Ball for the foreseeable future and now consider myself fortunate to have been involved in its organization…in fact, extremely fortunate to have been at the University of Cambridge from 2017 to 2019, the final years of normality pre-COVID-19.

I'd received many compliments throughout the evening for my efforts as food officer and all six hundred guests had been well-fed. I'd spent £18,000 on food, ice cream, and sweets for a party that ran for six hours, and the food concessions had made their own respective profits; everyone was happy.

The first food provider I'd contacted had been my friend and baker/*pizzaolo*, Michael, and I'd even managed to supply him with two staff members for the evening in the form of my good friend, Libei Wu, with a friend of hers she'd invited from London on short notice.

I'd met Libei on Facebook several months previously. She'd popped up as one of those "people you may know" on my feed. I didn't know her at all but, after flicking through her photos, I certainly wanted to. She accepted my friend request and I'd kind of forgotten about her until she waltzed into Darwin Bar's pool room with four Chinese guys in tow. Libei was definitely the leader of the gang and these guys all knew it.

Hailing from Wenzhou in southeast China, at that time she was a PhD candidate in Developmental Studies at Newnham College with a CV that reads like a Who's Who of the world's top universities—Zhejiang, Stanford, and Cambridge. She'd accompanied me as my guest to Homerton College's May Ball a couple of weeks before Darwin's and I'd obviously behaved myself because we've since become best friends.

Along with Big Pat, Michael's right hand man on the festival scene, Libei and her friend had made it four *pizzaoli* serving that evening.

Many Cambridge University May Balls employ the services of Aromi, a local Italian food shop, but I'd wanted to provide the guests with the experience of fresh pizza from a wood-fired oven. I'd allowed Michael to close the pizza stall at midnight so we could all party together for the last few hours. We'd managed to remain awake and vaguely *compos mentis* for the Survivor's Photo just before 3 a.m., and then we and all other guests headed off home or on to further parties—Darwin College is situated in a residential neighbourhood, hence such an early (and disappointing) cut-off point.

I'd handed in my notice to Ivan, the Darwin College catering manager, the previous week and, boy, was I glad to see the back of that career. It had served its purpose, however—I'd managed to remain at Darwin for an extra eight months and had paid off a substantial part of the money the college had loaned me.

* * *

I awoke next morning and met up with Michael and Big Pat for a beer at The Granta, the closest pub to Darwin College. These two couldn't be more dissimilar: Michael is the skinniest baker I've ever met with very little hair on his head while Big Pat, as his sobriquet denotes, is an enormous tank of a man with the wildest, frizziest dark hair one can imagine… complemented by an equal amount of facial hair and a generous smile.

It was a beautiful morning with cobalt blue skies, and the cold beer was a refreshing balm to my vague hangover. We were all three of us in pretty high spirits following such a successful evening, although I remember Pat complaining about the rough night's sleep on the floor of Michael's Transit van.

The beers were finished and the guys jumped into the van.

"Safe journey, man, I'll see you tonight or tomorrow," I said as they pulled out and headed off towards Trumpington and the M11.

I slowly walked to my Dodge 50 truck in Grantchester Meadows' car park and began the final packing of all my possessions. I'd already completed most of it in anticipation of this moment. I locked the back doors, jumped in the cab, fired up the engine, and allowed her to idle for ten minutes while I jumped down and said goodbye to this park-up that had been so good to me over the last nine months (an unheard of length of time to remain parked in the same spot, but then, the Universe always seems to favour me since I recalibrated my life). Climbing back into the cab, I strapped on the seat belt and started out on my road trip to far-off Georgia, 3,000 miles east.

That evening, I spent the night on Peacehaven's seafront, lulled to sleep by the repetitive crashing of waves and the wind rocking my truck. I was awakened by the heat of the rising sun blazing through the windscreen and lay in bed a while longer, smiling at the anticipation of the imminent adventure.

But remaining asleep in a truck in summer is never an option so I climbed out of bed, opened all doors and windows, made coffee, ate some breakfast then followed the directions to the farm Michael had given me. Pulling into the farmyard, I drove the Dodge round behind a barn and saw Michael tinkering about with the caravan he'd bought for the road trip.

"Morning, dude, how you doing?" Michael enquired.

"Yeah man, slept like a baby. The sea, the wind…was awesome. You?"

"Cool. Walked the dog pretty early then came to sort the caravan. Whatcha think?"

I took a walk around the caravan, checking it out. A Sprite, I seem to remember, around sixteen feet long and at least that may years old. Similar to a thousand trailers I'd seen hippies living in on sites and festivals for the past thirty years.

"You reckon she's good for a trek across Europe without falling to pieces?" I teased him. "How much did you pay?"

"She'd take us there and back, no problem; I paid a grand."

"Okay, where's my Dodge going?"

"Follow me, I'll show you."

I jumped back in the truck and followed him over to a low barn. This had been arranged in advance—somewhere sheltered from the elements for my truck. My plan at that point was to drive across Europe to Georgia, work with Michael selling pizzas for a few months (from a 1950's Russian school bus we'd be converting into a pizzeria) while saving money for a month's holiday visiting friends in different Chinese cities.

After loading all the pizza oven materials into Michael's Transit, we threw the remaining baggage into the caravan, then I hitched it up to the Transit. I raised the jockey wheel, plugged in the electrics, released the handbrake, then gave Michael the thumbs-up to confirm everything was hooked up.

Michael confidently pulled forwards way too fast, and I could see he wasn't going to clear the gate post.

"Whoa!" I screamed.

Nope, too late: as the Transit sped through the gate, the rear corner of the caravan clipped the metal post, and I heard the crunch of twisting aluminium, timber, and steel.

"What the fuck you doin', man?!"

It was evident Michael hadn't towed anything this long before. I was expecting him to await my instructions from where he could clearly see me in his mirrors. Now the rear corner of the caravan was in broken pieces before we'd even left the farm. Bits of aluminium, timber, insulation, and the rear light cluster were all hanging from a gaping hole. Fuck! Was it at this point I should've re-evaluated my decision to follow Michael the Baker across Europe to Georgia?

* * *

The gulls were screaming and careering above our heads in the wind, and the sun was glinting from the windscreens of the trucks secured to the deck below. I took another pull on the spliff before passing it to Michael and could feel a knot of excitement twist my stomach. Christ, how many times had I felt this before? The ferry pulling away from its berth, taking me away from the shores of my homeland—a homeland I was extremely angry with.

The Brexit vote had affected us both in the same way—a deep and sad sense of premonitory doom for our nation. I've never been much of a patriot and neither have I followed politics very much, but this felt like a betrayal of all I felt as a European traveller, while feeling like a victory for the xenophobic hordes believing the Daily Mail's headlines of "swarms of immigrants arriving on our shores to steal our jobs," believing the bullshit of the likes of Farage, Johnson, Rees-Mogg, et al. This had been a strong driver in my decision to get away from the UK for a while to gain some breathing space from the claustrophobia that was Brexit.

Vacillating between drinking a few beers in the bar and smoking in the wind on deck, we watched the white cliffs of Britannia recede into the distance from the stern while the uncertainty of our future approached from the bow. It didn't seem too long before we saw the church tower of Calais a few miles ahead.

* * *

The Transit began to slowly eat up the miles, Michael constantly checking the wing mirrors to ensure we hadn't left the caravan somewhere behind. He would also have been ensuring all our belongings weren't being scattered all over the road from a huge hole in the caravan's rear. We'd found a large piece of aluminium angle in one of the farm sheds and secured it vertically to the corner Michael had destroyed, and it was a good enough repair.

We were singing along to the sounds of Gil Scott-Heron's "B-Movie"—"Mandate, my ass" —and laughing together. This was often a feature of our trips to and from festivals, especially that song. Another tune we'd often destroy was one of my favourite road trip tunes: Neil Young's "Out on the Weekend," this being a song I'd busked around the South of France with Pierre and Marcos in my mid-twenties.

Belgian and French Autoroutes, service stations, and *péage* slowly morphed into Autobahns just as my language skills had to morph as we crossed each border—ironically, considering I'd learnt some German as a teenager, my French, Italian, and Polish skills had very much surpassed it over the intervening years.

Just as in life, a road trip is a steady stream of mundanity—i.e., driving for hours, stopping for fuel, food and coffee, sleeping, paying at tollbooths—with occasional bursts of excitement, wonderful sights, and memorable or hilarious moments. This was certainly the case as we slowly wended our way across Western Europe, towns and meadows blurring into one, architectural styles shifting and changing from one region to another, and place names becoming less familiar and more difficult to pronounce.

Signs for Düsseldorf, Essen, Dortmund, Kassel, Leipzig, and Dresden flashed past as we meandered our way through the German countryside coming ever closer to the Polish border. We had no desire to leave the Autobahn and explore any of these cities—our goal was Tbilisi, Georgia, and Michael wanted to arrive there and start work on the bus conversion as soon as possible.

He was happy to do most of the driving although occasionally I did take over to give him a break. We'd pull over and crash out in the caravan once we were both too tired and then rise in the morning to make fresh coffee and buy some croissant or similar from service stations. Showers aren't a problem on European trips because the majority of service stations have them available for all travellers, not just long-distance hauliers—they simply require a set of car keys as deposit.

We were heading for a German village that was off our direct route to Georgia via Ukraine because Michael had agreed to collect and transport a bun-making machine for his French baker friend, Jean-Jacques, who was resident in Tbilisi, Georgia; he was in the process of fitting out his own bakery and had purchased the machine.

Arriving at a tiny German hamlet, we searched for the address and soon introduced ourselves to the guy we'd been instructed to find, and he directed us to the bun-maker—it looked very heavy and didn't disappoint. With the help of three guys who worked at the premises—and some ingenuity—the five of us managed to manhandle it into the Transit and then Michael and I secured it with ratchet straps. The van wheel arches disappeared as the body sank with its weight, and the Transit immediately became more cumbersome to drive.

We found a supermarket across the street, bought some provisions and plenty of water to drink—the sun was high and the heat was impossible to escape in the cab of the van—then found the Autobahn and continued east.

We crossed another border and discovered the motorways in Poland were as smooth and fast-moving as those back home in England, so we continued to make good progress. I took a turn at driving while Michael tried to get some sleep, but the ambient temperature made it impossible.

I spotted a sign for Katowice. This town, I knew, wasn't far from Auschwitz.

I realised I may never again be as close as I was and felt morally obligated to go there. I suggested this to Michael and, although we both knew it would be a harrowing experience, he agreed on the small detour.

The first thing we saw was the infamous tower with its archway, the archway through which cattle cars filled with Jews, Gypsies, the handicapped, and POWs had passed through on their way to the sidings and selections. It looked just as it had in every image I'd ever seen in the history books. We pulled into the car park and both felt a sombre change in mood descend upon us.

Beyond this, I shall describe no more of our visit…the emotions that were elicited during those two hours will remain with me for as long as I breathe. This was the first of only two stops we made between Calais and Odessa.

Continuing our drive towards the border with Ukraine, the van was filled with our silence as we digested all we'd seen and felt.

* * *

It was dark when the traffic began to slow. An array of bright red brake lights began to glow and blink along both lanes before us. Michael and I thought there'd been an accident. However, after a short while, people began to exit their vehicles and formed small clusters, smoking, pouring tea, drinking beer, and eating. It slowly became obvious there was a wait ahead of us, so we followed suit. I wandered off to the roadside, clambered over the barrier, pissed down the embankment, then returned to the van and pulled open a can of beer.

The traffic was still for almost an hour before any movement and, even then, it merely crawled ahead ten yards. Then, the same again twenty minutes later—this was gonna be a long night. This stop/start/move ten yards/repeat continued for another two hours before we saw a lit gantry ahead indicating this was the Ukrainian border. The lanes funnelled into one single lane the border guards had left open, and this explained why progress had become so painfully slow, a thousand vehicles all passing through the eye of a needle.

As the cars approached this juncture, some drivers wouldn't give way to others, and these in turn became frustrated with those not giving way. The beeping of horns, raising of voices, and angry waving of arms were all to no avail. In reality, the waiting had only just begun. There really ought to have been a sign reading:

"Welcome to Krakovets—A Version of Hell"

How to describe the nighttime scene that welcomed us once we finally got through to customs? My first experience of Ukraine. This was a place from the Soviet era, surely? An enormous grey concrete gallery bathed in the kind of low wattage light you'd find in 1950's film noir. The border guards were wearing military fatigues or smart green uniforms straight out of the *Lubyanka*, the modernity of Europe was less than a kilometre behind, and we now inhabited an archaic and Kafkaesque world whose sole existence appeared to revolve around timelessness and *protokol.*

I consider myself quite well-travelled. I've spent plenty of time in several different European countries on many different occasions over thirty years. The world map I replaced my TV with a few months ago has twenty-seven pins denoting towns and cities I've visited in Europe alone. I've travelled around Thailand, I've been to Morocco, and I've been culturally shocked by some of the places I've visited...but nothing had prepared me for this Ukrainian border post after travelling across Western Europe. It literally felt like a reality shift—"surreal" is the word I'd use to describe it today and I'd have plenty of time to observe it more once the *protokol* really kicked in.

As Eugene Hütz says to Elijah Wood's character with a wry grin in the movie *Everything Is Illuminated*: "Welcome to Ukraine."

An interminable wait commenced. Our passports were required to be seen once, twice, three times over an hour or two while remaining parked in the same spot we'd initially halted at. Michael and I smoked cigarette after cigarette waiting for some form of progress, but none was forthcoming. We were surrounded by a novel scene of hawkers trying to sell anything from individual cigarettes to bread and cakes and refreshments, an entrepreneur's cavern where the women looked like *babushkas* draped in headscarves and the men all seemed to have stepped straight from an Emir Kusturica film set. Such an incredible shift from European to Slav culture in such a short distance, from the EU to a completely different planet.

Finally, one of the green-uniformed guys came and indicated to Michael he should follow him. They walked off together somewhere to my left and the long wait really began.

Again, one hour passed, then another...and another. By this time, I was beginning to wonder what the fuck was actually going on. I had some beers in the cab with me but distinctly remember thinking to myself, *But what if Michael doesn't return and I need to drive the Transit?* so I resisted. Any books I may have brought along were somewhere in the back of the van, no doubt impossible to retrieve due to the accursed bun-making machine.

As it turned out, the bun-making machine was the sole reason we weren't simply ushered through customs like many of those preceding us. Michael finally turned up after four long hours and explained he'd been sat in a waiting room full of truckers, all of whom endured a similar tedium awaiting transit papers. The authorities' concern was we may try and sell the machine within Ukraine's territory so therefore we couldn't proceed without authorization papers.

There was one final check before we'd be permitted to continue with our adventure: a search of the rear of the Transit van. Michael opened the back doors for the inspection but, after taking one look at the size and evident weight of the bastard machine, the border guards told him to close it back up and, basically, fuck off to wherever we were headed.

Fantastic—freedom at last!

35

Caravan
(Duke Ellington)

As we pulled out of the gallery of Babel and entered Ukraine proper, the sun was beginning to rise. We'd spent around seven hours crossing one border due to Jean-Jacques's bun-making machine.

After driving for ten minutes, we pulled over and took a celebratory photo to post on Facebook so our friends and followers could see we were making "good" progress. Little did I know at the time this same photo would be used on a crowdfunder page a couple of weeks later as I lay delirious with "pneumonia" in a Tbilisi hospital being pumped full of intravenous antibiotics.

We jumped back into the Transit, and I opened Google Maps on my iPhone to seek the fastest route to Odessa, where we needed to catch the ferry across the Black Sea to Batumi, Georgia. But, no, it wasn't having any of it. We'd left the EU, and my network provider was no longer providing. Using the maps without the search facility, I figured the quickest route was to head towards Lviv on the M10 and then pick up the E40 to Ternopil, then the E50 that would take us to the E95—the main route south to Odessa. One fact Michael and I noticed very quickly was the change in road surface. Basically, the route from Cambridge all the way to Krakovets had been driven on roads that were very well made. This would no longer be the case.

I took another turn at driving and plugged my own phone into the stereo—Leningrad. Not really Michael's cup of tea but he endured stoically while I pointed the Transit east and footed the accelerator.

"Is it just me or have we suddenly entered a Third World country?" I asked of Michael.

"Not just you, man, no, but more like a Second World country. You'll find many similarities in Georgia—they're both trying to join the EU but have too much governmental corruption to sort out before they're able; both ex-Russian federation and threatened by Russian occupation on a daily basis, and both fucked by their respective Orthodox Churches.

"Look over there, see that town? What do you notice about it?"

I followed the direction of Michael's pointing finger. To our south lay a small village or town that had a kind of run-down vibe to it.

"It looks dirt poor…?" I ventured.

"Exactly, but how about its church?"

"Well, that don't look so bad at all."

"No, because all the money goes to the church… it's like England a hundred years ago…or more. Georgia's the same, the church has a disproportionate amount of power and controls pretty much everything."

"Man, that sucks," I said and I meant it.

I wound up the volume on the next Leningrad track soon as it came on while Michael passed me a spliff. I continued driving for another thirty minutes.

"Where the fuck are we?" I heard Michael ask. He had a point, there was no sign of any town, village, or habitation anywhere around us, just the dirt track the road had transformed into and miles of flatland strewn with clumps of shrubbery and trees. I pulled over and a cloud of dust continued in the direction we'd been heading.

"Lemme look at the map," I said and opened my phone. "Okay, there's absolutely no signal…the map won't even open."

Michael checked his own phone and, likewise, nothing.

"Right, straight on is east, so let's just keep going until we see a sign, yeah?"

Michael began to laugh.

"'Til we see a sign? How's that gonna help, we don't know where the fuck we are."

"Speak for yourself, man. I know where we are…we're hundreds of miles from the UK and that's good enough for me. And if we keep driving east, we'll get some signal eventually, then come to the motorway down to Odessa, right? Simple. Now do something useful and skin up while I navigate our way out of here."

I pulled out onto the road while Michael made the spliff and, within twenty minutes, we were halted by some roadworks. A new bridge was being built to replace the old one and the road was closed. All that existed as a road now was evidently fit only for construction traffic or individual cars, not a Transit van towing an almost twenty-foot-long caravan.

"Aww, bollocks, I can't be arsed with driving around looking for a way around this without a bloody map," said Michael.

"So whatcha gonna do?"

"We'll make it," he answered.

"Are you kidding? You'll never make it. Look, the road's like a bowl… the trailer will bottom out."

"I'll do it. You stay outside and guide me and I'll make it," he insisted.

I wasn't as confident as he was but, fuck it—it wasn't my caravan that would be destroyed any more than it already had been.

I walked forwards a bit as Michael lined up the van and motioned him forwards but, as I'd suspected, the rear end of the caravan hit the dirt road and prevented any onwards movement. I was almost praying to the gods I'd been cursing for the past couple of hours the caravan wasn't stuck. Michael threw the van into gear and managed to reverse back to where he'd begun.

"Okay!" he shouted. "I'm gonna make a run for it. What d'ya reckon?"

"Ain't my caravan, man." I laughed. "It's up to you."

Michael pulled forwards and picked up speed enough to force the caravan beyond the point it had become stuck. I waited for the impact, not knowing whether the extra speed would allow it to make it or completely destroy it. The Transit raced forward, there was the sound of the rear end smashing onto the dirt road, a large cloud of dust and sparks, and then the caravan flew past me and up onto the solid road beyond. He'd made it but what was the damage?

The junction of the back wall and underside of the caravan was hanging loose, just as one corner had been back at the farm, and the offside light cluster was clinging on by its wires…other than that, we still had somewhere to sleep.

"Hahaha! Told you I'd make it!" Michael was out of the van, dancing in the dust, and I joined him in his dancing and laughter. I took photos of the caravan and the bridge he'd conquered for posterity, and we got the drill out for some impromptu repairs before continuing with the trip.

We continued for an hour or so re-living the events at the bridge, passing spliffs back and forth, laughing uproariously. Neither of us could believe the caravan hadn't simply exploded—that would come later. As I'd learned many times in my life, impunity has a shelf life.

As the van continued east, we spotted a large lake on our left-hand side. The sun was bouncing off the many ripples created by people taking turns diving from three or four staged platforms.

"Hey man, quick, pull over. Let's have a swim."

The sun was high and the air dry and dusty. No mirage in the desert would have been more welcome than this oasis in the middle of the arid plains we'd been driving through.

Michael pulled over and switched off the van. First thing I did was check our repairs to the back of the caravan—it wasn't good. The unevenness of the roads hadn't helped at all and the back was once again falling to bits. Michael's abuse was beginning to take its toll.

"Okay, let's swim. We can deal with that afterwards." I slammed the door and headed for the delightful lake and its cool promise.

Climbing the ladder to the first platform, I made a note of exactly where those preceding me were diving and joined the queue. It seemed to be plenty deep enough to dive without concern then it was my turn. I walked to the edge and dove. The water was perfect. The sun had been warming it all morning and it wasn't as cold as I'd anticipated. I broke the surface, swam back to the ladder, climbed out, and re-joined the queue as Michael leapt from the platform and disappeared in a huge splash. Awesome, this was exactly what we needed after baking in the tin can Transit nonstop for hours.

Feeling progressively braver after a few dives from the lowest platform, I tried the next-highest platform and took several dives from this one too. We both continued diving until we tired of it and then sat on the lakeside smoking a spliff before walking around the lake to a café. After coffees and some food, we were dry and refreshed and ready to hit the road again.

Before our departure, though, I once again lay on the dirt road beneath the caravan, drill in hand, trying to make a silk purse out of a pig's ear. The caravan's rear end was disintegrating badly and we had limited supplies of tools—a handful of screws, a few cable ties, and a roll of gaffer tape, no more. I gave it my best shot, and we waved goodbye to the lake, refreshed by its waters and feeling much cleaner.

We were off again—eastwards, then south. We followed the route and soon found signposts for Lviv, the next big town on our itinerary.

Ever so slowly and without our really noticing it, the roads began to deteriorate. Small potholes began to appear ahead of us and then became progressively larger. The traffic in both directions began to weave and wend its way around them, often causing opposing lanes to stop and allow oncoming traffic to negotiate these holes. We'd skirt one hole and the caravan would invariably drive over it, then we'd stop and allow someone ahead to negotiate the next hole in their turn. Then repeat the process. This stopping then trying to avoid a hole in the road continued for maybe thirty or forty minutes, the caravan heavily swaying from left to right every time it drove over a hole. In fairness to Michael, it was impossible to predict whether the caravan would skirt the holes as he'd tried to do or drive over them. Both directions of traffic at this point were moving at five miles an hour—lorries, buses, cars, everyone. I couldn't believe the roads had been allowed to reach this level of fucked-upness...this was the main road to Lviv from Krakovets.

Then, magically, a swathe of brand-new tarmacked road appeared and all traffic reverted to fifty or sixty miles per hour again, as if the potholed road had been a mirage. This brought us all the way to our first destination, Lviv.

We'd been driving through the town for fifteen minutes when I noticed a police car in the passenger wing mirror. It seemed to be following our progress.

"No way, man, they're gonna condemn the caravan." I laughed.

No sooner had I said this than the police car flashed its headlights at us, let out a short blast of its siren, and pulled us over. Shit, what now?

It turned out there was nothing to worry about. These guys were friendly and didn't seem concerned the caravan was held together with a piece of aluminium angle and a roll of gaffer tape. They spoke some English and simply asked us where we were headed, then offered to show us the road we needed for Odessa. They indicated we should follow them then pulled ahead and led the way. What a lovely surprise—we weren't being led off to Lviv's *Lubyanka* to have our fingernails pulled.

Once it was evident we'd seen the sign for Odessa, our escort flashed its hazard lights as a goodbye and left us to be on our way.

We left the town's suburbs behind and followed the dual carriageway taking us further east, a straight ribbon of wonderfully flat and smooth tarmac. Fantastic, it appeared we were going to make Odessa by this evening.

We were climbing a long hill and doing around fifty miles per hour. As we reached the top, Michael pulled over into a lay-by and switched off the engine. He wanted to grab something from the caravan before continuing. He climbed out and disappeared from sight while I took a look at the map on my phone.

I heard the sound of laughter from somewhere behind me. Then the laughter became harder and louder. *What the hell's up with him?* I wondered.

"Christian, come here, man. You gotta see this," Michael called between fits of laughter.

I jumped down from the van and went to join him. He was stood at the caravan's entrance door practically holding his stomach while still bursting with laughter and pointing at something in the caravan.

I walked closer and saw exactly what was so hilarious: the interior of the caravan was destroyed. All the cupboards at the top of the walls were now lying on the bed, the main cupboard to the left of the door was broken and misshapen and, after further inspection, we saw the caravan's huge front window was falling out of its frame ready to land in the road at the next big bump.

I too joined in the laughter. The disastrous Ukrainian roads had shaken the caravan to death, all that swaying from side to side and bouncing over huge potholes had finished it. I took photos of the trashed interior and closed the door. We did the best job we could of securing the front window in its frame and slowly set off again, this time with an awareness the caravan was slowly dying.

As Michael drove, I leant out of the passenger window and soon realised the biggest problem was the roof. The front of the roof was no longer attached to the front wall so, as the Transit pulled the caravan forwards, the roof was trying to free itself from the main body like the lid of a sardine can. Shit, this was really bad. If we continued, the roof would eventually be ripped off by the wind, fly onto the vehicle behind's windscreen, and cause a crash.

"Pull over, man," I urged Michael. "We need to have a think about this. We can't keep pulling this thing—it's lethal."

Michael obliged. I rolled a spliff in between my laughter and concern.

"What we gonna do? We can't keep driving or we'll cause an accident."

"Look, why don't we find a road in those woods over there? We can drive it in deep and set fire to it."

"Michael, are you out of your mind? We're in Ukraine, for fuck's sake! The border guards have taken an inventory of everything we've entered the country with—Transit van, two chancers, bun-making machine. You think they might have missed a small thing like a sixteen-foot caravan?

"I can just see us pulling up at the ferry in Odessa with a missing caravan. Meanwhile, there's a police bulletin about a caravan set on fire in the woods outside Lviv. You'd make a real shite criminal.

"No, what we have to do is unhitch the caravan, leave it here, and go back to Lviv in the Transit to find those nice policemen and tell them the caravan's fucked and we can't continue to Odessa with it. *They'll* need to come up with a solution."

"Burn it in the woods…Jeez."

We never did find the friendly guys from earlier. We did, however, manage to find another couple of policemen who helped us and the whole process took only a few hours (I'd been expecting reams of paperwork, a fuck-ton of *protokol,* and perhaps even a warm cell for the night as was my usual experience with the police).

These guys asked us to lead the way to the offending caravan and, upon arrival, agreed in Ukrainian, "This ain't going anywhere."

Next, they contacted a farmer friend who was more than happy to inherit a free chassis with brakes that could be turned into a farm trailer. We awaited the arrival of this farmer and a short while later he hitched the thing up and it disappeared from our lives.

These guys really were great. They indicated we should follow them once again, and a half mile down the road, they pulled into a guesthouse, explained to the proprietress an unfortunate experience had befallen these English travellers, and we were given a double room to share with the most enormous cuddly toys either of us had ever seen in our lives. Special rates were applied for the room because we had contacts in the Lviv police force, and we both enjoyed our first sleep in a real bed since leaving the UK almost a week ago.

I awoke in the morning feeling totally refreshed and, after coffee and croissants, stepped outside to be greeted by another glorious sunny day.

It was around nine or ten in the morning, and the temperature was rising nicely. It already felt like a great day to be driving without dragging dead weight behind us. Michael showed his face shortly afterwards and we hit the road again, laughing and marvelling at our good fortune.

"Those guys were so cool, man," I said to Michael, and he could only agree.

It actually took us more than seven hours to reach the E95 at Uman, which gave me an idea of the vastness of this country (the drive from Krakovets to Uman is 11.5 hours, which is probably only half the width of the country). Every few miles along this main route from Kyiv to Odessa were roadside stalls with men or women hiding from the sun's baking heat beneath awnings selling enormous green melons. Odessa was now within our reach, three hours away.

The surrounding countryside was mostly flat and the clearest memory I have of that drive is the sunflowers. I've never seen so many sunflowers—acres and acres of them—on both sides of the road. I think most of the world's sunflower seeds must come from the fertile lands between Uman and Odessa.

Shit, we were being pulled by the police again. Michael had been speeding through a section of motorway where the speed limit was 50 KPH. The police had waved at him to stop but he'd ignored them, so they came racing behind with flashing lights and pulled us. He pulled over and we both got out of the van—me to stretch my legs, Michael to get nicked.

These guys didn't have such great English, fortunately for Michael. They made some stern noises about his ignoring their gesture for him to stop, quickly scanned his driving licence, and then let us continue on our way. Thirty minutes later and we were entering Odessa.

We headed for the beach and found somewhere to park the van. Michael knew the spot from a previous visit. We found a bar on the seafront and found some new friends immediately. The girl serving was very funky wearing black leather gloves and a sexy vibe, playing some fantastic tunes really loud—if I were a bar owner, she'd be running my bar for me. The guys hovering around kept buying drinks and she kept serving them…

clever girl. This included me and Michael. I was smitten and saw no reason to change location.

This was where we met a friend who I'm still in touch with today: Bogdan Alexandrov (I don't think you could find a more typically Ukrainian name; there are probably thousands of guys with this name). He turned up at some point in the late afternoon, his English was very good, and he enjoyed a drink. What's not to like?

He invited us back to his place saying his partner would be home from work in an hour or two when we'd eat together, and then they would show us some places of interest. Like most people you meet when travelling, he was proud of his country and wished to share this national pride with us...a lovely guy with a wonderful smile. We drove the van back to his place following his directions, hitting a shop for beer and provisions *en route*.

As promised, Bogdan's partner, Daria, showed up a while later and she was as vivacious and lively as was he. Michael and I had been blessed with a pair of lovely friends on day one. We broke bread together and shared some nice food, they played us some of their favourite music (Bogdan is a big Joy Division fan), and then we headed out into the Odessa night to check out some sights.

We saw many monuments and statues that evening but the site I most wanted to visit was the Potemkin Stairs. Typical tourist, I know, but I'd watched the *Battleship Potemkin* movie two or three years previously and remembered the tension of the runaway pram hurtling down these steps, so I wished to see them.

It was quite late in the evening when we did see them and I ran from the first or second landing all the way to the top while Michael, Bogdan, and Daria casually walked up. They found me at the top feigning cool.

We spent a lovely evening with these two and I was extremely pleased to hear they married last year and am proud to still call them friends. Only last month I edited some English for Bogdan's business website, and I'm very much looking forward to seeing them again next time I'm there.

We were forced to remain in Odessa for three days due to ferry times and, it goes without saying, there was a fuck-ton of *protokol* to deal with at the ferry terminal during that time.

36

The Drugs Don't Work
(The Verve)

Muted music surrounded me as though filtered through a heavy thick drape, a theatre curtain. Its volume and density shifted and swirled in a way that made it difficult to pinpoint the direction of its source. Was it to my left? Was it before me? Coming from behind? Strange. It shifted again and then the music was joined by a guttural, almost-human voice sound…then another...above me.

And there was brightness. Again, above me. I was rising…surfacing from somewhere. I heard the voices again, a man's and a woman's voice but any meaning indistinguishable. As the light became more uncomfortably bright, the sound of the music shifted to a more familiar sound…familiar but as though from another time and place. It sounded like...like...

Like machines. That was it…

"Can you hear me?" The same guttural tones but this time in a language I understood. My own language? Yes. Weird. Why was everything weirdly different?

A shadow passed over the light and half covered it, lessening its glare, and I could see a tanned and bearded face. This person's hand was held above my face so I wasn't blinded by the light.

"You're in a hospital. Can you hear me?"

I heard myself make a sound that grated from my dry throat. I could feel my breath wasn't normal, as though something was pushing down on my chest. I drew in as much breath as I could and tried again.

"Yes. Where?" I rasped. My voice wasn't my own and the face didn't understand me.

"Don't try to speak anymore. It's okay. Give yourself time to wake. You've been suffering from a strong fever for days and have been with the delirium."

The music now revealed itself as the whirring and beeping of the medical equipment I was tethered to and something about been with the delirium bothered me, but I couldn't put my finger on it. My thought process seemed kind of mixed up, trippy.

* * *

I woke again. The room was empty. I lay on a bed with the machine noises now more recognisable for what they were. I had no idea how long ago the voices had been above me, it might have been a minute ago or a week ago; no idea. Light was streaming in through the window and the glare in my eyes was no longer as bright above me. I began to drift off and return to the strange dreamland I'd inhabited for I-don't-know-how-long when the door to the room opened and someone entered.

"Ah, you back now? I need to change your drip."

A nurse slowly drifted into view. I tried to sit up to see her better.

"Let me help," she offered, reaching for a remote on the bed and raising my upper body to a sitting position. I felt totally exhausted. Just trying to sit up took an incredible amount of effort.

"Why am I here? What happened to me?" I asked as she began fiddling with the clear tube running from a tall metal stand to my arm.

"You were admitted two days ago with pneumonia. You were being very crazy because of the fever. Shouting nonsense and waking everybody sleeping."

I realised she had the same heavy accent as the doctor from before and asked where she was from.

"I'm from here, Tbilisi. I live here all my whole life and study here to become nurse."

What the fuck happened? How the hell did I contract pneumonia? I'd never been hospitalised in my life before and couldn't get my half-functioning brain around this news.

"Get more rest," she instructed, "your body needs it to make better." She offered a warm smile then quietly left the room, leaving me with more questions than answers. I had no trouble returning to my otherworldly dream state.

* * *

The door opened again, and I thought the nurse had forgotten something but, no, it was Michael.

"Hey man, how's the patient?" he asked, gently closing the door.

"Yeah, okay," I rasped.

He proffered a plastic bottle of water realising my throat was parched and I couldn't speak. I drank a few sips and tried again.

"No, I'm confused! What the fuck happened?"

"You don't remember? You had a crazy fever, and you were in fucking Loopy Land…completely tripped out. The doctors tied your arms to the bed rails so they could insert a catheter. You were screaming at them and trying to bite them."

At these words, I had a sudden flashback of men in white coats pinning me to a bed while I tried to escape their grip. There was a shadowy figure behind them, a witness I guessed was Michael.

"Wow, okay. I just had a vision of that. I remember it, very…fucking… vaguely. But how? Why? I don't get it."

"Okay, do you remember us dropping off the bun-making machine at Jean-Jacques's place? You couldn't seem to stay awake. I thought it was coz of the ferry trip and all the vodka and weed but it must have been the onset of the fever.

"Then you went to bed but got up in the middle of the night and walked across the room towards the bathroom, peeing on the floor. You were reading from a book in German, it was on one of the bookshelves. I thought you were going mad! Really fucking strange, man."

"What the fuck?"

"Yeah, so I called an ambulance, and when they arrived, they asked what you'd been up to. I told them you'd been drinking homemade Russian vodka with those lorry drivers on the ferry for forty-eight hours. They did some tests, told me you had chronic liver disease, and said there was nothing they could do for you. Basically that you were fucked. Then they left.

"You just kept getting more and more delirious and crazy until my friend David and I brought you here, where they X-rayed your lungs and diagnosed you with pneumonia. Getting you here was an exercise in subterfuge as we sensed you might not wanna get into the ambulance… we said you had a gig and that the band was waiting for you.

"Now you need to rest and continue with the antibiotic drip until you're better. I brought a few things for you—some aubergine and walnut dish that these Georgians love, some khachapuri, and water. Oh yeah, and this."

Michael pulled a book from the bag and handed it to me. I turned it over so I could see its front cover.

"Perfect." I tried to laugh. "Let's hope it's not tolling for me."

It was Hemingway's For Whom the Bell Tolls. One of my favourites.

* * *

Picking up another party balloon, I gently blew into it until it was the size of an orange. I stopped for a few moments to take another breath because the first one was so weak and tried again. This time it swelled to the size of a grapefruit. My lungs were still affected and only seemed to be operating at half their normal capacity—not good for a saxophonist.

I'd stayed in the hospital for fourteen days. The IV drip filling me with antibiotics never left my arm in all that time and the doctors were perplexed by this "pneumonia" that wasn't responding to antibiotics. These symptoms resisting treatment eerily resembled what we'd come to know as COVID-19 some months later. It was a very long fourteen days, reminiscent of solitary confinement, with the doctors and nurses giving me the best care they could. Ironically, I had to offer them guidance when it came to finding a good vein to insert the IV line, as an ex-junkie's veins aren't the easiest to locate.

There'd been a problem with medical costs when I'd first been admitted. Michael had paid £150 from his own pocket for the first medical bill but, with me being in Loopy Land, he couldn't get any sense from me around my family's contact details or whether or not I'd secured medical insurance before travelling. I hadn't done it because I'd never been hospitalised for an illness before.

Michael posted a message on Facebook asking my friends for help and one of them launched a crowdfunder that garnered £2500 in three days. She knows who she is and I've expressed my eternal gratitude to her upon my return, just as all those beautiful friends who donated and thereby saved my life know who they are.

According to the media, the first recorded incident of COVID-19 occurred in Wuhan in December 2019. I don't have much truck with conspiracy theories but my own experience (along with that of my Tbilisi doctors and radiologists) tells me I contracted a mystery illness diagnosed as pneumonia while spending forty-eight hours crossing the Black Sea on a ferry jam-packed with mostly lorry drivers from France, Germany, Italy, Latvia, Russia, Georgia, and numerous other European countries—a veritable petri dish.

Three days before the doctors agreed to my discharge they said, "You're being discharged tomorrow." Then, in the morning, before releasing me, they took me for a chest X-ray and said, "No, it's still active, you can't go home."

This happened for the next two successive days. On the third day, the doctors were still scratching their heads but said, "It's still active. We're going to discharge you anyway."

I was instructed to buy some party balloons and to blow them up as lung exercise.

"What about saxophone? I'm a sax player."

"Even better," they responded. "Start with the balloons and then move on to the saxophone when you feel able to."

37

I'll Be Seeing You
(Francoise Hardy & Iggy Pop)

My mysterious pneumonia-like malady had left me with no desire to continue smoking cigarettes nor to drink any alcohol because, in my world, the one has always accompanied the other. I knew from experience if I drank, I'd smoke. This wouldn't last, but I did quit for a month, until I became immersed in Georgian society and culture, which has a strong tradition around both cigarettes and wine.

Michael and I landed on our feet immediately after my hospital discharge when we rented an Airbnb from a family in Tbilisi's suburbs. The father, Gio, played first trumpet with the Georgian Philharmonic Orchestra while two of his three sons played trombone and percussion, both aspiring to play the same stage as their father. The third son was still very young but his future place in the orchestra was as assured as that of his siblings. Their mother appeared to be the only family member who wasn't musical.

The three months we lived with these guys was a fantastic introduction to life in Georgia's capital city. Free tickets to Gio's concerts in the Rustaveli National Theatre with full orchestra on stage, balmy evenings in the garden drinking the family's home-brewed wine (a common theme in countries such as Georgia, Romania, Bulgaria, etc. due to their temperate climates and highly fertile soil) and mouth-watering homemade Georgian cuisine, a practice room in the basement where I could blow my sax as loudly and as long as I liked, and a household filled with both love and music.

We could have stayed longer, but another place became available in the courtyard where Jean-Jacques lived, a place where Michael had a double room to himself and I had a single room. We'd been sharing a twin room at Gio's so a new place with our own space located in Tbilisi centre was reason enough to change. Even more exciting, however, was our landlady's surname—Murat. And Mathilde Murat is a *bona fide* princess.

After reading possibly more books than anyone I know during my ten years' imprisonment, I'm left with two great historical figures to whom I've devoted the most time and research. The first of these is Ernest Shackleton, the last of the great adventurers and a man who, despite all the odds stacked against him, returned to Elephant Island three months after leaving it to save the entire almost-starved crew of his *Endurance*—in fact, Shackleton's family motto was "By endurance we conquer."

The second of these figures is Napoleon Bonaparte and, ironically, as I moved into my new room, I was halfway through reading Andrew Roberts's *Napoleon the Great*, the biography that inspired the latest Napoleon movie starring Joaquin Pheonix.

A very similar name to Pheonix's, Joachim, was the first name of one of Bonaparte's finest marshals, Prince Joachim Murat. This man was with Bonaparte from the very beginning, helping to suppress the royalist insurrection in Paris on 13 Vendémiaire and then accompanying him on many of the most successful campaigns.

Mathilde's father, Alain Murat, owned the property Michael and I were renting and joined us one evening for food and drinks as he was interested in these two Englishmen who'd driven across Europe to live in Georgia. I cooked a fantastic French dish called thirty-garlic chicken in his honour, and we sat around the kitchen table celebrating the anniversary of Napoleon's coronation while sharing a bottle of Scotch Whisky.

Alain carries himself as you would expect a genuine prince to carry himself. At seventy-three years old at the time of our meeting and standing at a comfortable six feet or more, he sports a moustache straight out of a Napoleonic painting and dark hair only slightly streaked with grey. His energy belies his age and the twinkle in his eye hints at the humour he is suffused with.

He and his wife, Princess Véronique Murat, had returned to Georgia after the fall of the Soviet Union where Alain's ancestor, Achille Murat, had married Princess Salomé Dadiani in 1868, linking the Murat family to the Georgian nobility. We were most definitely in good company.

We ended the evening with toasts of "*Vive L'Empereur*" as we drained our glasses of the last of the whisky. Alain discovered that evening he'd come across two of the most atypical Englishmen he'd ever be likely to encounter. And one such evening deserved an invitation to another.

* * *

"Jesus, six hours!"

Don't get me wrong, I was excited to be heading west at the invitation of Alain Murat, but a six-hour train journey seemed an awfully long time to travel.

Alain's wife, Véronique, while visiting Mathilde and her five grandchildren several days prior, had also spent some time tending the flowerbeds outside our little flat. I opened the door to leave and saw her kneeling and wielding a small garden trowel. She looked up from her gardening then said in heavily accented English, "You are Christian, the saxophone player?"

"Yes, I am, and I love the way you say my name. It reminds me of my travels in France many years ago."

"Fabulous! You are invited to a grand soiree at Château Chkadouache in Zugdidi. Bring your friend." Véronique then gave me the time and date Michael and I were expected at the chateau and she reverted to her gardening.

As long train journeys do, this one finally came to its end and the train slowed as it approached Zugdidi station. It screeched to a final halt, so Michael and I grabbed our bags and headed for the exit.

Alain was there to greet us. He was standing in a long, dark greatcoat looking as imperious as ever. But there was something else, a look I discerned in his eye, as though he were looking for someone else with us.

"*Où est ton saxophone?*"

I perfectly understood the words but was instantly confused. Where's my saxophone?

Alain began to look behind me, he looked at Michael, then spread his hands palms up in a gesture of disbelief.

"I've had flyers printed for all the guests tonight saying an English saxophonist will be playing for us all. Where's your saxophone?"

"Alain, nobody said anything about a saxophone. Véronique asked me if I was Christian. I said yes, then she told me about the invitation and said to bring my friend. She didn't say I was playing nor that I needed to bring my saxophone…otherwise, I'd have brought it with me."

"*Un désastre,*" he said.

"Well, we must get to the house and think of some way to recover. Mm, I wonder, do I know anybody with a saxophone?" I could almost hear the thought process working in Alain's mind as he tried to figure some way to overcome the disaster.

Michael and I were shown to the bedroom we'd be sharing so we could change. Me into my tuxedo, Michael into a dinner suit.

I shan't pretend my memory is so good I remember what we were served to eat that evening; it was five years ago, after all. I am certain, however, it was three courses of delicious *haute cuisine* spread over a few hours accompanied by wonderful conversation and delicious wine. We were served by a young dark-haired butler sporting a waistcoat adorned with thin horizontal yellow and black stripes that left an unsettling impression of a wasp.

Looking at the photographs today, the clothing, the faces, and the decor all conjure a scene from the Russian Federation. The beige wallpaper embossed with burgundy velvet alongside pea-green painted wood panelling is a strange contrast. One of the ladies has a faux fabric tiara at the top of her forehead, and there's definitely something made from the fur of an animal sat on the back of one of the sofas, perhaps one of those warmers ladies fold both arms into to stay warm. Christmas decorations hang from the high walls that indicates when the party was held (I believe it was around my birthday so mid-January). There are eight women and only three men—me, Michael, and Alain.

Suddenly, amidst all the guests' talking, a sweep of headlights and the sound of a car on gravel entered the room from beyond the window. The waspy butler headed for the front door, opened it, and a cold draft entered the warm room as he left it.

He returned a moment later carrying my saxophone case that I thought I wouldn't be setting eyes on again until I returned home. The sound of a car pulling away across the gravel outside disappeared once he closed the front door and he then brought the saxophone over and passed it to me. I looked immediately towards Alain who was standing across the table from me with that inimitable twinkle in his eye and a wide grin spreading over his features.

"Who was that?" I asked.

"That was the president of Georgia," he replied.

* * *

"Christian. You okay?"

I could feel Leo's genuine concern over the phone and also sensed an urgency in his tone.

"Course I'm okay. Why wouldn't I be? What's the matter, man?"

"I thought you'd have attended the Learning Together event at London Bridge with Karen and everyone else. I was worried you'd been stabbed, too."

"Stabbed? Who's been stabbed? What're you talking about?"

"Shit, you haven't heard about it…two of your friends were killed at Karen's event."

"I dunno what the hell you're on about," I said, trying to make sense of Leo's words, struggling to imagine two of my friends had been killed. Which two?

"I'm in Georgia with Michael, driving into Tbilisi. Let's backtrack a little, okay? What happened?"

"Okay, right, you know Karen's Learning Together programme? They were holding an event, a five-year anniversary…birthday kind of event in London…near London Bridge, when one of the participants began stabbing people. Some prisoners chased him from the building, and he was shot dead by the police on the bridge. I called to make sure you were safe coz I guessed Karen would have invited you."

"Fuck! Is Karen alright?" I asked, my stomach clenching, anticipating the worst.

"Yes, she's fine. She wasn't injured at all but two of your fellow students were killed."

"Do you know who?"

"No, man, no idea. It's all over the news but no names yet."

We said goodbye and I stared numbly at the blinking red taillights of the cars ahead of us. I wound down the car window a little to help me breathe, the cold November air biting into my lungs while my thoughts threw me back to seminars I'd attended at the Institute of Criminology, the laughing faces of friends half my age, passionate about creating change. I struggled to comprehend the awful news of what had befallen two of these comrades while silently—selfishly—hoping they wouldn't be two I'd been close to.

I placed the phone back on the dashboard and reached for a cigarette, my mind numb from Leo's call.

"You okay? What was that about?" Michael asked.

The awful news came through the following day that the two victims were Jack Merritt and Saskia Jones, the former being a PhD candidate who'd given us fledgling criminologists several lectures, the latter being my friend and drinking partner from Queens' College.

I remembered Jack well because his aura wasn't something one could easily forget. He was blessed with good looks and high intelligence; he was athletic and had equal amounts of humour and charm. He was confident and his future successful career as a criminologist was assured...until one of those he was trying to help turned on him. I've read the inquiry transcripts and they're not easy reading. Jack had gone outside for a break after the morning session and then re-entered the building's toilets before the afternoon session began. Unknown to Jack, his murderer was inside one of the toilet cubicles taping kitchen knives to his wrists in order to destroy all the hope and charity within the Learning Together programme. Jack's assailant came out of the booth and attacked him with both knives. Many of Jack's wounds were defensive and I cry to think of his last moments. Next this monster left the toilets and stabbed Saskia in the neck. It was at this point some members of the programme took it upon themselves to set upon the attacker and force him from the building where he was eventually shot by the Met Police—an end too swift and not just enough for him in my opinion. He represented everything Jack and Saskia stood against. Meanwhile, Karen was inside Fishmonger's Hall trying to stem the flow of blood from Saskia's neck wound. Saskia, my friend, whose sole focus was on becoming a support worker for rape victims within the police force. Saskia, my drinking buddy who was so caring and bright but could also be hilariously funny while doing the dumbest things. I'll never forget the moment she told me she'd lost her laptop...that contained half of her dissertation with no copies or backups anywhere. Now gone, murdered at an event celebrating hope and rehabilitation. As if these murders weren't terrible enough, Karen and her Learning Together team would ultimately be held responsible for the tragedy. Apparently, their risk assessments weren't robust enough, so they were to blame. Never mind the fact the London Bridge attacker was on parole and was granted permission to attend the event by the police and probation services. A scapegoat was required.

The English judiciary struggles to look itself in the eye when things go awry, whether accidental police shootings of innocent victims, point-blank shootings of unarmed guilty criminals, or paedophile gangs that have existed for decades, nobody within that system is held accountable and the blame will always be deflected, apportioned to an outsider. I can't imagine the trauma Karen must still be holding inside today, the woman who saw something in me that engendered enough trust to invite me to study for a master's at the institute that taught her so much. Thankfully, she has her family and a very strong faith.

* * *

The bus from Tbilisi to Gudauri airport contained around twenty people of varying ages, mostly Georgians. It also contained a strong atmosphere of tension and fear. Ironically, when it came to buying face masks and hand gel, I'd struggled to find any. The reason for this irony was my having sent boxes filled with both items to mainland China for some of my Cambridge friends whom I knew were having difficulty sourcing sufficient supplies of them. Media outlets were claiming a new virus had been discovered in a Wuhan city wet market while I and my doctors at Tbilisi hospital supposed otherwise. A week prior to my stepping onto this bus, I'd had a conversation with a friend I'd met at the Into the Wild festival while erecting marquees. We'd encountered one another at the festival each year and she was now living in the southwest of France with her husband and two teenage children.

"Christian, you need to come here and write your book."

I'd mentioned to her many friends in DarBar had suggested I write my life story but, as yet, I hadn't written a single word. My days of playing music with Levan in Tbilisi bars and restaurants were over because the pandemic was forcing venues to close their doors. My other option might have been construction, but I wasn't keen on earning Georgian wages and, besides, there'd be a wide language barrier. "Wow, really?" I said. "Whereabouts in France are you? And do you have room for me?"

"We're in a place called Montreal du Gers, between Bordeaux and Toulouse. We can see the Pyrenees from here. And we have a five-bedroom guesthouse for our nonexistent guests so, yeah, plenty of room for you."

"Ah, yeah, I know where you are. I've spent time around that area before…busking and living la vie en rose."

Mags laughed at my reference, then asked, "So, how about it? Fancy some more la vie en rose near the Pyrenees?"

"Well, it seems my time here in Georgia is up so, yeah, why not? I'll book a flight and keep you updated."

I've never flown on such a sparsely populated plane before, which came as enormous comfort after sharing the bus with such a cramped cargo of people. I slept across three seats all the way to Paris, then caught a train down to Toulouse. I had some concerns around catching this virus, which was sweeping the world but, in some ways, felt I probably already had antibodies to it in my system. Mags and Stephen's property in Montbrun was perfectly situated in near seclusion, surrounded by wine and Armagnac vineyards and little else. They'd bought it with a view to running yoga and meditation retreats—hence the five-bedroom guesthouse—and, had COVID not threatened, who knows whether it would've proved a viable business model. Its isolation worked to our advantage during the COVID lockdown, and I was able to take long countryside walks, go jogging, and take regular dips in the swimming pool. I wrote the first 250 pages of this memoir during the three months I lived there, and it really was a wonderful experience. Mags, Stephen, and their two teenagers (a sixteen-year-old boy and eighteen-year-old girl) all shared the family home while I shared the guesthouse with another friend of Mags's she also knew from the UK festival scene. As per our agreement, I paid rent and earned a small income by doing various maintenance jobs around the house. I fitted a chimney to the wood burner in the yurt, replaced the wooden railings around a small staircase on the guesthouse, and helped Stephen build some raised beds for growing vegetables. We'd also share stories and an evening meal together each day in the family house. I was able to borrow the family car for shopping trips and would also take my solo self on trips to places of historical interest and, fortunately, was never stopped and questioned by the police; we were that isolated. My living quarters were perfect with a kitchen I cooked in most days, a patio with a large table for eating and writing, and a fireplace where I'd sit and play guitar before its flickering flames in the evenings when not writing on my laptop in my upstairs bedroom. It was a great place for reflection and was perfect for getting into the necessary headspace for writing…as well as drinking the local victuals. Despite an ongoing pandemic, we made the most of our situation and I have fond memories of those months we spent together. However, the days of those months felt a lot like *Groundhog Day* as there wasn't much change in routine.

The lockdown restrictions in France were lifted, so I was able to travel once again. Stephen drove me to my next destination, so, with bags and saxophone packed into his car, we headed an hour east and he dropped me off at a place called Montbrun-Bocage. I watched his car recede into the distance back the way we'd come and turned to face my next adventure: a place where writing ceased and partying resumed.

Ben pulled the car up outside the address we'd been given, cut the engine, the music on the stereo quitting with it, and we both climbed out. I pulled my sax case from the rear seat, then looked at the imposing stone house we'd landed outside. In England, we'd call this type of house a mansion or a stately home. It was huge. There was music coming from the other side of the building, so we followed the sound and discovered a colourful medley of musicians and a small audience, some of whom were dancing. I counted three saxophones, one trumpet, a trombone, drum kit, electric and bass guitars, a mic stand, and an accordion. There was a woman singing into the mic and the band were giving her room to sing.

What lockdown?

This wasn't anything like where I'd spent the past three months and the change felt exhilarating. I could see tables behind the crowd set with a large buffet along with many different types of wine and large buckets filled with ice and cans of beer.

"You know what, Ben?!" I shouted into his ear so he could hear me above the music.

"What?!" he shouted back.

"The French are extremely good at two absolutely vital aspects of life: appreciation of music and protest!"

And this was my kind of protest. Fuck being locked down. There was still life to be had.

I met Ben at the same festival I'd met Mags. While he lives in southern France, he travels for work...and he works as a clown, magician, and musician. A wonderful *smorgasbord* of skills designed to keep himself as far away as possible from more conventional forms of employment. And the next several weeks' staying at his place in Montbrun-Bocage would cement our friendship.

It's a tiny little village, this Montbrun. Typically French with its market square, quaint side streets with obligatory shuttered house facades, a ruined chateau, and an eclectic population gathered from all corners of the world. It resides in the L'Ariège region, which I like to joke has the most number of dreadlocks per square kilometre in all of France.

Having lived in this place for a fairly long time, Ben knew practically everyone...and vice versa. The reason for this renown is La Grangette, a small yet personable venue nestled behind Ben's house consisting of an old barn converted into a creative space, sometime musical venue, sometime workshop for a variety of skills—juggling, Latin dancing, clowning, theatre, anything goes—where Ben presides as compère. Beside La Grangette was a large caravan similar in size to the one destroyed by Ukrainian roads, although in much better shape, and this was my home during my stay in Montbrun.

Six weeks of fantastic food and drink while meeting gentle, lovely, generous folk I now count among my friends; naked swimming in a small cool lake several miles from the village; special meals cooked by me or Ben and shared with his fifteen-year-old daughter; the Saturday market—a huge communal *affaire* where everybody meets everybody else, swaps or buys provisions, catches up on local gossip, plots the next event at La

Grangette; a bustling and lively community in a village that suited me well mid-pandemic but was, in reality, too small for my personal ambitions.

* * *

The car horn competed in a crescendo then a diminuendo as it approached and then receded from me at speed. Another scared fucker not stopping to pick me up. Memories flooded my mind, memories of 1 June 1984, swirling within my mind, taking me back to the time I'd been stood on the side of the M3 roundabout heading for my first Stonehenge festival when Scott had given me a lift.

Only this time, the world had been certified insane and was wearing a face mask.

The musical notes emanating from my own horn as I blew into the wind of this infected world became audible once again as the car's horn moved too far away to hear. I carried on playing and awaited the next car in the hope it would stop.

There's no quicker way to get a lift than blowing a sax at the side of the road. I'd discovered this over many years' hitchhiking. However, now that COVID-19 had landed, it wasn't proving such an effective strategy… My train of thought was interrupted by a car pulling up and the window slowly sliding down to reveal a young girl in, I'd guess, her early twenties.

"Bonjour…"

"Hey, bonjour…" I responded.

"You're English? Cool, I speak English. Where you going?"

"I'm headed East, Nice, Genoa, Venice…can you take me some of the way?"

"Sure, I'm going as far as Fréjus, this side of Cannes. It will help you."

"Perfect," I said. I quickly disassembled the sax and put it inside its case, then threw it in the back and jumped in the passenger seat.

"Oh, hang on, you want me to wear a mask?"

"No, it's fine."

"Cool…and *merci. Je m'appelle Christian.*"

"*Je m'appelle Sylvie*. Nice to meet you. So, tell me, what is an Englishman doing playing sax on the side of the road and heading for Italy in these crazy times?"

I laughed at Sylvie's comment and agreed, "Yeah, crazy times is right! I was living in Georgia when the pandemic hit, then I came here and have been staying with different friends around the Toulouse area. I'm now travelling to see another friend in Vicenza, an hour this side of Venice. She's a singer and a good friend."

"How long have you been playing saxophone?"

"Around twenty-five years, but I also play guitar and sing. What about you? Do you play?"

Sylvie threw back her head and laughed. "No, not at all. I'm training to be a pilot. That's where I've just been, flying a small plane with my instructor. I'm now headed to see my mother in Fréjus. She always wanted me to play piano. I tried for a while, but I guess I'm more, how would you say…? What's it called when a girl acts like a boy?"

"Tomboy?"

"*Oui, c'est le mot!* I'm a tomboy."

"Well, Sylvie, despite forgetting the word tomboy, your English is fantastic."

"Thanks, I worked in a bar in Marseilles to pay for flight school and there were always a lot of English came in. I got a lot of practice."

We drifted into silence, both watching the kilometres and the scenery quickly flashing past. We became Facebook friends, and I still see her posts occasionally…always in a cockpit with a set of headphones on her ears.

* * *

The alarm on my phone entered my dreamscape and slowly became intrusive enough to swipe the dream memory away. I realised I was sweating uncomfortably and reached over to unzip the flap door. It was five in the morning, and the sun had already created a sauna inside my tent. I climbed out into the dry heat of a Nice morning and drank some water.

Pitching a tent on a roundabout in central Nice probably isn't a great idea, but I've had worse. I set the alarm early because I know from experience, if you're not careful, the automatic sprinklers give you a good soaking, and the police might wake you and give you some hassle.

I quickly dismantled the tent, then headed for the nearest bakery for croissant and coffee. After splashing some water on my face inside the café's toilet, I set out to find a decent lay-by and assembled my sax. It didn't take too long.

This time, a guy from Sardinia driving a van who invited me to meet his mother and sister, uncle, auntie, and everybody else in his village whenever I liked. He also didn't seem overly concerned about the global emergency. I graciously accepted his address, and he dropped me off on a dual carriageway approaching a town called Vermiglio. I waved my goodbyes and resumed playing sax, awaiting another kind soul to help me in my quest to visit Isabella in Malo and Patrizia in Vicenza.

The next van to pull over was filled with several roadworkers wearing orange high-visibility vests. They all began shouting at me in Italian until I realised their *vietatos* meant it was forbidden to hitchhike on this stretch of road. With some confusing gestures and a few *per favores,* I begged them to give me a lift farther down the road to a place where hitchhiking wasn't *vietato*. They somehow understood and made room for me in the crew cab of their van.

Upon reaching Genoa, I knew I'd now need to head south because I'd discovered Isabella wasn't currently in Malo. I'd spoken with her and she'd fled to her place in Riparbella to escape the hordes of potentially infected people in her hometown.

Before going anywhere, though, I was famished so, after being dropped near the city centre, I chose a restaurant on the main drag and decided on people watching accompanied by a plate of pasta and a glass or two of Montepulciano d'Abruzzo. After this welcome interlude, I headed for the train station.

Once in a city centre, you can forget hitchhiking. I caught the train down to Riparbella and awaited Isabella once I arrived.

* * *

"Ciao, Christian...I'm home."

I have a video of this on my Instagram. It's Patrizia returning to her house from a concert she'd performed in Bologna the previous evening. I'd last seen her jump into a car with the guitarist of her band and I'd spent an evening alone cooking provisions I'd bought from the local supermarket and drinking lots of good Italian wine. In the video, my saxophone can be heard getting louder and louder as I answer Patrizia's call and come closer to the window. I'd spent a few days with Isabella helping her tend her patch of land in Tuscany, and we'd then shared the driving from west to east until we'd landed in Vicenza. She dropped me off at Patrizia's, and we'd said our goodbyes. It was fantastic to see Patrizia once again, although there was a slightly subdued note due to the possibility of either of us carrying a virus and infecting the other without knowing.

Despite this undercurrent, Patrizia cooked food for me and poured wine while asking me about my experiences at Cambridge. She then sang for me and showed me where to sleep while her co-musicians arrived and whisked her away for her Bologna gig. And now she was back.

She was also tired after the concert and the drive home. There was a hammock hanging in the lounge and she fell into it.

"Sing for me, Christian, please? I'm so tired."

I picked up the guitar, checked its tuning then began singing a Tom Waits ballad I loved, "Soldier's Things," with its lilting lullaby and beautiful chord structure. Patrizia closed her eyes, and I sensed she was enjoying my rendition.

I had a great sensation sweep over me as I played. Patrizia had won a talent show at a very young age—in her late teens—and had then garnered a huge fan base over the years, and here I was playing saxophone in this famous singer's house, playing guitar to her, and being invited into her house as a great friend...an equal.

She knew my history, I'd related it to her in Vicenza's Piazza dei Signori when I'd first met her during my French, Italian, and Swiss adventure back in 2016. It felt wonderful to be staying at her house and playing for her.

However, the time had come to return home to the UK. The great adventure was over. I'd checked my bank balance, and it said in huge Caps Lock letters: YOU ARE SKINT.

I needed to return home and find employment so I could refill the coffers for more adventures. I explained this to Patrizia, paid for the flight online, then spent another day enjoying her company. She drove me to Marco Polo Airport in Venice the following morning.

We stopped for coffee at a service station en route and I got out my sax and assembled it.

"This is for you, Patrizia," I told her and blew a sensual version of the Godfather theme, *Speak Softly Love*. I knew she was born in Sicily, which was why I chose to play this beautiful and melancholy piece.

She walked me to the departure desk, a memory I still cherish, and then, after saying goodbye, I was alone in Marco Polo Airport with time to spare before my plane departure.

I noticed a cashpoint machine that got me thinking about how skint I was. I'd been in this position before in Calais and I'm convinced there's some kind of glitch between European ATMs and UK banks. My instinct was right; I successfully pulled a hundred euros from the machine, then another hundred.

"That'll keep me going for a bit," I said to myself while placing the notes in my wallet.

38

That's Life
(Frank Sinatra)

The day promised warmth and a cloudless blue sky. Perfect. The alternative didn't bear thinking about on such an exceptional day. I was feeling uncomfortable in black suit and gown, white shirt paired with a ridiculous white bow tie, and blue hood I was required to wear. I'd had to buy a new suit for the occasion as I'd left my own suit and tuxedo in Georgia before returning to the UK. I also soon came to realise I'd be sweating every moment I was required to stay in it.

The date was 24 July 2021, and today I was to graduate in the Senate House of Cambridge University. I completed my master's in 2018, but a £3000 debt to my college delayed my graduation.

The morning required me to attend a dress rehearsal in Darwin College's Old Library where all graduands were instructed in the protocols of the morning's ceremony replete with Latin gibberish and much doffing of a mortar board by the college praelector. Recent pandemic restrictions rendered the ceremony less tactile than former years, which suited me just fine. There is usually an archaic practice of four graduands holding the four fingers of their college's praelector, who then presents the graduands to the college master. I was extremely pleased COVID-19 had made such practice redundant.

The time to gather outside college arrived, and I couldn't help smirking at the memory of almost a hundred pyjama-clad students similarly lining up after my fire alarm *faux pas* three years previously. A slow march along Silver Street past Queens' College, left past its front gates on Queens' Lane, then King's Lane, and we arrived on King's Parade—probably the most famous road in Cambridge city for both students and tourists.

We continued, King's College on our left, bringing more memories of my incredible time playing their May Ball with the Galapagogos. On our right the Corpus Clock with its time-eating insect followed by a long parade of shops touting different Cambridge University-themed trinkets.

King's College Chapel's enormous façade with its marvellous stained-glass depictions sailed past on our right giving way to the Old Schools building. This brought vivid memories of the students' support of the teachers' strike in the summer of 2019. I'd arrived with my saxophone to join the protest little knowing I'd be in the newspapers the following day: "To a backing track of live saxophone music, students then pounded on the Old School's doors, crowding around the entrance and chanting: 'Whose university? Our university.'"

We arrived outside the Senate House and joined a long queue of black-gowned graduands all wearing different coloured hoods according to their major—while a fluffy white hood denoted graduands of Anglia Ruskin University, Cambridge City's own university not affiliated with Cambridge University (us Cambridge students jokingly referred to it as the Early Learning Centre).

Closer and closer, I was now only a few metres from the imposing wooden entrance door. My friend beside me, Matt, gave me a huge grin and I reciprocated. This was the moment we'd given so much of our time and sweat to. Hours, days, weeks, months of insane cramming to achieve the seemingly unachievable. We'd made it!

I walked through the doors into the building and was ushered to a spot on the highly polished chequered floor. I was introduced to the system by an usher and moved forwards a step as each graduand before me moved. Another step, then another.

The air felt heavy and cold inside the cavernous stone building, the scent of old wooden benches and many years of tradition filled my nostrils. I'd heard the expression 'standing on the shoulders of giants' uttered many times during my time at Cambridge but here now, standing among my fellow graduands with the slanting sunlight, our gowns and mortar boards, I sensed exactly that—a continuum of academic lineage with me, Christian Austin, among that pantheon; incredible.

The graduand in front of me was called to stand before Darwin College's Master who was sitting on an ornate chair.

Darwin College's praelector uttered a long monotonous line in Latin of which I understood little, my name was called out, and I then slowly walked ahead until I was standing before Darwin's Master. I gave a small bow as I'd been instructed, then left the building where I was photographed as a graduate before descending the stone staircase.

And that is how after half a life spent as a criminal, a drug dependent, a fugitive and a prisoner, I became a Cantabrigian, the term given to a graduate of Cambridge University.

* * *

Oh, Cambridge! What an incredible two years of my life…two years never to be repeated yet filled with memories that will be cherished forever. Each time I return and walk its streets, recollections of my time spent there flood my mind. A period seemingly snatched from a destiny I could so easily never have lived to see. How on Earth did I survive all these years while watching so many friends perish to overdoses, stabbings, disease, or incredibly long prison sentences?

The day wasn't over yet, though, nor was my facility for flouting college tradition—albeit unintentionally. I hurried back to Darwin College so I could change out of the stuffy gown and suit and back into my shorts and T-shirt as fast as possible, and that's how I presented myself at the formal graduation dinner. I was placed almost opposite the Master and, happily, he didn't utter a word. He knew my history and that I'd worked in the college catering department after my master's degree and I guess you could say he wasn't surprised at my being unorthodox. I'm certain, however, that my fellow graduate's friends and families will be scanning the photos of the day asking why just one guy at the dinner isn't dressed in gown and suit.

* * *

The following Saturday, I entered my local Marks and Spencer's store with the suit I'd worn for the graduation inside its protective plastic cover and approached the teller.

"Good morning. I bought this suit last week, but it's not really for me. I'd like a refund, please."

"I'm sure I can help with that. Do you have the receipt?"

"Yes, here it is," I responded, handing it to her.

She gave the suit a cursory inspection and then refunded me the £250 I'd paid for it.

"Thank you very much."

I gave her a smile, turned, and then walked slowly towards the exit.

Cambridge may have given me a degree, but the streets gave me an education.

Thank you for reading *RESILIENT - Childhood Adversity to Cambridge University*.

If something in these pages spoke to you—if you felt seen, challenged, or moved—I'd be truly grateful if you could take a moment to leave a review on Amazon or Goodreads.

Your words don't need to be long or polished. Just honest. Reviews help others find the book, especially those who might be walking a similar path and need to know they're not alone.

Thank you for sharing in this journey.

—CHRISTIAN

Acknowledgements

This book could not have been written—or lived—without the support, wisdom, and belief of many people across different stages of my life. Some offered me shelter when I was barely surviving; others challenged me to grow, or simply refused to give up on me when I was close to giving up on myself.

To the social workers and probation officers who saw the human being beneath the chaos—Christine Giles, Colin Mitchell, and Barbara Pegler—thank you for treating me with dignity when I hadn't yet learned to give it to myself.

To the drug counsellors who held space for my pain while nudging me toward the possibility of healing: Bill Brown and Charlie Fuggle, I owe you more than you know.

To the educators who lit small fires that kept me moving forward—Stephen King, Adrian Kendon, Rob Milner, Dave Murrell, Julian Nicholas, Robert Smith, Alun Tomos, Ruth Armstrong, and Ben Crewe—thank you for seeing potential even when I didn't.

To Debbie at Queen Esther Publishing, thank you for guiding this manuscript with skill, patience, and care—from raw pages to finished book.

To my beta readers, Duncan Koerber and Duxicus Dux, thank you for your time, insight, and belief in this story.

To my mother, and to Camilla, Serena, and Raven—your presence in my life, however complex or brief, has shaped who I am.

To Seb, Alfie, Rosie, and Liam—I wrote this book with you in my heart. I hope you'll read it one day and understand how much I love you, and how hard I fought to become someone you could be proud of.

And finally, to every soul out there who's been counted out, written off, or forgotten: this book is also for you. Keep going. You never know what's possible.

About the Author

Christian Austin is a writer, musician, and speaker who turned his life around after surviving childhood trauma, heroin addiction, and nearly two decades in and out of prison. After entering recovery, he pursued education relentlessly—eventually earning a master's degree in Criminology from Cambridge University. Christian now gives talks at universities and prisons, inspiring others through his lived experience.

His debut memoir, *RESILIENT: Childhood Adversity to Cambridge University*, chronicles a raw and redemptive path through chaos, music, and personal transformation. He splits his time between the UK, France, Italy, and Georgia.

www.ingramcontent.com/pod-product-compliance
Ingram Content Group UK Ltd.
Pitfield, Milton Keynes, MK11 3LW, UK
UKHW021504300925
463415UK00015B/14

9 781068 168109